Gillian Ishlove.

1945.

MAJOR ENGLISH ROMANTIC POETS

Edited By

Clarence D. Thorpe,
Carlos Baker,
and
Bennett Weaver

 FORUM HOUSE

© COPYRIGHT 1968, 1969 AND PUBLISHED BY
FORUM HOUSE PUBLISHING COMPANY
TORONTO – LONDON – SYDNEY
AUCKLAND – CAPETOWN – SINGAPORE
PRINTED IN CANADA

CONTENTS

III. Coleridge

IV. Byron

V. Shelley

VI. Keats

INTRODUCTION

THIS VOLUME was planned as a symposium of present-day critical estimates of the chief English Romantic poets. It was intended neither as a defense nor a justification of these poets or of the period to which they belong, but as a cross-section of opinion and appraisal by as many qualified scholars and critics as could be conveniently included in one book. The scheme of the project called for frank evaluation, in terms of present-day standards and needs, of the English Romantic period as a whole and of each of its five leading poets. Readers will find three longer articles on the period, and one on the thought, one on the art of each poet, with one or more "capsule" essays on each, running from 1,200 to 2,500 words in length. Except for the fact that some of our capsulers happily exceeded the prescribed word limits, the original plan has been followed.

We have been fortunate in enlisting the aid of twenty leading scholars and critics of three great English-speaking countries, Canada, Great Britain, and the United States. These writers furnish a considerable range of view and practice. Not all are academic men and not all are specialists in Romantic literature or on the author of whom they write. Not all are friendly to the Romantic period, and some have anything but a partisan bias for their immediate subject: thus Hoxie Fairchild may scarcely be reckoned as a true apostle of Romanticism; Raymond D. Havens, whose last long literary essay is here posthumously published, had distinct reservations about Shelley's poetic art; Cleanth Brooks has high praise for Keats, and on occasion for Wordsworth, but his acceptance of Romantic writers in general is a highly selective and qualified

one. The more valuable all these for our purpose: a representative and
diversified set of opinions on the period and its chief poets.

The questions asked our contributors were these: How do English
Romanticism and the leading English Romantic poets stand with us today? What has endured in them and is likely to endure? What is there
of value in this body of writing for men and women living in this time
and in this present kind of world? In what ways do the Romantic writers speak to this world as men of thought? How do they stand up under
modern scrutiny as literary artists? In putting these questions there was
no idea on the part of the editorial committee of influencing opinion
one way or another; no suggestion went to any contributor that this was
to be either an attack on or a defense of the Romantics.

The question may be asked, Why the division between thought
and art; in good poetry is not thought essentially inseparable from the
artist's performance? This is a valid point; it is in effect an argument
for organic unity, a principle in which the editors firmly believe. It is
an interesting fact, however, that there has been for a long time a distinct tendency in our academic and critical journals and books toward
a sort of specialization either in ideas or in artistry; those who emphasize thought say little about art, those whose interest lies in artistry are
likely to neglect thought. Mr. Ransom writes brilliantly of *Lycidas* as
a formal construct but says no word about its meaning; Kenneth Muir
writes brilliantly on *Hyperion* in an essay which concentrates on meaning but pays small attention to art. Whatever the merits of this situation,
it exists—and in a more decisive way than the mere statement reveals: for
the division is far from an equal one, with the balance so heavy on the
thought side, especially among academic writers, that the quest for those
willing to deal with the artistry of a poet may be far from an easy one.
So merely as a practical matter, the editors found it advisable to make
assignments in the light of this observed tendency. As a further consideration they saw value in a wider cross-section of opinion, with
greater diversity in point of view, than could be secured under a more
concentrated authorship.

All good criticism of past work is an exercise in revaluation, and
the wise critic is bound to examine the author or poem before him in
terms of values and principles current in his day. But there is also a
special reason for a new attempt to assess the merits of the writers of
the Romantic period. For a generation now, Romanticism itself has

been under fire, though it has not by any means lacked for sturdy de-
fenders. As for writers of the period some have fallen into disfavor or
have been vigorously attacked; others have been widely praised, with an
observable tendency to give them higher ranking than formerly.

Such facts alone are abundant justification for a volume of scholarly opinion and reappraisal. There is, however, an even stronger motivation: the fact that Romantic poetry touches contemporary literature
at so many vital points. Like our own poets of the past generation, the
Romantics found themselves in the midst of a sharp conflict between
the claims of the spiritual and those of the physical and materialistic.
And in facing this cleavage, poets of each period have had their ups
and downs of hope and despair. It is no accident surely that T. S. Eliot
was attracted in his earlier criticism to *The Triumph of Life* as perhaps
the work containing Shelley's best poetry: *The Waste Land* and *The
Triumph of Life* are apparently born of a similar tragic consciousness
of the actualities of human society as each poet sees them in his own
day, set against the concept of an ideal society in which love, justice,
goodness, and truth might prevail.

English and American poetry, literature in general, of the past three
decades has gone through the Waste Land phase; much of it still takes
a dismal view of life, though one frequently observes a strong recru-
descence of the poet's urge to free himself from disillusion and despair.
But Shelley's gloom was not characteristic of him or his age. He had
his dark hours as did Coleridge, Byron, and Keats, even Wordsworth;
but deep down in his best, more habitual poetic self he believed that
bad as things are, wrongs may be righted and evils banished: the way
was through cultivation of the imagination, the special instrument of
love and understanding, and dedication to the power of truth and beauty
as exemplified in the spirit of Intellectual Beauty.

If Keats sometimes walked in the night of despair, he also found
the road to acceptance and explanation. His own revered Spenser saw
no remedy for the ills of human mutability but in a final escape to a perfect future existence; but Keats could point to the fall and rise of dy-
nasties as a natural mode of progress:

> *So on our heels a fresh perfection treads,*
> *A power more strong in beauty*

—a power, as the context of this passage in *Hyperion* shows, more highly developed in the physical graces, in mental and social capabilities, and in a thousand other ways. So, too, rejecting the concept of the world as "a vale of tears," Keats manfully works through to a philosophy of the world as "A Vale of Soul-Making," a school in which "the human heart must suffer in a thousand diverse ways," to bring forth a soul with individual identity. It was such a creative philosophy of acceptance that enabled Keats to write odes that, in the words of one critic in this book, "are tough-minded, not soft and self-indulgent or prettified," and to insist in his *Fall of Hyperion* that the true poet must know and feel "the miseries of the world," and yet be able, quite objectively we may assume, "to see as a god sees" into "the depth of things."

Byron could be both sentimental and pessimistic, but he outgrew his sentimentalism, while his uncertainty and revolt never broke his will to reform or overmastered his belief that the cure for the evils of his day was truth. So he worked with all his might to expose cant and hypocrisy, misgovernment and oppression in all their unpleasant reality, and he came to his death in an act of affirmation of his belief in freedom. Coleridge in turn mourned the loss of creative imagination, then went on to continual demonstrations of steadfast religious faith that embraced belief in God and the universe and, perhaps most notably, in man's mind with its godlike and God-given powers to create and do. Wordsworth's Waste Land came early, through disillusion with the excesses of the French Revolution and with England's selfish, even, in Wordsworth's view, perfidious, response to that revolution, as well as through despair in his personal Gethsemane of the Godwinian conflict. But his temporary loss of faith in the power of nature and God and in the basic integrity and goodness of man was superseded by a recovery in which, with triumphant confidence, he went on to write his finest poems about common humankind in a world exquisitely fitted to the Mind, where Mind in turn is exquisitely fitted to the external world.

Students of the Romantic movement in recent years have continually emphasized the positive attitudes developed by the Romantic poets and the positive quality of their aspirations and efforts. The terms in which such scholar-critics as Arthur O. Lovejoy, René Wellek, Newton Stallknecht, D. G. James, C. M. Bowra, Morse Peckham, and W. J. Bate have sought to describe the uniqueness of the movement are significant: among them are "dynamism," "organicism," "dynamic organicism," "organic vitalism," "positive romanticism," all expressive of vitality, confidence, largeness of view; others less cryptic are "imaginative inquiry into . . . the mystery of things," imaginative penetration to the "abiding reality" thereby to understand "more clearly what life means and what it is worth," the establishment of "the sentiment of being in England."

Goethe, of course, saw Romanticism as a sickness, in contrast with the health of Classicism. Other critics have since agreed wholly or in part with Goethe. And not always without justification. For usually the things they have decried belong to "negative romanticism," unacceptable elements like sentimentalism and escapism that no one can approve or admire, though it may be argued that these qualities are at a minimum among the major English Romantics.

Readers of this book will be interested to see how many of our contributors have in one way or another commented on the positive qualities of the Romantic poets, on their confidence in the power of man to meet his problems, to bridge the gap between the seen and unseen, the material and the spiritual, to do something to remedy the ills of the world; all this, too, with a hopeful view of the power of poetry as a prime agency for doing good. It is just here perhaps, as is intimated more than once in the following essays, that our own generation may derive much from the Romantics. We find the injunction "Accentuate the Positive" in a popular song; but many of our writers embody only those negative convictions which Karl Shapiro has called the trademark of modernism.

Meeting points of the Romantic period with our own on matters of literary artistry are numerous and important. The poets of each age were initially confronted with the necessity of finding a language and style suitable to the mood and ideas of the day. Each group, too, had to face up to the dilemma posed by the pressures of traditionalism against those of modernity. Each is rightfully seen as owing great debts to the past, as the recipient of handsome largesse from gifted predecessors. The Romantics utilized, in one way or another and with remarkable thoroughness, about all the resources their past had to offer. Their success lay in the fact that in this utilization they did much more than borrow: at their best, they recreated what they took and made it into something new. Coleridge used the ballad form, but no one before or since has written such another ballad as his *Rime of the Ancient Mari-*

ner; Keats in his *Lamia* used basically Dryden's couplet and the ideas of poetic romance, but the verse and the poem he wrote are such as only Keats could write. The theory of a simple, inartificial literary language was old long before Wordsworth was born, but in his hands it became an instrument of quiet power capable at need of sounding as true notes as have ever been heard on the profoundest experiences of man in contact with his world.

Similarities with modern poetry appear also when we come to more specific qualities of Romantic verse. Symbolism did not have its birth with the Romantics, but who among past poets has used it more pervasively and more effectively than Coleridge, Keats, and Shelley? Paradox, contrast, irony had appeared before, but had they ever been more richly exemplified than in Keats and Byron? The wonderful music of Coleridge, Shelley, and Keats is surely comparable to the finest ever produced by others—not excluding Shakespeare. And in some respects it seems to stand by itself, with its magic sound-patterns, its fitness and diversity of rhythms, its subtle chordal effects: charming, faintly defined chromatic variations, likeness in difference, nearly imperceptible half-steps in the vowel scale. Music is linked with imagery of rarest sort, capable of creating in the mind of the reader or listener large-scale organic impressions, unity of tone and effect, or at times suggestions of long-buried workings of the subconscious mind. One might cite in illustration the first over-all image, with its lesser component images, in Keats's *Hyperion,* or the *vox humana* of *The Ancient Mariner.*

As the critics concerned with literary artistry in this book have in one way or another made clear, the presence of such qualities has made Romantic verse meaningful to our age, and these virtues have frequently come to us with fuller impact because our contemporary writers in both verse and prose have demonstrated anew their utility and significance for poetic purposes. Except for the Romantics themselves, probably no generation of poets has drawn more heavily on the past than those of our own age; consciously or not, they appear to have assimilated much from the greater Romantic poetry. So too with modern critics. Though they have rejected much they have also accepted much, through either simple retention or transformation of the more durable parts of Romantic criticism. The writings of I. A. Richards, T. S. Eliot, and Cleanth Brooks, for example, bear indelible marks of Coleridge. This is as it should be and is to the honor of all parties concerned. The relevant remark just here is that such facts corroborate the conclusion reached by various writers in the present volume that our time still has appreciable need for the Romantics.

C. D. T.
C. B.
B. W.

1: The Romantic
Movement

Form in Romantic Poetry

I

ELIZABETH NITCHIE

THE CRITIC, says Mr. F. R. Leavis, "endeavours, where the poetry of the past is concerned, to realize to the full the implications of the truism that its life is in the present or nowhere; it is alive in so far as it is alive for us." [1] This is not the place to argue whether this is a truism or not. I merely accept the statement as a directive for thinking about the Romantic poets in the middle of the twentieth century. There is, of course, more than one way in which the poetry of the past may be alive for us. It may live because we have sufficient historical imagination to project ourselves into that past and to read the poetry as its contemporaries read it. [2] Or we can say, with Virginia Woolf, that the poet is always our contemporary, [3] that his work, being universal, is as alive in our own century as in his. It is in this second sense that I shall try to show that the Romantic poets, no matter how we respond to their ideas, are alive for us by reason of a formal excellence in their work that knows no restriction to time or place.

There is ample evidence that for modern critics as for modern readers Romantic poetry is alive. They are aware not only of breathing and heart-

[1] *Revaluations* (London: Chatto & Windus, 1936), p. 2.

[2] Cf. J. C. Ransom, *The World's Body* (New York: Scribner's, 1938), p. 70: "We sometimes pore over an old piece of poetry for so long that we fall under its spell and forget that its spirit is not our spirit. . . . By means of one of the ripest and subtlest powers in us, that is, the historical sense, we made an adaptation of our minds to its mind, and we were able to suspend those centuries which had intervened. . . . Yet it is not exactly with our own minds that we are reading the old poetry; otherwise we could not read it."

[3] *The Second Common Reader* (New York: Harcourt, Brace, 1932), p. 289.

3

beat but of a vital energy that cannot be ignored, an energy not peculiar to the twentieth century but characteristic of all great poetry. Like all vital energy it rises from deep within the body and gives to it shape and action. Miss Edith Sitwell, quoting Blake ("Energy is the only life, and is from the Body"), says: "All technical achievement is, as it were, the Etheric Body of the poet." [4] This Etheric Body cannot be denied to the Romantic poets.

Even the men commonly known as the new critics, who charge the Romantics with unreality and escapism, with adolescent thinking, especially with formlessness, recognize many of those technical virtues which they admire as they turn to examine individual poems. Cleanth Brooks includes Wordsworth's *Ode: Intimations of Immortality* and Keats's *On a Grecian Urn* among the well wrought works of art. And Keats's *To a Nightingale* Mr. Leavis says "has the structure of a fine and complex organism." [5] Mr. Kenneth Burke and Mr. R. P. Warren seek and find a unifying symbolism in the *Rime of the Ancient Mariner*. Although they differ on the symbols, and although they go to extremes of Freudian and theological interpretation, they agree that it is a well constructed poem. The attacks of the new critics are most often directed at those poems which, popular anthology pieces though they be, most scholars and critics would recognize as inferior. Shelley, for example, suffers under the analysis of *The Indian Serenade* or *When the Lamp Is Shattered*. But what poet is always at his structural best?

The new critics have done us a signal service in stressing the importance of form. For the old critical mistake probably was to evaluate too largely in terms of content. How far it is possible to dissociate ideas or content and form is a debatable point. Wallace Stevens maintained in a recent lecture that "the style of a poem and the poem itself are one." [6] And Mr. John Crowe Ransom has said, "The union of beauty with goodness and truth has been common enough to be regarded as natural. It is the dissociation which is unnatural and painful." [7] Surely form itself is good only if it is organically unified with content, if it is the skin of the hand rather than the glove.

Mr. Allen Tate, however, says: "From my point of view the formal qualities of a poem are the focus of the specifically critical judgment because they partake of an objectivity that the subject matter, abstracted

[4] *A Poet's Notebook* (London: Macmillan, 1943), p. 21.
[5] *Op. cit.,* p. 245.
[6] "Two or Three Ideas," *Chap Book:*
Supplement to *The CEA Critic,* XIII, No. 7 (October, 1951).
[7] *The World's Body,* p. 72.

from the form, wholly lacks." [8] His is a good point of view from which to consider Romantic poetry, one on which good critics, teachers, and scholars (even though they may not make the complete dissociation between content and form) have always taken their stand.

The modern critic's conception of form and its function differs little upon examination from that which we inherit from the Romantics. Form is a control—the "bridle of Pegasus," Mr. I. A. Richards calls it.[9] Its function, says Mr. Ransom, is "to frustrate the natural man and induce the aesthetic one . . . ; it wants us to enjoy life, to taste and reflect as we drink." [10] It controls also in the sense that it unifies all the diverse parts of the poetic structure, including the content, the meaning, the argument. "The composition of a poem is an operation in which the argument fights to displace the meter, and the meter fights to displace the argument," a fight in which the terms of peace "are the dispositions in the finished poem." [11] Indeed the moral intelligence gets into poetry "not as moral abstractions but as form, coherence of image and metaphor, control of tone and of rhythm, the union of these features." [12]

We should not find anything shockingly new in these statements. They remind us of Wordsworth's

> *function kindred to organic power,*
> *The vital spirit of a perfect form;* [13]

or of Coleridge's definition of a poem as "proposing to itself such delight from the *whole,* as is compatible with a distinct gratification from each component *part*," and of his entire discussion of meter in the eighteenth chapter of the *Biographia Literaria*. Even Mr. Cleanth Brooks's insistence on paradox as the language of poetry should not startle those who remember Wordsworth's recognition of "the pleasure which the mind derives from the perception of similitude in dissimilitude" as a principle of the arts. In the familiar passage on the imagination in his *Biographia Literaria* Coleridge anticipated Mr. Brooks by more than a century:

[8] *Reason in Madness* (New York: G. P. Putnam's Sons, 1941), p. 110.

[9] *Coleridge on Imagination* (New York: Harcourt, Brace, 1935), Chapter IX.

[10] *The World's Body*, p. 39.

[11] J. C. Ransom, *The New Criticism* (Norfolk, Conn.: New Directions, 1941), p. 295.

[12] Allen Tate, *Reason in Madness*, pp. 109–10.

[13] See Ernest de Selincourt, *The Prelude* (London: Oxford University Press, 1932), p. xliii, note 1.

This power . . . reveals itself in the balance or reconcilement of opposite or discordant qualities: of sameness, with difference; of the general with the concrete; the idea with the image; the individual with the representative; the sense of novelty and freshness with old and familiar objects; a more than usual state of emotion with more than usual order; judgment ever awake and steady self-possession with enthusiasm and feeling profound or vehement; and while it blends and harmonizes the natural and the artificial, still subordinates art to nature; the manner to the matter; and our admiration of the poet to our sympathy with the poetry.

Indeed the modern critics often seem to have echoed the Romantic critics. Signor Croce, for example, sounds much like Wordsworth when he defines a poet or draws a distinction between imagination and fancy. They recognize their indebtedness. Miss Sitwell, the technician, fills her notebook with quotations from Blake, Coleridge, Wordsworth, and Shelley. The advocates of paradox and wit appeal to Coleridge by name and by quotation. Mr. I. A. Richards comments on a letter from Coleridge to Godwin: "I can think of no passage in which so many of the fundamental problems of what is now known as semasiology are so brought together or so clearly stated." [14] Coleridge is, in fact, the father of many modern theories.[15]

Another proof that the Romantic poets have a voice to which the twentieth century listens is to be found in the admiration of the neo-romantic poets of England. In revolt against the hard intellectualism and cynicism shown in argument and language by their immediate elders, especially the earlier Eliot and Auden, the poets who grew to young manhood between the two wars saw themselves as a new anticlassical, romantic generation. George Barker in his *Vision of England '38* summoned the ghosts of Blake and Shelley and

> took Shelley's tear which like a single rain
> Dropped into the blood that murmured at my feet.

David Daiches has compared the imagery, the poet's attitude and approach to his object, in *The Amazons* to those of Coleridge.[16] Dylan

---

[14] *Coleridge on Imagination*, p. 12.
[15] Mr. Tate, to be sure, thinks that it is a "false legacy" that Coleridge has passed on to us in his "failure to get out of the dilemma of Intellect-or-Feeling." See *Reason in Madness*, pp. 45–51.
[16] "The Lyricism of George Barker," *Poetry*, LXIX, No. 6 (March, 1947), 338.

Thomas, in his inner vision, his symbolism, his imagery, whether the sexual and Freudian or the pastoral of his "five and country senses," shows his heritage from Coleridge and Blake and Wordsworth. The group that derived from Barker and Thomas and called itself the Apocalypse published a manifesto whose terms remind us of the 1800 Preface in the revulsion from the machine age and the emphasis on the "individual development of Man." One of their number, J. F. Hendry, using Coleridge's word *organic,* writes that art is "the recognition, the communication of organic experience, experience with personal shape, experience which (however wild and startling in content) is a formal whole." [17] Although their subjects are not strikingly different from those of the later Auden and Spender, their language is romantic. Of Henry Treece it has been said: "His poetry represents . . . a kind of contemporary romanticism, a romanticism of language." [18] He has indeed been charged with the same formal sins as those of which his Romantic ancestors are often supposed to be guilty: lack of specific observation, use of literary imagery, structural failure resulting from the use of a mere stream of images.

Modern critics, as Mr. Barzun has pointed out,[19] seem to contradict themselves by accusing Romantic poetry now of formlessness, now of too great concern for form. Yet the first charge is really implicit in the second. This second charge involves three alleged faults: too great insistence on conventional verse forms and on metrical rhythms for their own sake; too much use of language that is beautiful only by reason of sound or of vague suggestion and trite association; too frequent use of images and figures of speech for their individual beauty, so that the result in a poem is a failure in close-knit architectural structure.

If these things are so, the poets are untrue to their own critical theory. They furnish rebuttal in their statements on prosody, diction, imagery, and the organic structure of a poem.

Writing of prosody in his *Defence of Poetry,* Shelley said that "every great poet must inevitably innovate upon the example of his predecessors in the exact structure of his peculiar versification." Coleridge, explaining the variations in the meter of *Christabel,* said that they

[17] See Francis Scarfe, *Auden and After* (London: Routledge & Sons, 1942), pp. 155, 158.
[18] H. R. Hays, "Hypnotic Words," a review of Treece's *Collected Poems, Poetry,* LXIX, No. 6 (March, 1947), 347.

[19] *Romanticism and the Modern Ego* (Boston: Little, Brown, 1943), p. 275. It is difficult to say anything about Romanticism and the modern ego half so well as Mr. Barzun.

occurred only "in correspondence with some transition, in the nature of the imagery or passion." Blake said of his septenaries: "Every word and every letter is studied and put into its fit place; the terrific numbers are reserved for the terrific parts, and the prosaic for the inferior parts; all are necessary to each other."

Similarly diction must be the organic outgrowth of thought. In *Style* DeQuincey recognized that Wordsworth was profoundly right in saying "that it is in the highest degree unphilosophic to call language or diction 'the *dress* of thoughts.' . . . [H]e would call it the *'incarnation* of thoughts.' " Blake wrote: "I have heard many people say, 'Give me the ideas, it is no matter what words you put them into.' . . . These people knew enough of artifice, but nothing of art. Ideas cannot be given but in their minutely appropriate words."

For Coleridge, "images, however beautiful . . . do not of themselves characterize the poet." The poetic image must have, among other qualities, "the effect of reducing multitude to unity, or succession to an instant." And Wordsworth has shown how the parts of a successfully imaginative figure of speech interact to produce the unity and concentration of poetic structure. For Keats the organization of imagery was that which gave shape and form to a poem. To him it is axiomatic that "Its touches of beauty should never be half-way, thereby making the reader breathless instead of content. The rise, the progress, the setting of Imagery should, like the sun, come natural to him, shine over him, and set soberly, although in magnificence, leaving him in the luxury of twilight." He wrote to Clarke of

> *the sonnet swelling loudly*
> *Up to its climax, and then dying proudly.*

On the whole matter of organic form one may quote Coleridge:

> The true . . . mistake lies in the confounding mechanical regularity with organic form. The form is mechanic, when on any given material we impress a pre-determined form, not necessarily arising out of the properties of the material; as when to a mass of wet clay we give whatever shape we wish it to retain when hardened. The organic form, on the other hand, is innate; it shapes, as it develops, itself from within, and the fullness of its development is one and the same with . . . its outward form.

Lest we think Coleridge unique in his generation, we can turn to DeQuincey on *Style,* or to Keats's third axiom, that like the leaves of a tree poetry must come from the poet's very life-sap.

Theory may be one thing, however, and practice another. These principles should be considered in the light of Romantic poetry, not merely of Romantic criticism.

With a real concern for verse form and an unwillingness to be confined to the couplet the Romantic poets revived earlier English patterns— blank verse, the tetrameter couplet, the ballad stanza, the Spenserian stanza, the sonnet—and introduced from Italian verse the terza rima and the ottava rima. Of these strict forms the poets were not slavishly observant. Byron was unconventional in his occasional lyrical ottava rima and his freely overrunning Spenserian stanzas, as well as in his loose dramatic blank verse. Coleridge experimented with tetrameters in *Christabel,* with the ballad stanza, with quantitative verse, and with rhythmic prose. Blake used blank verse in lyric poems, revived, with infinite variations and substitutions, the old fourteeners or septenaries in his prophetic books, and in many of his shorter poems achieved the kind of supple, clipped "prose" rhythms that we associate with modern innovators. Keats and Shelley both experimented with the sonnet. Keats developed his own form of the ode; Wordsworth freely adapted both the irregular and the regular patterns. Although, except for blank verse and Blake's septenaries, the emphasis is on end rhyme and regularly recurrent internal rhyme, there is no lack of assonance and suspension. And the sound patterns are as intricate and as highly unified in the work of Shelley or of Coleridge as in any poem by Archibald MacLeish or Dylan Thomas.[20] The result is a rich variety of versification, with a range as wide as that of the twentieth century, except that the rhythms are those of music rather than of speech.

This music, though admittedly pleasing to the ear for its own sake, is primarily the music which belongs to the poem. The west wind sweeps through the terza rima; the cloud ever changes and shifts as the vowels and consonants shift, ever remains undying as the rhymes recur in Shelley's closely-patterned stanzas; the heavy, long-drawn sounds of grief wail for the world's wrong in *A Dirge.* Biblical cadences dignify the blank verse in Wordsworth's tragic idyll of the Cumberland Abraham and

[20] See Kenneth Burke, *The Philosophy of Literary Form* (Baton Rouge, La.: The State University Press, 1941), pp. 369 ff.

Isaac. The visions in *Kubla Khan* melt one into another in hypnotic rhythms. The blank verse of *Hyperion* takes the shape of antique sculpture; the short lines of the *Ode to a Nightingale* have the sound of caught breath. The mocking colloquial tone of *Don Juan* is heard in the insistent, humorous reiterated rhymes of the ottava rima and the clinching finality of its couplet; a haunting regret lingers in the long vowels and feminine endings of *So We'll Go No More a-Roving*. The lament for fleeting beauty sighs in the echoes of *The Book of Thel;* the exciting hammer strokes of the Creator sound in the stresses and repetitions of *The Tiger*. The same principle obtains as that laid down by a modern critic for modern poetry: "So long as his form allows him to make the utmost of what he has to say, it does its work, and no more need be required of it." [21]

The same principle applies also to language. To quote Wordsworth again, "Language is the *incarnation* of thought." The diction of the Romantic poet—when he is writing his great poems, of course—does not lose touch with reality. It is concrete—a quality which Mr. Albert Gerard says "a large section of the poetry-reading public of the present day chiefly values." [22] It puts flesh on the objects upon which he steadily fixes his eye. Whether the poet looks at the dancing daffodils or the swift cloud shadows, the inner nature and the thoughts of Michael or of Prometheus, the world of classic art and literature or of contemporary politics and society, the drab and evil present or the ideal future, he sees what is real and he uses the "real language of men." This point is made especially clear for Wordsworth by a study of his first choices, the passages in the 1805 version of *The Prelude,* for example, instead of the 1850 version. And yet who has surpassed the reality of vision and of language in the 1850 lines about Newton's bust,

> *The marble index of a mind for ever*
> *Voyaging through strange seas of thought, alone?*

Romantic diction is not vague: it is precise.

Neither is it shallow or single: it is richly suggestive. "Ambiguity" was not unknown in the early nineteenth century, though Mr. Empson had not yet given it a name. What, for instance, of the two meanings of *closing* in the *Ode to the West Wind*—

---

[21] C. M. Bowra, *The Creative Experiment* (London: Macmillan & Co., 1949), p. 22.

[22] "Coleridge, Keats, and the Modern Mind," *Essays in Criticism,* I, No. 3 (July, 1951), 251.

> *this closing night*
> *Shall be the dome of a vast sepulchre—*

one, *enclosing,* related to *dome,* the other, *ending,* to *sepulchre?* The word pulls together the whole image and links it with the main theme of the poem: the enclosing cycle of death and rebirth. Mr. Brooks has pointed out possible ambiguities in the diction of Wordsworth's *Ode.* But has anyone really interpreted the word *piety* in *My Heart Leaps Up?* Its usual religious sense, reverence for God and His laws, is linked with the exaltation of the opening words and the Biblical symbolism of the rainbow. But it also means reverence for parents, one aspect of the *pietas* of Vergil's Aeneas.[23] And so the poet wishes the days of the man to be bound by natural piety to the days of the child who is his father. The ultimate, climactic, "ambiguous" word unifies the poem.

Like Romantic diction, the Romantic image is precise, often highly concentrated, wide in range, and structurally important to the poem.

The imagery of Shelley in particular is frequently said to be abstract and vague. There is perhaps some excuse for this charge. His images are often bewilderingly profuse: he slips, with a music which may lull the critical intelligence into inattention, from image to image, from metaphor to metaphor until, in terms of one of his favorite symbols, we ship our oars and float down the stream of sound. Yet upon the examination which the reader owes to good and difficult poetry, the images may prove to be as cunningly nested as Chinese boxes; or a series of metaphors is seen to be climaxed by a unifying line:

> *Even as a vapor fed with golden beams*
> *That ministered on sunlight, ere the west*
> *Eclipses it, was now that wondrous frame—*
> *No sense, no motion, no divinity—*
> *A fragile lute, on whose harmonious strings*
> *The breath of heaven did wander—a bright stream*
> *Once fed with many-voiced waves—a dream*
> *Of youth, which night and time have quenched for ever—*
> *Still, dark, and dry, and unremembered now.*

[23] Cf. Herbert J. C. Grierson, *Criticism and Creation* (London: Chatto & Windus, 1949), p. 118: "Virgil and Wordsworth were both poets of *pietas* in an age of revolution . . . . Wordsworth learned his reverence, his *pietas,* from intercourse with Nature."

It should be clear too that images that seem abstract are the result of his expressed intention to draw them from the operations of the human mind: an avalanche is like a great truth loosened in a heaven-defying mind; the sun is like "thought-winged Liberty"; it is the spirits that come from the mind of humankind who comfort Prometheus and celebrate the millennium. His belief in "life's unquiet dream"—that mutability is the law of life and that men know only the imperfect, unreal, half-seen forms of ideal beauty—is expressed and reflected by his repeated images of things that shift and change and of the light of eternity stained by life or half-hidden, imperfectly revealed, behind a veil:

> *Child of Light! thy limbs are burning*
> *Through the vest which seems to hide them;*
> *As the radiant lines of morning*
> *Through the clouds, ere they divide them;*
> *And this atmosphere divinest*
> *Shrouds thee wheresoe'er thou shinest.*

This is the kind of precision which exactly expresses an idea. Shelley is capable also of the precision resulting from accurate observation: the "azure moss" submerged in the "intenser day" of the blue Mediterranean; the swift departure of Mercury over the eastern horizon:

> *See where the child of Heaven, with winged feet,*
> *Runs down the slanted sunlight of the dawn.*

The precision of Wordsworth, who looked steadily at his subject, is rarely questioned, or that of Coleridge, or of Keats, or of Byron, who, as Keats said, described what he saw.

Of himself in contrast Keats said that he described what he imagined, meaning, of course, that he exercised that abstracting and modifying power which Wordsworth ascribed to the imagination. The concentration that results from this activity is rare in Byron's poetry (though he occasionally startles us as by the image of the "arches on arches" of the Coliseum, where "the stars twinkle through the loops of time") and he is said to have asked Shelley what Keats meant by "a beaker full of the warm South." It is frequent in Keats's best poems. The development of an image can sometimes be traced from the lax assembling of details in the first draft to the poetic fusion in the published lines: from, for example,

The Oaks stand charmed by the earnest stars

to

Tall oaks, branch-charmed by the earnest stars.

As Robert Bridges said, Keats had "the power of concentrating all the far-reaching resources of language on one point, so that a single and apparently effortless expression rejoices the aesthetic imagination at the moment when it is most expectant and exacting, and at the same time astonishes the intellect with a new aspect of truth." [24] Blake too knows the secret of creating the image that astonishes by its truth and rejoices by its fulfillment of aesthetic expectations and exactions:

> *And the hapless soldier's sigh*
> *Runs in blood down palace walls.*

These lines of Blake's show something of the range of Romantic imagery. Although many of the images of the period are drawn from what are commonly regarded as beautiful natural objects, they are by no means confined to bird songs and boughs breaking with honey-buds. Nature herself is not always beautiful: the dead wind stinks in Shelley's ruined garden. In the chartered streets of Blake's London are heard not only the soldier's sigh but the cries of the chimney-sweeper and the new-born infant, the curse of the harlot, the rumbling of the marriage-hearse. To these poets, as to those of other ages, the intellectual developments of the time furnished subject matter and images: new philosophical and psychological systems, innovations in social and political thinking, technological and scientific advances. As Lucretius used the atom, or Donne the compasses, or Tennyson the railroad, or our contemporaries the airplane or the bombsight, so Shelley, for example, that "Newton among poets," used electricity. E. L. Mayo, justifying his use of the bombsight as an image in a mid–twentieth-century poem, writes that how an A-bomb and a flying saucer

> are employed as imagery must depend on how we feel about them
> *now,* not on what the future holds. . . . In my 'The Pool,' for ex-
> ample, I allude to Leonardo's Madonna of the Rocks and comment:

[24] "John Keats, an Essay," quoted by   (London: Oxford   University   Press,
J. M. Murry, *Keats and Shakespeare*   1925), p. 10.

> *The rock she sits among*
> *Waits in a bombsight to be otherwise.*

The 'Bombsight' in this instance is a metonymy for the whole technology of modern war and its threat to human values. Few of us have seen a modern bombsight but most of us have heard, or read, of its uncanny, superhuman accuracy. That is, enough of us have a definite attitude toward it to make it accessible as poetic imagery.[25]

A hundred and fifty years ago Wordsworth wrote:

> The remotest discoveries of the Chemist, the Botanist, or Mineralogist, will be as proper objects of the Poet's art as any upon which it can be employed, if the time should ever come when these things shall be familiar to us, and the relations under which they are contemplated by the followers of these respective sciences shall be manifestly and palpably material to us as enjoying and suffering beings.

The imaginal structure of the best poems of the Romantic period is tight and balanced and unified. It is no mere series of exquisite, flashing images. The sustained and intricate metaphor of *On First Looking into Chapman's Homer* determines and is determined by the structure of the Petrarchan sonnet. The images of death (Death and his brother Sleep) in the *Ode to a Nightingale,* from the word *hemlock* in the first stanza to the word *buried* in the last, are interlocked with those of eternal life to culminate in the exaltation of the seventh stanza and be resolved in the fading uncertainty of the last. In *To a Skylark* images of the ascending bird and the overflowing, descending sound—the "rain of melody"—blend in the emotional identification of bird and poet. *The Solitary Reaper* is constructed on the contradictions in the girl's song which is both natural and mysterious, near and distant, symbolic of eternal beauty. The images of power and daring mount in *The Tiger* to a point where they explode in a heavenly cataclysm and return through the wondering contrast with the lamb to the slight modification of the first question. Often the images are symbols which hold the meaning of the poem: the light in Wordsworth's *Ode,* the unfinished sheepfold in his *Michael,* the albatross and the watersnakes in the *Ancient Mariner* —whether or not we accept them as symbols for Sara Coleridge and opium. These images fulfill the requirements of Keats's second axiom. They help the imagination to reveal itself in "the balance or reconcile-

---

[25] See John Ciardi (ed.), *Mid-Century American Poets,* (New York: Twayne, 1950), pp. 143–44.

ment of opposite or discordant qualities." Through arching movement and often paradoxical tension they build the organically unified poem.

There is also in these poems a unity of logical or narrative structure. Even the reflective poems like *Tintern Abbey* or *Frost at Midnight* move along a line of somewhat free association to a conclusion which echoes the beginning and completes the circle of the poem. The structure is as strict as that of many similar contemporary poems, such as *The Love Song of J. Alfred Prufrock*—and infinitely clearer to the reader. The *Ancient Mariner* has in its very narrative that fine circular movement which Coleridge himself compared to the symbol of unity and eternity, the snake with its tail in its mouth. The Mariner's voyage begins and ends in reality, which both surrounds and is penetrated by the mystery. The albatross closes each arc of the circle as it closes each division of the poem. Even the moral, I believe, is part of the dynamic circle.[26] Similar structure marks Keats's *Eve of St. Agnes*. Youth and love and warmth and quiet are set in a frame of age and hate and cold and noise. Yet there is no sharp demarcation: old Angela ministers to youth and love; the noise of the revelry penetrates Madeline's chamber; the sleet patters against her window panes. The quiet of Madeline's azure-lidded sleep in blanched linen is in contrast with that of the Beadsman's eternal sleep among his ashes cold. Her vespers balance his thousand aves. All is fused in a rich intricate pattern and is set in a verse form which has always seemed perfect for the "golden broideries" on the pages of "legends old." [27]

As Sir Herbert Grierson summarizes the Romantic theory of unity, "It is a harmony of all the elements, sensuous, intellectual, imaginative, none of which would be what it is apart from the others—diction, thought, imagery, rhythm, all are interdependent." [28] The Romantics—indeed all good poets—knew and acted upon the principle that Stephen Spender seems to have discovered, with some surprise, for himself, "that form

[26] See Elizabeth Nitchie, "The Moral of the *Ancient Mariner* Reconsidered," *PMLA*, Vol. XLVIII (1933).

[27] These comments on the imaginal and structural unity of Romantic poems are by no means entirely his own. See, for example, Cleanth Brooks, *The Well Wrought Urn* (1947); Richard Fogle, *Imagery in Keats and Shelley* (1949), as well as a number of his articles; M. R. Ridley, *Keats' Craftsmanship* (1935); J. M. Murry, "When Keats Discovered Homer," in *Essays and*

Studies in Keats (1930); Kenneth Burke, "Symbolic Action in a Poem by Keats," in *Accent*, Autumn, 1943; R. D. Havens, "Structure and Periodic Pattern in Shelley's Lyrics," *PMLA*, December, 1950; Frederick A. Pottle, "The Eye and the Object in the Poetry of Wordsworth," in *Wordsworth: Centenary Studies* (1951). For further titles, see *The English Romantic Poets. A Review of Research* (New York, 1956).

[28] *Criticism and Creation*, pp. 24–25.

does not lie simply in the correct observance of rules. It lies in the struggle of certain living material to achieve itself within a pattern." [29] By imposing artistic discipline upon their living material and enabling it so to achieve itself, these poets attained "the inward balance and fulness which was, to a larger extent than is commonly realized, the ultimate ideal of English romanticism." [30]

[29] *World within World* (New York: Harcourt, Brace, 1951), p. 284.

[30] Albert Gerard, *Essays and Studies,* I, 249.

A Note on Romantic Oppositions

2 | and Reconciliations

RICHARD HARTER FOGLE

ROMANTICISM IS undoubtedly susceptible of comprehensive, even universal definition. I am thinking of it here, however, as the creative impulse of the most considerable English poets—Wordsworth, Coleridge, Byron, Shelley, and Keats—of the late eighteenth and early nineteenth centuries. A compendious label for this impulse is "vitalist idealism"; if the label is a little forbidding, perhaps it may be allowed for the sake of its neat summing-up of apparently opposite notions. It suggests the difficulties which the Romantic is seeking to reconcile, and it implies the manner of the reconciliation itself.

Vitalist idealism infuses the world with life, and at the same time considers this life as divine and transcendent. Reality is both material and ideal. Taken separately, as the Romantic poet was forced and as we are still perhaps forced to take them, the material is sheer mass, meaningless and dead, while the ideal is a formless glimmer. The Romantic tried, however, to catch and hold them together in his imagination: to suffuse the material with meaning, to clothe the ideal with form. This is the purpose of Wordsworth's lines, which explains the apparent incompleteness of his comparison:

> . . . a sense sublime
> Of something far more deeply interfused,
> Whose dwelling is the light of setting suns,
> And the round ocean and the living air,
> And the blue sky, and in the mind of man . . . .

"Far more deeply interfused" than what? one would like to know. But the phrase expresses Wordsworth's imaginative struggle to realize as unity what can only be worded as a dualism of matter and spirit. The unfinished comparison is his expedient and device.

If "vitalist idealism" is an acceptable formula, the problems it raises still remain. It contains within itself more or less significant oppositions. Then, too, we need to bear in mind a truism which we strangely but persistently tend to forget: a poem is never identical with its informing idea or principle, since this idea is forced to submit to the test of artistic practice. The idea of life, with its corollary or organic relationship, is in itself too uncontrolled, while by itself the ideal promises too swift results, for either to be a sufficient cause for literary form. Likewise, a literary movement is not completely accounted for by any idea. It would be juster and certainly far more interesting to think of it as a reconciliation of opposites, which contains an idea and also the difficulties, the countercurrents which an idea has to face in either life or art, and without which, as a matter of fact, it would never be realized. For these reasons it seems politic to treat the work of the great English Romantics as a series of oppositions, all stemming from the single source of vitalist idealism. The prime reconciler of oppositions is as we all know the Romantic imagination.

In so brief an essay as this it seems pretentious to call attention to basic assumptions. I am about to take some liberties, however, which it is doubtless expedient as well as candid to point out. These liberties seem to me justifiable, but I would not force them unnoticed upon readers of different opinions from mine. Briefly, then, I am assuming that there is a body of doctrine common to the great English Romantic poets. Whatever the individual differences, the similarities predominate. Correspondingly, one man's terms will fit another man's theory and practice; Coleridge and Wordsworth do not make such play as Keats with Truth and Beauty, yet Truth and Beauty are perhaps the most appropriate single words to apply to the subject-object problems which preoccupy them.

Through the agency of poetic imagination, the Romantic poet reconciles the opposites of Beauty and Truth. The Beauty-Truth equation in turn has two aspects; in one the Truth acts as a check upon the daring of the imagination in its quest for the greatest imaginable beauty and potentiality, while in the other considerations of truth tend to disappear or be subsumed in pure aestheticism. Keats's "Beauty is Truth,

Truth Beauty," and his "What the imagination seizes as beauty must be truth" are of the second sort; beauty is empirically true because what is felt to be supremely valuable must be true. The result justifies itself. Keats is making a serious epistemological statement, arrived at by introspection and meditation. His conclusion is predominantly aesthetic, but it is backed by all his experience, and it is central to Romantic theory.

In the other formulation of Truth-Beauty, Truth is first conceived as the check of the actual upon imagination—a struggle in which the opposites are reconciled and interfused so that Truth finally becomes the agent through which Beauty is embodied in form. "The actual" here is generally external nature, and the check is faithfulness to its outline and detail. Thus Wordsworth's "I have at all times endeavored to look steadily at my subject"; and thus too his insistence upon "the necessity of producing immediate pleasure," since pleasure for the Romantic derives from the contemplation of objective beauty. The appropriateness at this point of the doctrine of "emotion recollected in tranquillity" would seem to be evident. Emotion and imagination are checked and modified by reflection upon their objects. C. M. Bowra comments upon the peculiar Romantic ability to achieve a world of the ideal from particular actuality:

> In their vivid perception of sensible things, they were able almost in the same moment to have a vision of another world, and this illuminates and gives significance to sensible things in such a way that we can hardly distinguish them from the mysteries which they have opened and with which they are inextricably connected. The result is that they shed a celestial light on the objects of sense and make them examples of something else much more wonderful.

Our excellent formalist critics have accepted the Romantic identification of Beauty and Truth, but have preferred to shift its terms to form and content, and to divest it of its psychological and metaphysical implications in the service of a strict poetics in which the work itself is absolute. Thus form and content are identical, and while in Keats Truth tends to be absorbed in Beauty, at present content tends to be lost in form. There is a difference, however. Keats applies the criterion of reality, and therefore, as with the other Romantics, Truth manages to retain its power and identity. For the pure formalist there is no reality outside the literary work, and therefore Truth (or content) vanishes.

Romantic poetry endeavors to lay bare the unusualness of the usual, and conversely the usual in the unusual. In either case the end is the same—to reveal the hidden, wondrous vitality of the world, obscured to us by deadening custom. This twin endeavor is the extension of the Beauty-Truth equation into more practical and limited criticism and poetics. "To find no contradiction in the union of old and new; to contemplate the ANCIENT of days and all his works with feelings as fresh, as if all had then sprang forth at the first creative fiat; characterizes the mind that feels the riddle of the world, and may help to unravel it." Wordsworth's and Coleridge's respective parts in the *Lyrical Ballads* represent the two versions of the union of usual and unusual. Wordsworth was "to give the charm of novelty to things of every day, and to excite a feeling analogous to the supernatural, by awakening the mind to the lethargy of custom, and directing it to the loveliness and the wonders of the world before us"; Coleridge, of course, was to deal with "persons and characters supernatural, or at least romantic; yet so as to transfer from our inward nature a human interest and a semblance of truth . . . ." Almost all of Wordsworth is of the first variety; *The Ancient Mariner, Christabel, Kubla Khan, The Eve of St. Agnes,* and *Lamia,* to offer the minimum of examples, are of the second. Again, Coleridge's "conversation poems," like *Frost at Midnight* and *The Eolian Harp,* are of the first sort. Shelley offers us both, and his "Poetry lifts the veil from the hidden beauty of the world, and makes familiar objects be as if they were not familiar," along with his observation that "We want the creative faculty to imagine that which we know," shows that he has the same end of uncovering hidden truth and beauty.

Both the Romantic equation of beauty-truth and the Romantic synthesis of usual and unusual are efforts to encompass *all* conceivable issues, which establish wholeness itself as a standard of excellence. This standard of plenitude is in accord with vitalist idealism—the metaphor of life leads to the conception of organic unity, itself a means of reconciling unity with the greatest conceivable diversity and fullness, while idealism produces the necessity of reconciling the material and ideal in an all-inclusive scheme. As a specifically literary theory the Romantic doctrine of wholeness emerges as *intensity.* Many contemporary critics are perhaps even more insistent than the Romantics upon the value of wholeness, but it appears in them as irony, identical in its components with intensity yet significantly different in its treatment of their relationships. The poetry of irony—T. S. Eliot's poetry of metaphysical wit, and I. A. Richards' poetry of inclusion—is "a poetry which does not leave out what is apparently hostile to its dominant tone, and which, because it is able to fuse the irrelevant and discordant, has come to terms with itself and is invulnerable to irony." Set against this Keats's "The excellence of every art is its intensity, capable of making all disagreeables evaporate, from their being in close relationship with Beauty and Truth." The same elements are present in both statements: "able to fuse the irrelevant and discordant" is very close to "capable of making all disagreeables evaporate." There is a difference, however. The first statement emphasizes the irrelevant and discordant elements which must be fused, the second the intensity which fuses them.

It is possible to fit the same poem or interpretation to either standard. The famous passage in Longinus on Sappho's Ode is in Romantic terms an affirmation of the standard of intensity: intensity of imaginative vision mirrored in intensity of technique, revealing the essential beneath the accidental. Allen Tate, on the other hand, has treated it as an exposition of the doctrine of irony: that is, as a reconciliation of opposites in which the opposites are more heavily stressed than the reconciliation.

The literary standard of irony is powerful because it represents a genuine contemporary attitude and problem. Very likely all contemporary literature must in a sense be ironical. Irony, however, is not necessarily the fullest conceivable attitude. One might argue, indeed, that Keats's "intensity" is not an avoidance but an acceptance of the discordant and irrelevant, and that it goes beyond irony by a superior power of unification.

From the Romantic conception of life, of organic unity, and of wholeness comes also the notion of continuity. Continuity, like organic unity, raises a fundamental problem, for it demands that a continuum be rendered accessible to discursive analysis without altering its nature (one may not murder to dissect), as if a river were to be cut into segments without disturbing its flow. Put otherwise, a continuum or organic whole is of itself unintelligible, but if it is subjected to analysis it dies. Wordsworth is confronted with the difficulty in the *Prelude* and in the *Ode on Intimations of Immortality*. The mind with its experience in time is an indivisible whole, in which no one event is really separable from the rest; the roots of the conscious lie deep in the unconscious; the child is father of the man beyond the capacity of memory to recall. Coleridge's conception of the mind as a unit, while his account of it depends upon separate faculties, might well appear an insoluble contradiction. But the solution, of course, lies in the imagination as reconciler of opposites; or, from another point of view, the transcendental reality for which imagination is the appointed organ of vision. Wordsworth does succeed in making intelligible the growth of a poet's mind, while also preserving the sense of its living unity and continuity; and Coleridge is able to do justice both to unit and faculties. W. H. Auden has placed the center of Romanticism in consciousness itself, with the artist the Romantic hero because of all beings his consciousness is most intense. Consciousness to the Romantics, as it is to the twentieth century, was a continuum of overlapping, inseparable images, ideas, events, feelings, and states of mind; but to the Romantic this complex organism had a center in the unity of the individual mind, which based itself in turn upon a transcendental unity. Thus the play of association in a Romantic poem, however apparently free and spontaneous, is always ordered by values beyond and above association itself.

Finally, the central Romantic metaphor of life extends itself into the antitheses of organic and mechanical unity, or the opposing visions of a living and a dead world, the world of imagination and the world of the isolated understanding:

> . . . *that inanimate cold world allowed*
> *To the poor loveless ever-anxious crowd* . . . .

This distinction is so nearly omnipresent in Romantic poetry and thought that it is unnecessary to illustrate it. It is fundamental to Coleridge and Wordsworth, and a starting assumption with the younger Romantics, including Byron. This distinction appears in three ways: as between two visions of reality, as between aesthetic theories of unity, and as between standards of literary value. In the first the living world, in which mass is given unity and meaning by a substance of ideal life, is opposed to the dead world of material ("all objects *as* objects are essentially dead"). The second distinction separates an inner organic unity from a unity external and superimposed, in which separate parts are arranged into order by an act of the intellect. In the first, the whole is more than the sum of its parts, in the second the whole *is* the sum of its parts. In the third version of the antithesis, which directly imports the first into literary judgment, the distinction is between the original and the derivative, Coleridge's distinction between imitation and copy, as old as Longinus on The Sublime. The original imitation catches the essential spirit and reclothes it in a novel and vital form; the copy achieves a superficial likeness, but totally misses essentials.

All three distinctions are powerfully operative in twentieth-century criticism and poetry. The wasteland or the modern city of T. S. Eliot is a dead world awaiting the revivifying touch of the spirit. The mythology and the symbolism of Yeats are expedients to transform a world in which nobility and significance are lost, as Blake envisions the fallen and petrified world of Urizen, which will become Jerusalem only after unceasing mental strife. Our present wide interest in myth is actuated by the same gloomy vision of the machine ("these dark Satanic mills") and the modern city, the basic units of modern society. We would escape them and return to our deep-covered vital origins.

Likewise, the notion of organic unity has perhaps never passed so current as now in aesthetic criticism. And the third aspect of the division is also present in our interesting attempt to reconcile a revolutionary spirit of experiment with a thoroughgoing traditionalism, which requires of the poet originality combined with knowledge of the past. There can never have been a greater scorn of the derivative, nor a greater respect for the traditional, than has been shown in English and American poetry since the rise of Eliot and Pound, both avowed anti-Romantics, yet nonetheless Romantic despite themselves.

3 | *Romanticism: Devil's Advocate*

HOXIE N. FAIRCHILD

REVALUATION OF English romantic literature as a whole implies the existence of a whole which can be revaluated; if no common denominator unites the particulars, there can be no hope of a valid generalization. I agree with those who find the taproot of romanticism in man's desire to feel independently good, strong, wise, and creative, his thirst for boundless expansion of being in a universe which echoes back to him his assertion of self-sufficient power. All the achievements and shortcomings of romanticism are direct or indirect manifestations of this ineradicable human impulse.

This familiar interpretation implies no hostile prejudgment of the case: it has proved no less acceptable to friends than to foes of romanticism. Indeed it renders impossible any unqualified condemnation of the Movement. A man totally devoid of the romantic impulse would be no man at all. Romanticism has contributed much to individual happiness, to social progress, to every sort of creative achievement. One may nevertheless argue that in the long run the drive of human self-trust produces more harm than good unless it is tempered by awareness of the aesthetic, social, and spiritual necessity of external limitation; that the Romantic Movement failed to achieve equilibrium; and that the twentieth century is desperately struggling to repair the consequences of this failure.

This brief discussion may fairly be confined to poetry, in which romanticism is seen at its purest and most successful. The culminating exploit of the romantic imagination is a universe in which God, man,

24

and nature, finite and infinite, objective and subjective are so completely interfused that no distinctions, negations, or limits oppose the outrush of desire. Romantic poetry exploits every possibility of human enlargement offered by this interfusion. It scrutinizes the present, revivifies the past, dreams about the future; it searches the depths of nature and the depths of the heart. Other contributors to this volume will emphasize the beneficial results of this enrichment and deepening of imaginative experience. The task of the Devil's Advocate is to show that these good things are bought at a heavy price.

To be romantic is to reject that finitude which is inherent in all pattern. The universe must always be in process of creation, but it must never be created: just as there must be no boundaries within it, so there must be no boundary around it. And this universe, though the poet wants everybody to live in it, must be completely individual and private, since to share the vision of other men is to limit one's own. Hence romantic poetry is seldom characterized by impersonality and architectonic largeness. Since the romantic artist is an artist as well as a romanticist he can usually impose aesthetic wholeness upon his lyrical responses to bits of emotional experience without overtly defying the law of lawlessness. When he essays a longer flight, however, he is torn between the desire to make a pattern and the desire to transcend limitation, producing a loose sequence of more or less effective parts rather than an integrated work of art.

If the true aim of these poets were to achieve delightful smallness, one would be wholly content to admire their attainment. What they yearn toward, on the contrary, is illimitable vastness. The ideal romantic poem would be the romantic universe itself. What the romantic poet accomplishes not merely falls below his aspiration but seems radically different from it. We may say that the famous lyrics are beautiful in themselves; but in relation to the ultimate romantic purpose they do not exist in themselves at all. They are delightful fragments of a pleasure-dome which the poet has not built in air, and which he could never build without stultifying his own insatiability. As the nineteenth century moves onward, the conflict between art and infinitude sets up an oscillation between pretty but meaningless craftsmanship and passionate but inchoate outcry. Romantic poetry expresses more beautifully than twentieth-century poetry the fitful and evanescent quality of modern man's emotional life. It seems illogical, however, to rebuke the contemporary chaos by glorifying the source of that chaos.

These poets have often been praised for establishing an "ennobling interchange" between the external world and the inward world of thought and feeling. It cannot be said, however, that we have lost this integration merely through our disloyalty to romantic insight, for in this respect also romanticism nourishes the seeds of its own dissolution. Influenced at first by the sentimental naturalism of the eighteenth century, the romanticist would like to assume, as an essential element of the universal interfusion, a harmonious relationship between the two parts of the Cartesian dichotomy. He soon discovers, however, that the world of eye and ear is not the partner of the romantic impulse but its deadly enemy. The poet then abandons any genuine attempt to establish the objective-subjective nexus and investigates merely himself, defining reality as the product of the imaginative will. The shift is not difficult, for he had never cared greatly about nature except as raw material for the feats of the esemplastic power. As early as Book III of *The Prelude* Wordsworth declares:

> . . . *Of Genius, Power,*
> *Creation and Divinity itself*
> *I have been speaking, for my theme has been*
> *What pass'd within me.*[1]

Withdrawing deeper and deeper into the stronghold of his inward uniqueness, the romantic widens the gap between himself and other men and between life and art. As he forgets the original gospel of "Come forth into the light of things," his images tend to become mere fabricated symbols of his subjective feelings. This rejection of reality in the interests of an illusion of creativity generates a naturalistic reaction which in turn produces either a dreamily neoromantic counterreaction or a vain attempt to externalize romantic feeling through incongruously naturalistic media. Eventually, then, the struggle to express the inexpressible by uniting the concrete particularity of descendentalism and the quasi-mystical vagueness of transcendentalism ends in defeat. The collapse of the "ennobling interchange," rendered inevitable by the passion for human infinitude, is largely responsible for the present-day medley of naturalism, symbolism, and post-impressionism.

Aesthetic criticism is inadequate for the revaluation of romantic poetry because the poet's own motives are so far from being purely aesthetic. The ideal romantic poet is a prophet with a passion for trans-

---

[1] *Prelude* (1805–6), III, 171–74.

forming the world. He is Los, the builder of Jerusalem and the eternal foe of Urizen. His highest office is not to compose verses but to dream the world of interfusion. Poetry is the appropriate but not completely adequate vehicle for conveying the vision to mankind. The vision must not merely be shown in images as a beautiful thing (the business of poetry) but must be argued out in propositions as a metaphysical or religious system (the business of rhetoric). Hence his poems are somewhat uneasily divided between aesthetic and didactic considerations. It is not surprising that the romantic tradition split under the pressure of Victorian problems, turning on the one hand toward overt preachment and on the other hand toward art-for-art's-sake.

In the Romantic period proper this disintegration is merely latent; the rhetoric is so passionate and melodious that it almost seems to be part of the poetry. At all events few of the present-day academic champions of romanticism are inclined to argue their case on strictly aesthetic grounds. They may analyze the images of this poem or that in a praiseworthy endeavor to confute the bigotry of the new criticism; but when they speak of the "beauty" of romantic poetry they are thinking chiefly of its spiritual and moral efficacy as a means of revivifying the desiccated ego of modern man.

Nowadays, however, it is dubious strategy to glorify the romantic poets solely as seers and mystics: they must also be honored at our MLA conventions for their "realism." Were they not precursors of the most advanced modern thought in substituting an organic for a mechanistic conception of science? Perhaps they were, but one feels that Professor Whitehead read a great deal between the lines when he found his own philosophy in their poems. The earlier Wordsworth based his "ennobling interchange" upon a very forward-looking reinterpretation of eighteenth-century psychology, but for reasons which have already been explained he soon fell back upon the transcendental doctrine that "The mind is lord and master" and in so doing bade farewell to science. Coleridge may well have been right in holding that intellectual energy is the *prius* of the physical universe, but when he identifies this energy with the imagination of the romantic poet he deprives science of one of its essential functions—that of enforcing belief in a real universe which imposes limits upon human self-will. One may grant all that scholars have said about electricity in *Prometheus Unbound* and the correct meteorology of *The Cloud* and yet insist that Shelley was as passionate a foe of the scientific spirit as ever lived.

Romanticized science becomes merely one more means of flattering that desire for independent human power which genuine science denies.

Nor are we justified in associating romanticism with any scientifically respectable conception of the doctrine of evolution. To most intelligent Victorians, Darwinism was repugnant not because it denied a literalistic interpretation of Genesis but because it denied the romantic view of nature and of man. Next to supernaturalistic religion, science is the chief obstacle to the lust for infinitude. Hence romanticism has thrown its weight on the antiscientific side of the cleavage between experimental and intuitional thinking which runs through the nineteenth century to our own day. It has fought science sometimes with sentimental anti-intellectualism, but more often with some variety of that transcendentalism which has created so disastrous a chasm between fact and vision. Unquestionably the writings and the lives of the romantic poets have enriched the documentary resources of psychology and psychiatry, but this does not mean that romanticism and science are firm friends.

There is less reason to question the common opinion that the Romantic Movement helped to establish that great liberalizing force, the historical outlook. But has this contribution proved an unmixed blessing? As early as 1874 the simon-pure liberal John Morley laments that the historical method has produced "a tendency . . . to make men shrink from importing anything like absolute quality into their propositions." Since, he continues, all truth is now regarded as relative to time, place, and circumstance, it seems rather absurd to insist that any idea is really true or false.[2] Romantics have found in historical relativism one more way of evading those restrictions which objective truth imposes upon their desire for boundlessness. If any real truth exists, it lies not in the past or present but in the ever-receding future; hence there is no danger of being cramped by it. All conclusion is limitation. One sees the romantic influence in the incapacity of modern liberalism to make up its mind about anything.

This does not imply that the romanticist is always a liberal in the sense of being an idealistic champion of democracy and humanitarianism. What he wants is personal enjoyment of the romantic experience; a man-centered benevolism is inevitably a self-centered benevolism. Since it

[2] John Morley, *On Compromise* (London, 1903), pp. 31, 32.

is easier for him to feel boundless in a free, fluid, individualistic society in which other men seem to mirror his own self-trust, he is usually attracted by liberal causes. But when such causes acquire a rationalistic, utilitarian, scientific tinge, he senses the threat to his infinitude; and even a liberalism purely sentimental and inconclusive cannot satisfy a desire which is doomed to frustration by the very terms of human existence.

The disillusioned romantic liberal may turn in almost any direction. His confidence may invert itself into cynicism or despair, or it may sink still further into a dull indifference to all higher values. He may find a feeble substitute for the romantic dream in occultist superstitions, or drink and drugs, or eccentricities of conduct. If he is a more titanic personality, he may try to regain the romantic illusion through an exaggerated and hysterical assertion of his personal lust for power; that is, he may seek to become a Carlylean hero, a Nietzschean superman, or a Fuehrer. Weaker spirits—the huge majority—will derive vicarious bigness from some tradition, theory, or personality which is bigger than they. No one will deny that the romantic spirit has sometimes furthered human freedom. It has also furthered *laissez-faire* competition, sentimental Toryism, nationalism, imperialism, racialism, and fascism. It is far too protean to be invoked as an ideal by those who would preserve and purify the democratic tradition.

On the whole, then, contemporary champions of romanticism are more impressive when they emphasize its spiritual rather than its realistic merits. Some influential veterans in this field of scholarship revere these poets as the inspired seers of a religion which is capable of solving the predicament of modern man. With less solemn piety, several younger scholars who think that what the world needs is more stallions admire the great romantics not because they are so "inspirational" but because they are so vital. Although perhaps they fall below Nietzsche and D. H. Lawrence as apostles of the life-force, they are rich in the desirable dark energy. The chasm between those who believe that man makes God and those who believe that God makes man is too wide to be bridged by argument, but the respective historical consequences of the two positions may be studied. The religious bearings of romanticism are described at length in the third volume of my *Religious Trends in English Poetry,* where abundant evidence forces me to conclude that the "genuinely religious aspirations" of the poets

are frustrated by their reluctance to believe in any force superior
to the force of their own genius. The divine universal interfusion is
merely the goal of their personal creativity. Nature, love, brotherhood, liberty, beauty—all the objects of their devotion—become so
many ways of expressing the spiritual sufficiency and independence
of man.[3]

For those who believe, as I do, that it takes the superhuman to keep the
human from becoming subhuman, this fact explains why even the
noblest fruits of romanticism are doomed to decay. (May I observe
parenthetically that the radical antihumanism of this position should prevent my opponents from describing me as a disciple of Irving Babbitt?)

But although the substitute religion of human self-sufficiency has
been severely battered by the twentieth century, many believe that the
future of civilization depends upon our ability to revive it. The fact that
it is diametrically opposed to Christianity will be irrelevant for those who
have either rejected Christianity or transformed it into an expression of
the romantic impulse. Has the twentieth-century chaos been produced by
our desertion of a *true* faith in independent human power, or by the
inevitable collapse of a *false* faith in such power? The answer, on which
our judgment of romanticism hinges, need not imply acceptance or
rejection of any fixed dogmatic assumptions. It demands only that we
make a rational choice between two antithetical readings of modern
history.

The twentieth century terribly needs to believe in the existence of
a real external world completely independent of human powers and
wishes; a world bristling with solid objective truths, not figments of our
thought, concerning religion, science, art, politics, and everything else.
This absolutism will, of course, be no less disastrous than the most
extravagant romanticism unless, believing that such truths exist, we
acknowledge that we can never be certain of what they are. We must
make up our minds if we are to survive, but we must not try to make up
the minds of others by any sort of coercive authority. There need
be no fear of totalitarianism among us if we grant that, although the
universe is absolutistic, man must be content to live in it pragmatically.
It is more dangerous to live absolutistically in a pragmatic universe.
The fact of human limitation is inescapable. If a man is not limited by
his belief in suprapersonal truth, he will be limited far less nobly by
his own passions and by those of his fellow-animals.

[3] *Religious Trends in English Poetry,* III (New York, 1949), p. 509.

Romanticism, being inherently man-centered and hostile to limitation, runs directly counter to these principles. Its spirit is summed up in Emerson's *Self-Reliance:*

> To believe your own thought, to believe that what is true for you in your private heart is true for all men,—that is genius. Speak your latent conviction, and it shall be the universal sense; for the inmost in due time becomes the outmost, and our first thought is rendered back to us by the trumpets of the Last Judgment.[4]

Those who hold, on the contrary, that the twentieth-century predicament is largely the result of man's attempt to subject the outmost to the inmost, find in the poetry of the English Romantic Period so many danger signals that they cannot regard it with the enthusiasm which its beauty and vitality would otherwise deserve. Emerson's man-made "trumpets of the Last Judgment" remind them of Shelley's West Wind, which solely "by the incantation of this verse" becomes "the trumpet of a prophecy"—a prophecy not of spring, but of the winter of our present discontent.

This antiromantic position is not inconsistent with admiration for all that is best in the romantic poets. They were much more than mere embodiments of a single *ism:* any complete treatment of their work should duly recognize its non-romantic values. Nor did they invent those tendencies which force us to distrust their ultimate influence. They represent the climactic phase in that rise and fall of human pride which constitutes the main theme of modern history. Splendidly expressing the most vital feelings of their age, they remind us that every sincere impulse of the mind deserves the noblest externalization that art can give it. And since the romantic aspiration will never vanish from our hearts, their poems remain permanently valuable in helping us to understand ourselves. These great poets should be regarded not with malice or scorn or rigid disapproval, but with the pity and fear which we experience in beholding some profound tragedy of hybris. But no—our relation to this tragedy is not that of spectators, for we ourselves are playing little parts in what may be the last act.

[4] Ralph Waldo Emerson, *Essays,* First Series (Boston, 1885), p. 47.

11: Wordsworth

Wordsworth:

4 The Mind's Excursive Power

JOSEPHINE MILES

WILLIAM WORDSWORTH gave poetry the power to generalize about human nature subtly and consistently. A century of poets before him had tried with all sorts of crudity of device. Desiring to speak of a general humanity, they had struggled with the appurtenances of its nobility, a lofty language, a cosmic simile, a heroic couplet, a basic psychological antithesis and balance, a sublimity of invocation and epithet. Everything got out of hand. It was either too laborious, as for Crabbe, or too elaborate, as for Blake; it rose out of sight or lay heavy and inert. Wordsworth and Coleridge undertook to remedy these extremes; Coleridge, by a deeper implication in metaphor and meter of the soaring soul; Wordsworth, by a serious refining of the literal and earthly. Wordsworth's was the force of consolidation; he gave not only hints toward a new realm as Coleridge did, but the fullness of a matured power to a familiar realm needing comprehension. All the stumblings of Addison and Akenside toward the achievement of psychological statement, all the gross niceties of Pope in his perception of complexity, all the shadings of Gray's exploration and the smoothness of Goldsmith's certainty came to win an eventual triumph in Wordsworth's articulation of their concern, the quality of human thought and feeling in the natural world.

Today poetry is working as it was in the eighteenth century, with a great deal of stiff effort and unease, toward the assimilation of consequences and the articulation of human concerns in an impressively large universe. It shares the difficulties of Pope and Thomson, the stifling amount of device to deal with a stifling amount of objects and

35

sensations, and it needs a Wordsworth of its own to be the generalizer and steadfast interpreter of its own terms.

This is the integral Wordsworth of *The Prelude,* the sonnets, *The Excursion,* the odes, from one end of his life to the other, the Wordsworth of faith as well as glee, the classicist in an effort toward a difficult synthesis of human perceptions. This is the Wordsworth whose particularity of ego and observation is turned to a poetry as general in abstraction as any we have, with its even proportions, its sustained contours of meditation, its vocabulary of emotional abstraction, its repeated patterns of association. Such poetry attempts to tell men about themselves, how they feel, how they arrive at moral judgments, as these feelings and judgments are common and shared. It appears early for Wordsworth, as in *The Borderers:*

> *Action is transitory—a step, a blow,*
> *The motion of a muscle—this way or that—*
> *'Tis done, and in the after-vacancy*
> *We wonder at ourselves like men betrayed:*
> *Suffering is permanent, obscure and dark,*
> *And shares the nature of infinity.*

It continues in the very beginning of *The Prelude:*

> *For I, methought, while the sweet breath of heaven*
> *Was blowing on my body, felt within*
> *A corresponding breeze that gently moved*
> *With quickening virtue, but is now become*
> *A tempest, a redundant energy,*
> *Vexing its own creation.*

And throughout *The Excursion:*

> *As the ample moon,*
> *In the deep stillness of a summer even*
> *Rising behind a thick and lofty grove,*
> *Burns, like an unconsuming fire of light,*
> *In the green tree; and, kindling on all sides*
> *Their leafy umbrage, turns the dusky veil*
> *Into a substance glorious as her own,*
> *Yea, with her own incorporated, by power*
> *Capacious and serene. Like power abides*
> *In man's celestial spirit; virtue thus*
> *Sets forth and magnifies herself; thus feeds*
> *A calm, a beautiful, and silent fire,*

From the encumbrances of mortal life,
From error, disappointment—nay, from guilt;
And sometimes, so relenting justice wills,
From palpable oppressions of despair.

And again in mid-1830's, *The Foregoing Subject Resumed:*

To a like salutary sense of awe
Or sacred wonder, growing with the power
Of meditation that attempts to weigh,
In faithful scales, things and their opposites,
Can thy enduring quiet gently raise
A household small and sensitive . . . .

This mode of speech and thought endures through all Wordsworth's experiments: through the ballad narratives, which *Tintern Abbey* encompasses, through the high originality of the Immortality ode, which later odes conventionalize, through the restrictive couplet and sonnet forms and orthodox feelings of the later years, in which the mind still ponders its security in delicately meditative iambic pentameters:

bees that soar for bloom,
High as the highest Peak of Furness-fells,
Will murmur by the hour in foxglove bells:
In truth the prison, unto which we doom
Ourselves, no prison is.

The confines of the steady and flexible pentameter, rhymed or unrhymed, and the steady literal analogy between nature and man, pressed Wordsworth to bring all his musings home to his own plot of ground. And the range of these musings was vast, through the processes of human thought and feeling, through the sympathetic powers of nature, through revolutionary force and social institution, through liberty, evil, justice, individuality, fear, death, and the horizons of mystery where he grew to see Heaven. He cannot now tell us what we want to know about these matters, for they are subjects, they have changed in context for us; but he can remind us how much we do want to know about them, from our own perspective but in his patiently meditative terms; with our own answers, but in his skillful and graceful modes of excursion. The poetry of a thinking process need not be limited to any one half-century, now that we have got it clear and can see the power of its workings.

This high seriousness which a century ago gave Wordsworth rank

with Chaucer, Shakespeare, and Milton, most of the critics of our own
century have tended merely to excuse him for, or not even to excuse
him for. We remember how hateful his style seemed to George Moore
and W. B. Yeats—a harping on generalization when pure objects would
do—and how to the Imagists he seemed a very model of mistaken
cosmic abstraction. Their stress on the image as an emotional complex
in an instant of time directly opposed Wordsworth's encouragement
of the tendency of perceptions to generalize themselves. Less specialized
critics today still try to ignore the mass of Wordsworth's work, the while
they give him credit for the fresh and natural particularity which he
helped to foster and which has become the major poetic substance of
our era. Herbert Read selects *The Solitary Reaper,* and George Rylands
a line like "These bright blue eggs together laid" as characteristic of the
best Wordsworthian style. F. R. Leavis and Helen Darbishire agree on
the supremacy of the brief lyric *A slumber did my spirit seal,* and in the
recent collection of centennial lectures on Wordsworth at Princeton
and Cornell this is the poem quoted by three of the lecturers:

> *No motion has she now, no force;*
> *She neither hears nor sees;*
> *Rolled round in earth's diurnal course*
> *With rocks, and stones, and trees.*

These are of course the terms, this the poetry, of our own era,
and therefore the selection of it may reflect us primarily, Wordsworth
only secondarily. Rocks and stones and trees—they draw their primacy
from our own great concreteness, which had only some of its tentative
beginnings in Wordsworth's work. Even Mark Van Doren, listening
for a "Noble Voice" finds nothing in poetry better than Wordsworth's
reality and fact of scenes; but fears that "the voice of the prophet is a different matter" (p. 313).

One should hesitate then to suggest that it is not only the special
modern part but also the traditional whole of Wordsworth that can be
important to us. One should not wish to deny the long dull stretches
of verse which the author of over fifty thousand lines is apt to write,
nor try to disregard the stiffening of forms and creeds which beset the
aging poet.

On the other hand, our own forms and creeds of objectivity and
particularity have aged and stiffened also, and tradition may recall to
us other modes of value. The small celandines to which Wordsworth

gave happy infancy we have outworn and outdone, but the structures
of deliberation to which he gave maturity we have yet to make our own.

I shall try to describe the Wordsworthian mode as specifically
as possible in brief space, in order to justify my sense of it in its power
for our day. The need is, first to recognize its basic materials, the terms
and structures of language in which it works. Second, to note the
temporal matrix of these materials. Third, to see how style shapes them,
how Wordsworth's habit of work in selection and arrangement gives
pattern and tone to them and conveys ideas through them. These three
questions imply an observation of all the poetry. They imply a kind
of neutrality, which may turn to partisanship if one favors the answers
he finds.

The basic importance to Wordsworth of the iambic pentameter
line is clear from its persistence in his work. Early, when he was still
reciting Gray and Goldsmith to himself, he tried not the freer meters
of Gray, but the more conventionally coupled pentameter, for his
own *Evening Walk* and *Sketches*. His first long narrative used the line
in stanza form; his first dramatic poem, in blank verse. Even before the
Lyrical Ballads grew famous, the early *Prelude* fragments and *Tintern
Abbey* itself showed the quick mastery of the sustained blank verse
motion. Marmaduke alone in the wood on the edge of the moor in Act
III of *The Borderers* says,

> *Deep, deep and vast, vast beyond human thought,*
> *Yet calm.—I could believe, that there was here*
> *The only quiet heart on earth. In terror,*
> *Remembered terror, there is peace and rest.*

And the beginning of *Tintern Abbey,*

>   *Once again*
> *Do I behold these steep and lofty cliffs,*
> *That on a wild secluded scene impress*
> *Thoughts of more deep seclusion; and connect*
> *The landscape with the quiet of the sky.*

These share the traits of sound-structure which Wordsworth was to
continue: an iambic beat strongly sustained under the surface variation,
as the alliteration of *Yet calm.—I could* strengthens what was not yet
established in *Deep, deep and vast;* a five-accented norm, breaking at
any point in the line, and easily run on, yet constantly bringing in a line

like "the landscape with the quiet of the sky," which, while not complete in itself grammatically, adds a phrasal poise to the pentameter; and finally a use of tonal rhyming which may be final as in couplet or stanza but is usually subordinate and often inward, as in the sounds of *remembered* and *rest* above, or in the hard *c* linkage of *connect* with *landscape, quiet,* and *sky.*

Prelude, Recluse, Excursion and later descriptions of tours led Wordsworth to develop blank verse as discursively as possible, to pause and rest and then go on again with impressions or arguments. Often in middle years he used couplet or sonnet rhyme for shaping, but not I think to any very different effect line by line. He wrote in 1832, for example,

> *Calm is the fragrant air, and loth to lose*
> *Day's grateful warmth, tho' moist with falling dews.*
> *Look for the stars, you'll say that there are none;*
> *Look up a second time, and, one by one,*
> *You mark them twinkling out with silvery light,*
> *And wonder how they could elude the sight!*

And in 1842 as prelude to his *Poems Chiefly of Early and Late Years,*

> *In desultory walk through orchard grounds,*
> *Or some deep chestnut grove, oft have I paused*
> *The while a Thrush, urged rather than restrained*
> *By gusts of vernal storm, attuned his song*
> *To his own genial instincts; . . .*

In both of these beginnings is the sort of phrasal stiffening which Darbishire and de Selincourt have vividly pointed out in the *Prelude* revisions, yet both keep too the direct and personal forward motion of the earliest pentameters.

Except for a few unsustained experiments with longer lines, or longer feet, Wordsworth's two serious experiments outside pentameter were the tetrameters of the ballads, with their abrupt obvious rhyming, and the free improvisations of the Immortality Ode. Both of these have a sort of magic which he could not later manage: in the first, a literalness of downright measure, in the second a tenuosity and flexibility, both of which were extremes perhaps inspired by Coleridge or extremes of youth and rebellion and unsettled skill. At any rate, by 1802 Wordsworth tried and was resigned to the confines of the sonnet, which he had once disdained, and from then on in his least excursive pieces his prevailing pentameter took this shapely form, a tonal pattern within predictable structure.

His prevailing sentence structure may best be noted in such a form, where progress from beginning to end is visible upon one page. One may remember how the early poems begin with the statement that a traveler sets forth, and then list items which he sees. The Ballads are similarly declarative: I met a girl . . . I have a boy . . . There is a Thorn . . . Her eyes are wild . . . It is the first mild day of March . . . In distant countries have I been . . . 'Tis eight oclock . . . Five years have passed . . . These are the declarative beginnings, and the conclusions, drawn out of carefully observed and listed instances, are exclamations of moral significance. *The Old Cumberland Beggar* is a good example, beginning, "I saw an aged Beggar in my walk;/ And he was seated, by the highway side, / On a low structure of rude masonry," proceeding through his observations as a traveler to people's view of him and a general analysis of his social and moral status, to the concluding exclamation, "As in the eye of Nature he has lived,/ So in the eye of Nature let him die!" In a sonnet the whole process is concentrated, sometimes to be sure in reverse, from judgment to descriptive statement, but more often in order like *The River Duddon*, V:

> *Sole listener, Duddon! to the breeze that played*
> *With thy clear voice, I caught the fitful sound*
> *Wafted o'er sullen moss and craggy mound—*
> *Unfruitful solitudes, that seemed to upbraid*
> *The sun in heaven!—but now, to form a shade*
> *For Thee, green alders have together wound*
> *Their foliage; ashes flung their arms around;*
> *And birch-trees risen in silver colonnade.*
> *And thou hast also tempted here to rise,*
> *'Mid sheltering pines, this Cottage rude and grey;*
> *Whose ruddy children, by the mother's eyes*
> *Carelessly watched, sport through the summer day,*
> *Thy pleased associates:—light as endless May*
> *On infant bosoms lonely Nature lies.*

This is the normal structure of statement for Wordsworth early and late—the interconnection of particular declarative statement and of phrasal and clausal series with a framing general declaration or exclamation, and, especially in later years, an accompanying invocation.

Such a pattern makes for a classical proportioning of terms, a balance between adjectives and verbs, qualities and actions, and a moderate subordination of verbs to substantives. Wordsworth thought, in other words, not complexly as metaphysical poets would, nor yet fully descriptively as Milton or Keats would, but rather discursively, drawing a constant statement from quality and quality from statement. Even in the *Lyrical Ballads,* for which the sources and models showed a great stress on action, which Coleridge adopted, Wordsworth mildly persisted in his own standard eighteenth-century proportioning of ten adjectives to sixteen nouns to ten verbs in ten lines, a proportion which he maintained closely in such various work as the 1806 and 1807 poems, *The Prelude,* and the poems of his last decade, increasing substantives a little, especially adjectives as in the Duddon sonnets where description was central. So we see the arrangement in the poem above: the nouns of *river, breeze, sounds, solitudes, sun, shade* and kinds of *trees,* moving to *cottage, children,* associates and Nature, while the verbs stress interconnection in *played, caught, seemed, flung, risen, sport, lies,* and the adjectives, *sole, clear, fitful, sullen, green, silver, sheltering, pleased, light, lonely,* do the work of interpretation by the setting of emotional atmosphere and responsiveness.

Wordsworth's major terms, like his sound and sentence patterns, work steadily throughout his poetry. The Duddon terms suggest their quality: adjectives of emotional atmosphere, nouns of scene and concept, verbs of spatial motion and connection. *See* is the primary action, with *look* and *hear* and *come* and *feel* and *die* and *love,* also, verbs of responsiveness. And the common nouns make human generalization— *man, life, love, heart, thought, eye, mind, hand, hope, soul, spirit, joy,* along with outer *day, nature, earth, heaven, light, power, time,* and the most clearly objective *mountain.* While they describe, in *bright, deep, high, old, little, long,* the adjectives also evaluate, in *good, dear, poor,* and *sweet.* In the combination of these terms, used more than any others, except of course the common particles and auxiliaries, all through Wordsworth's poetic lifetime, we can sense even in abstraction from context the special quality of his thought—his concern with the process of the reception and interpretation of sensation by feeling, in verbs of perception, in adjectives of size, scope, age, and affection, and in nouns of bodily and emotional sense combined with concept and atmosphere.

The differences as well as likenesses between early and late years are reflected in vocabulary stress. The Ballads used *cold* and *warm, trees* and *woods, praying* and *weeping* more than they were to be later used. The Ballads were, that is, more specifically objective, though they also introduced most of the major later sorts of terms, like *little* and *old* and *love* and *joy* and *mountain, sun, thought, spirit.* The materials of the 1806 poems, the sonnets of 1820, and the poems of the last decade differed mainly in small details—the increase of interpretive terms like *calm, divine, happy, silent,* the increase and return of *prayer* and *spirit,* the addition of *child* and *mother, fear* and *faith, sea* and *star,* as particularizations of earlier observations and relationships in a more stabilized state of mind.

In all these ways, in all these materials of language, its reference, sound, and statement structure, Wordsworth worked along with other poets of his time. He shared a common substance, a common selectivity and sense of style. We may see, for example, that the poets of the 1790's were like him in trying ballad measures but remaining faithful in the main to pentameters; that they tried very hard for an objective sort of tracing of objects and dispositions, in declarative statement; that they used abundantly a vocabulary of attitude, and tentatively one of observation. Burns, Campbell, Rogers, Southey, and others were stronger for epithets like *sad* and *weary* than Wordsworth was, more for eighteenth-century *friend, scene, tears, sorrow, virtue, crying* and *mourning,* but quicker, on the other hand, to take up emphases he would later adopt, like those on *mother* and *child, mountain, sea,* and *spirit.* Their proportionings were balanced like his, their modes seriously devoted to explication and understanding of man in his situation.

Changed as matters were by his last decade of poetry, with Tennyson, Browning, Arnold, and Clough, the mode Wordsworth wrote in was still maintained. As he had differed from his early associates in concreteness and affirmation, *green trees* and *joy,* he differed from the late in the abstractness of the affirmation, in *faith* and *truth, calm, silent,* and *divine;* yet the basic pattern of abstract and concrete terms did not, in the fifty years, greatly alter. It was rather the mode of sound and statement which altered for Tennyson, Poe, Clough and the younger poets, away from Wordsworthian declaration toward implication and symbolizing, and away from Wordsworthian flexibility within the pentameter and the iambic, to much more experimentation like Coleridge's, with implicative timing in metrical feet. In other words, by 1850 poetry had moved farther from its Laureate in its measures than in its references; it was still deeply concerned with the statement of human sensitivity to atmosphere, though by odd syllables and phrases it was trying to temper the downrightness of such statement. Later, the general human terms themselves grew suspect, and an increasingly concrete vocabulary enforced the other forms of implication in poetry.

No wonder then that today critics praise the most modern Wordsworth of the "bright blue eggs" and the "single stone" and the "reflex of a star." Indeed he was one of the first to foster such detail and suffered at the hands of his own contemporary critics for such fostering. It seems just that what he was most blamed for he be now admired for. The course of poetic history has moved steadily toward more and more implicative references, measures, and sentence structures, and Wordsworth's has been part of that progress. He prepared, as Cowper and Campbell did, for the flexible pentameters of a Shelley and a Browning, and, as Blake and Burns did, for the significant concreteness of a Keats and a Tennyson. But we lose him if we bring him down all this way in terms of what he has given us that we have used and approved. Central to his own style is what he used and approved from his own eighteenth century, what he perfected as well as what he invented. And what he perfected we have a chance to learn again; not the diverse particularity of images which, as in *Ossian,* he abhorred as "isolated," but the continuities and connections of perception, the wise passiveness, the smooth and steady assertion.

The complex of Wordsworth's materials was not a radical but a traditional one: terms of human feeling and thought allied to sense; meters outwardly regular, inwardly toned and shaded in the manner of his day; structures exclamatory yet deliberative. All were familiar enough so that he could assume and thus simplify them, let them work directly and literally, as his beliefs allowed. Most were opposed to the particular, irregular, presentative, figurative materials of present day poetry: they were general, regular, discursive, literal; their effect of literalness was Wordsworth's especial contribution. Whereas the modern poet feels the need to invent and struggle with connections in tension and irony, Wordsworth had only, against the equal struggles of his predecessors, to observe and declare them in the synthesis of imagination.

Wordsworth himself has clearly set forth in Prefaces, Supplements, and Essays the description of his style, and a few fragments of quotation may serve to recall the tenor of his well-known argument. He wanted to deal with "manners connected with the permanent objects of nature and partaking of the simplicity of those objects" (*Early Letters,* p. 221). He wanted to increase our knowledge of human nature "by shewing that our best qualities are possessed by men whom we are too apt to consider, not with reference to points in which they resemble us, but to those in which they manifestly differ from us" (*Early Letters,* p. 260); he was more interested in likeness than distinction. "There is scarcely one of my Poems which does not aim to direct the attention to some moral sentiment, or to some general principle, or law of thought, or of our intellectual constitution" (*Middle Letters,* p. 128–29). ". . . I have endeavoured to dwell with truth upon those points of human nature in which all men resemble each other, rather than on those accidents of manners and character produced by times and circumstances . . ." (*Later Letters,* p 127). And, ". . . our business is not so much with objects as with the law under which they are contemplated" (*Later Letters,* p. 184).

These beliefs and intentions made for the special relation of observation to generalization which was Wordsworth's own. In his note on the early *Evening Walk,* he reports his "consciousness of the infinite variety of natural appearances which had been unnoticed by the poets of any age or country, so far as I was acquainted with them." He states of the poem, "There is not an image in it which I have not observed"; yet he states also that "the plan of it has not been confined to a particular walk or an individual place,—a proof (of which I was unconscious at the time) of my unwillingness to submit the poetic spirit to the chains of fact and real circumstance." In the note to a much later poem, *This Lawn A Carpet* (1829), he develops the stress on the combination, on the need for fact as well as generality: "Admiration and love, to which all knowledge truly vital must tend, are felt by men of real genius in proportion as their discoveries in natural Philosophy are enlarged; and the beauty in form of a plant or an animal is not made less but more apparent as a whole by more accurate insight into its constituent proportions and powers." So Wordsworth articulates the tendencies of his era, to know more facts, and to draw wider inferences from them, and above all to feel more deeply with and about them, directly and explicitly. Truth is available to human perception.

Such an attitude, such a sense of straightforward poetic power, gives us no hint of that fictionalizing which for many throughout history had been the essence of poetry. Aristotle named metaphor as the key creative device of poetic style: Wordsworth says almost nothing about metaphor except to warn against some sorts like personification. Genre and device proper to genre have little meaning for him; one notes that he makes his own groupings of poems in his own terms, the sorts of affections they deal with. And one notes that his recurrent names for the parts of poetizing, assuming some metrical form, are "thought, feeling, image"— the names not of device but of subject, in terms of human response. The image, a record of sight, sound, or impression; the feeling, an emotional association; the thought, a resultant influential complex—these are the general human, and thus the poetic essences for Wordsworth. Therefore the devices of trope, generic propriety, metrical irony, and so on, though present in his verse by long convention, are secondary, often as if accidental, and not usually even essential to the frame of the whole.

Consider as an example of such characteristic directness the poem *Written in Very Early Youth,* so much like what Wordsworth would write all his life:

> *Calm is all nature as a resting wheel.*
> *The kine are couched upon the dewy grass;*
> *The horse alone, seen dimly as I pass,*
> *Is cropping audibly his later meal:*
> *Dark is the ground; a slumber seems to steal*
> *O'er vale, and mountain, and the starless sky.*
> *Now, in this blank of things, a harmony,*
> *Home-felt, and home-created, comes to heal*
> *That grief for which the senses still supply*
> *Fresh food; for only then, when memory*
> *Is hushed, am I at rest. My Friends! restrain*
> *Those busy cares that would allay my pain;*
> *Oh! leave me to myself, nor let me feel*
> *The officious touch that makes me droop again.*

The theme here is the need for human harmony with the calmness of nature; it is conveyed directly through all the major substance, the selection and spread of natural examples in the octave, the threat of the obverse in the sestet, and the human response in *heal* and *rest.* Is there essential trope? Not the odd *wheel,* which moves no further, nor the *food,* which works very abstractly. Rather, the concept which lies behind the description, not as poetic ornament at all, but as belief. "Now, in this blank of things, a harmony / Home-felt, and home-created, comes to heal" we may take as figurative language in terms of our belief, but for Wordsworth it was a direct reporting of how he felt, how sensitive human beings would feel, in such a situation. "Blank" means "blank for him," and "to heal" is literal. As he says explicitly, objects should be reported not as they are but as they seem (*Prose* II, 226; 1815), and it is the seeming that is literally reported.

In one sense then, one could call Wordsworth's poetry a single vast metaphor of natural-human-divine harmony in terms of *breath, stream, spirit, power, flow, feeling, love, soul, light.* The primary terms of receptive emotion and descriptive concept work together toward this metaphor, and it infuses every single poem. For this very reason of pervasiveness, however, it is not to be taken as a literary device but rather as a philosophical view, a conditioning of reality as the statement "The sun rises in the east" is a conditioning. Within this frame, Wordsworth's literalness magnificently operates. His by-the-way figurativeness seems controlled, more accidental and unintegrated with the whole of the imagery, as is the "wheel" above, or nature as both "anchor" and "nurse" in one line of *Tintern Abbey.* Few poems are as thoroughly worked out in figures as "Hopes, what are they?—Beads of morning" in the 1818 *Inscriptions.* Few on the other hand are as objectively descriptive, without spiritual interfusion, as the *Water-Fowl* of 1812. Most make a literal general study of reflection like the poem of *Early Youth,* and like the late Tours, or, in between, *The Prelude* with its great unfinished work, and such small characteristic pieces as *My Heart Leaps Up* and the poems on flowers. Thus directly Wordsworth thought art should function, as he wrote in 1811, *Upon the Sight of a Beautiful Picture:*

> *Praised be the Art whose subtle power could stay*
> *Yon cloud, and fix it in that glorious shape;*
> *Nor would permit the thin smoke to escape,*
> *Nor those bright sunbeams to forsake the day;*
> *Which stopped that band of travellers on their way,*
> *Ere they were lost within the shady wood;*
> *And showed the Bark upon the glassy flood*
> *For ever anchored in her sheltering bay.*
> *Soul-soothing Art! whom Morning, Noontide, Even,*
> *Do serve with all their changeful pageantry;*
> *Thou, with ambition modest yet sublime,*
> *Here, for the sight of mortal man, hast given*
> *To one brief moment caught from fleeting time*
> *The appropriate calm of blest eternity.*

Thus art symbolizes, by preserving the timeless moment, and symbol like metaphor is, for Wordsworth, implied in the whole structure of the relation of time to eternity, not a literary device to be used in the indirection of idea.

It has often been said, and my own studies of statement of feeling have shown in one set of materials at least, that Wordsworth became in later years more fond of art, more "literary," and therefore more explicitly a user of figure and symbol as modes of statement. It is true that his later work used less of fine original abstraction and more of the personification, metaphysical metaphor which he had at first mistrusted, and that some of the result seemed mechanical rather than natural. But such poems as *Papal Abuses* or *Mutability* from the *Ecclesiastical Sonnets* should remind us of the power Wordsworth sometimes gained from such artfulness, his ability to subordinate a rich trope to lofty statement. The last River Duddon poem may serve as example:

> *I thought of Thee, my partner and my guide,*
> *As being past away.—Vain sympathies!*
> *For, backward, Duddon, as I cast my eyes,*
> *I see what was, and is, and will abide;*
> *Still glides the Stream, and shall forever glide;*
> *The Form remains, the Function never dies ;*
> *While we, the brave, the mighty, and the wise,*
> *We Men, who in our morn of youth defied*
> *The elements, must vanish;—be it so!*
> *Enough, if something from our hands have power*
> *To live, and act, and serve the future hour;*
> *And if, as toward the silent tomb we go,*
> *Through love, through hope, and faith's transcendent dower,*
> *We feel that we are greater than we know.*

The form and function, the morning of youth and transcendent dower, all are absorbed into the imagery of transcience and persistence and into the cumulative abstraction of the ending.

Wordsworth offers us then a style of poetry to which modern poets are unaccustomed. In the hundred years since his laureateship, endings have become concrete and implicative, exclamations have been subdued, the human situation has become an instant of time, image has become symbol, and explication has become antipoetic. Nevertheless it seems to me possible to admire Wordsworth's complex in its own nineteenth century terms, the explicit association of natural particularity with general human truth in a meditative pentameter and a vocabulary of pleasure. Wordsworth had his own version of this complex, more subtle, more understated, more "silent" as Miss Darbishire and others have made plain, at once joyful and calm, and steadily more direct than either the pedestrians from Campbell to Lowell or the inventors from Blake to Poe would have cared to manage. This deliberation we have turned away from we may well turn back to, though at the moment few of Wordsworth's key terms or measures are primary for us, except perhaps the abstract *truth* and *mind* of a few didactic poets like Auden; an echo of smooth metrics; and the enduring idea of humanity.

Probably in the realm of idea we must most question Wordsworth's import for us. As his recent critics have pointed out, he has a very great deal to say about nature, a deal of description, attribution, and personification, to which we are numb. What he has worked out to tell us, we have long learned and do not want to know. Grant, if we may, the possible renewal of his familiarly literal and explicative style, we must ask what attitude or theme of value can be conveyed through such a style. We tend to favor irony as attitude and conflict as theme and drama as mode. Wordsworth said rather that the poet might well be predominant over the dramatist. ". . . then let him see if there are no victories in the world of spirit, no changes, no commotions, no revolutions there, no fluxes and refluxes of the thoughts which may be made interesting by modest combination with the stiller actions of the bodily frame . . ." (*Middle Letters*, p. 198).

And here he provides us with themes we can use philosophically as well as dramatically, downrightly as well as ironically—the victories, changes, commotions, revolutions in the world of spirit. Our Nature need not be his and cannot be his, but our human nature has still its commotions and victories, about which we in our poetry are as yet deeply unlearned. Miss Darbishire and others have told us that "belief in the greatness of the human mind is at the very center of Wordsworth's thought" (*The Poet Wordsworth*, p. 139), and indeed this is what the sympathetic reviews were saying in the early decades (for example, *Blackwood's* in 1822; cf. Smith, p. 344). It is a belief we may well accept. The powers of sense, reason, intuition—as *The Excursion* says—of hope, faith, and love—are powers still our concern, as are equally the early themes of revolution, the late of institution, and the whole of science.

Relationship is what matters for Wordsworth, and in this theme he is our kin. But we are still tentative and oblique about the relationships we celebrate, and are not to be hurried. Douglas Bush thinks that because Wordsworth's prophecy for science has not come true it will not. But it seems to me the very future toward which we move, the "if" of the second Preface: "If the time should ever come when what is now called science, thus familiarised to men, shall be ready to put on, as it were, a form of flesh and blood, the Poet will lend his divine spirit to aid the transfiguration and will welcome the Being thus produced, as a dear and genuine inmate of the household of man." This domesticity does not seem to me too explicit for us, nor too plain in sentiment.

As for politics, there the poetic again can make good sense, ecclesiastical and civil, and the exclamatory literal pentameter say what needs ever directly to be said:

> *Toussaint, the most unhappy man of men!*
> *Whether the whistling Rustic tend his plough*
> *Within thy hearing, or thy head be now*
> *Pillowed in some deep dungeon's earless den;—*
> *O miserable Chieftain! where and when*
> *Wilt thou find patience? yet die not; do thou*
> *Wear rather in thy bonds a cheerful brow:*
> *Though fallen thyself, never to rise again,*
> *Live, and take comfort. Thou hast left behind*
> *Powers that will work for thee; earth, air, and skies;*
> *There's not a breathing of the common wind*
> *That will forget thee; thou hast great allies;*
> *Thy friends are exultations, agonies,*
> *And love, and man's unconquerable mind.*

Such a theme may prevail not only for the individual psychology of *The Prelude* and the sober institutionalizing of the mid-century sonnets, but for twentieth-century poetry to come.

As for the art, that we come back to as the be-all of what the poet has to tell—it is for Wordsworth, as he has said, a force for preserving and making serene what knowledge of life might otherwise be rough, transitory, and obscure. "Language, if it do not uphold, and feed, and leave in quiet, like the power of gravitation or the air we breathe, is a counter-spirit, unremittingly and noiselessly at work, to subvert, to lay waste, to vitiate, and to dissolve" (*Essay on Epitaphs*).

The art for Wordsworth speaks in sentence and line, in culminating phrase, in harmony of accent, and in literal statement, "sympathy with man's substantial griefs," "a blazing intellectual deity," "the dignities of plain occurrence," and "clear guidance . . . to the mind's excursive power." These in their accord of accent, emphasis, and understanding represent the aimed-for power of language which should uphold, and feed, and leave in quiet. Not variety of tone, complexity of structure, brilliance of metaphor are primary to his art, but rather the process which leads to concord of thoughts, feelings, images, the process which made all the poems one poem.

The power of the Wordsworthian mode for our day is the mind's excursive power, the change and commotion in the world of spirit. In its harmonious regularity and cumulative stress it demands meditation; in its accords, sympathy; in its literalness, a steady observation. All these are difficult for us. An age of symbol, passion, and irony is not much good at a common view or a general concern or even a strong abstract statement in a determined meter. But we can learn. And Wordsworth's can be the poetry not only from which, but toward which, we proceed.

Wordsworth and the

5 | ## Quality of Man

NEWTON P. STALLKNECHT

FOR MANY of his readers, the Wordsworth of *The Prelude* clearly deserves a place "first by the throne" in the ideology of our century. In the English-speaking world of today, Wordsworth might be thought to stand as a long acknowledged "legislator of mankind," whose many programs and ideals, although now perhaps commonplace through their familiarity, are almost everywhere respected and, indeed, often carried into practice. This is true of all the causes which the younger Wordsworth so thoughtfully espoused and so eloquently defended. It is true of his contributions to the theory and practice of the poet's art, of his political convictions, and even of his views on education. Thus, we may ask, should we not turn to Wordsworth in gratitude and in reverence as Wordsworth himself turned to Milton, recognizing him as an author and champion of our ways of art, of thought, and of life? The fault may seem ours if we do not do so with a generous enthusiasm comparable to Wordsworth's own.

The situation is complicated, however, and our attitude toward Wordsworth is confused by the very wealth of his contribution. Thus, today some students fail to emphasize our debt to Wordsworth's political liberalism and to his humanitarian ideals. This is because they think of him—in marked contrast with such liberal theorists as Locke and Jefferson—as essentially a mystical pantheist, the prophet of a natural religion, which they often consider out of place upon the stage of modern thought. They have perhaps grown too accustomed to a sophisticated liberalism founded upon a very cautious, almost a skeptical, philosophy, that surveys with a weary and suspicious, albeit an urbane, toleration the many grounds of contention, moral, religious, or economic, which prevent or delay the effective unity of our civilization. Wordsworth's liberalism is not of this sort. It contains no irony and no contempt, and it is rooted in convictions far more intense than those with which the *philosophe* is acquainted.

> . . . *in the People was my trust*
> *And in the virtues which mine eyes had seen.*

Indeed, Wordsworth inspired by recognition of the "godhead which is ours" founded his belief upon something firmer than an open mind and a generous willingness to compromise. These latter virtues were most welcome in the Europe that had painfully survived the Thirty Years War and the English Revolution; but they are by themselves hardly sufficient as a foundation for a social progress involving the profound transformations to which the sincere liberal looks forward. A natural religion such as Wordsworth's may serve, along with Christianity itself, as a source and as an enduring support of humanitarian liberalism. Since Wordsworth's time, we have learned to our cost that such support is indispensable.

But there are those who would prefer to ignore this, feeling that Wordsworth's world view is too irrational, too "unscientific," to be of much aid in establishing an ethics of democracy. Then again, even those who find more in Wordsworth's vision than mere sentimentalism are inclined to think of his natural religion as an unusual insight open only to a few rarely gifted people, whose ideas can hardly be expected to influence a large public or to establish and cogently defend a way of life.

Such criticism, which could also be directed toward much of Christian thought, is after all, the last shadow of the rather brittle materialism of the late nineteenth century, and there are signs that Wordsworth's contribution is becoming more at home in recent thinking than it was, say, fifty or sixty years ago. We may even argue today that Wordsworth's contribution, direct and indirect, to modern thought is a powerful one and that it is actually furthering the very ideals which he cherished and is indeed still capable of advancing them. Today we feel as acutely as in Wordsworth's time the need of a positive, rather than a positivist or skeptical, philosophy of democracy. This philosophy has not yet been formulated in any finally systematic way and thus any statement concerning its possible origins must be recognized as speculative. Yet Wordsworth's *Prelude* may someday be seen as standing, not the least important, among the sources of democratic thought and feeling. Here Wordsworth will appear more moving than Locke, more modest and sober than Shelley or Rousseau, more comprehensive than Emerson, and more scholarly than Whitman. I believe that something of this influence is already felt and recognized by people who do not find it necessary to apologize for the natural religion from which Wordsworth's contributions spring.

In defending this position, it will be necessary to distinguish between those utterances of Wordsworth's which are philosophically radical in orientation and those which, although equally Wordsworthian in origin, fall into a more conventional mode of expression. We must remember that Wordsworth's thought is primarily a naturalism, and the fact that nature is interpreted in idealist or panpsychist terms does not alter this. The supranatural is out of place in Wordsworth and when, at times, he plays with supranatural concepts he fails to do full justice to his profoundest insights. Thus, we must recognize that much of the doctrine of *The Excursion* and some of that of *The Prelude* takes on a neo-Platonic aspect, traditionally conventional in that it involves reference to an order of being which is thought to transcend space and time, a supranatural reality, opposed to the obvious appearances of things.

This dualism of natural and supranatural must be contrasted with other utterances more original in mode of expression and less doctrinaire which have appealed strongly to some twentieth-century thinkers. In certain passages, as often in *The Prelude,* and in *The Recluse* fragment, the imagery opens to us an interpretation of nature and of man's place in nature that avoids any appeal to the supranatural. Here God, man, and nature, are seen together as interpenetrating features of one universal life. Wordsworth's chief strength lies in that his greatest verse heightens our sense of community with nature and humanity and thus offers a compelling motivation of democratic loyalties, making other ways of thought seem shabby, even inhuman, by contrast. The consequences of this insight are important and have not been exhausted today.

In this, his happiest mood, Wordsworth finds the ultimate truths immediately at hand and "nearer" to us than the distorted or oversimplified schemes of a pragmatic common sense, based on use and wont.

Thus, Wordsworth seeks to eliminate the supranatural—unless perhaps we should reserve this term to describe the "shades of the prison house" —and to emphasize as the source of our existence and the matrix of all human values the "one life within us and abroad," which is identical with nature.

Such emphasis upon a "life of things," obvious to all of us who will look for it, has led some students of Wordsworth to think of him as an empiricist or a philosopher of experience and to suggest that his attitude is essentially that of the British sensationalists. But for Wordsworth, human experience is not a composite of sensations and associations. It is something very different upon which both sensuous observation and rational insight are founded.

Before turning to these central questions, let us consider an adverse criticism of Wordsworthian philosophy: namely, that his view of nature is a figment of sentimental escapism. On the contrary, we may argue that the insight shared by Wordsworth and Coleridge into that "one life within us and abroad" is compatible with the thinking of many biological theorists, among whom, for example, Mr. Julian Huxley and the late J. S. Haldane are to be included. In the background looms the great figure of Claude Bernard, the pioneer physiologist of the past century, for whom the continuity of life and nature never seemed to reduce the living into a function of a non-living material. Bernard reopened on scientific grounds the possibility of another interpretation according to which "life" includes both organism and environment.

> The living being does not form an exception to the great natural harmony which makes things adapt themselves to one another; it breaks no concord; it is neither in contradiction to, nor struggling against, general cosmic forces. Far from that, it is a member of the universal concert of things, and the life of the animal, for example, is only a fragment of the total life of the universe.

Today, we hear from more recent scientists, like the elder Haldane, that the line between organism and environment cannot be very sharply drawn. Thus, blood is the "environment" of the cells which it nourishes and purifies, and the fertile soil upon which we depend for nourishment, from which our lives emerge and to which they return, is, perhaps unlike the "dust" of the Psalmist, replete with life. Again, life and its entelechy, consciousness, can hardly be said to "belong" to the body of a particular organism except in the fullest context of that body's world.

This full context may even be conceived as the "great body" to which our consciousness does indeed truly "belong." This idea, at first bewildering in its implications, enters the tradition of modern thought with Spinoza and is emphatically underwritten by Bergson in his theory of creative evolution.

People are never tired of saying that man is but a minute speck on the face of the earth, the earth a speck in the universe. Yet, even physically, man is far from merely occupying the tiny place allotted to him, and with which Pascal himself was content when he condemned the "thinking reed" to be, materially, only a reed. For if our body is the matter to which our consciousness applies itself it is coextensive with our consciousness, it comprises all we perceive, it reaches to the stars. But this vast body is changing continually, sometimes radically, at the slightest shifting of one part of itself which is at its centre and occupies a small fraction of space. This inner and central body, relatively invariable, is ever present. It is not merely present, it is operative; it is through this body, and through it alone, that we can move other parts of the large body. And, since action is what matters, since it is an understood thing that we are present where we act, the habit has grown of *limiting consciousness to the small body and ignoring the vast one.* The habit appears, moreover, to be justified by science, which holds outward perception to be an epiphenomenon of corresponding intracerebral processes: so that all we perceive of the larger body is regarded as being a mere phantom externalized by the smaller one. We have previously exposed the illusion contained in this metaphysical theory. If the surface of *our organized small body* (organized precisely with a view to immediate action) is the seat of all our actual movements, *our huge inorganic body* is the seat of our potential or theoretically possible actions: the perceptive centres of the brain being the pioneers that prepare the way for subsequent actions and plan them from within, everything happens *as though* our external perceptions were built up by our brain and launched by it into space. But the truth is quite different, and we are really present in everything we perceive, although through ever varying parts of ourselves which are the abode of no more than potential actions. Let us take matters from this angle and we shall cease to say, even of our body, that it is lost in the immensity of the universe.[1]

[1] Henri Bergson, *The Two Sources of Morality and Religion* (New York, 1935), pp. 246–47. Italics mine, except for last phrase.

If, as Pascal, shaken by the vast silences of celestial space, once thought, the universe is a "sphere whose center is everywhere and whose circumference is nowhere," then the same may be said of man's "body" or the physical conditions of his existence and "in our life [at least] does nature live."

In a sense, we do not *depend* on physical nature: we *are* or we participate in "earth's diurnal course," the whole solar system in its cosmic background. We *are* our evolutionary ancestry and our cosmic past of which this ancestral development is but an aspect. Most important of all, we *are,* or essentially participate in, the full community of contemporary human life. We *are* the life and thought in which we participate and yet, most crucial point, this life and this thought are not our exclusively private possessions. And if we think of them as divorced from their larger context, we are guilty of a vicious abstraction: "we murder to dissect."

Thus, modern biological emphasis upon the unity of life in nature and the continuity of life with nature rather shares than conflicts with Wordsworth's attitude. Dover Wilson has done well to insist that a true Wordsworthian may accept a theory of organic evolution, even when it includes a Darwinian version of natural selection, since this can deepen our "sense of the oneness of man with nature, and of the 'whole creation groaning and travailing in pain together.' " [2] Certainly Wordsworth recognized that man's place in the physical world is precarious, and that his achievements may easily be swept away.[3]

The all-environing unity of nature within which we live and move will suffer no fundamental dualism or "bifurcation." Man's bodily life, his total heredity, his sensibility, his emotion, his intelligence, and his will belong equally within the scope of nature and there can appear no final lines of demarcation between soul, organism, and environment. In this respect, Wordsworth reminds us of certain recent naturalists who insist upon the unity of nature without subjecting this unity to a traditionally materialist or mechanist interpretation. This attitude has called in recent years for a radical redefinition of "matter," as Santayana often argued:

In popular speech the word matter continues to suggest the popular aspects of natural things; in scientific speech, at each stage of it,

[2] Dover Wilson, *Leslie Stephen and Matthew Arnold as Critics of Words-* worth (Cambridge, 1939), pp. 49–50. [3] *The Prelude,* V, 18–49.

the word comes to denote such aspects of those same things as have become calculable at that stage. Thus to a stonecutter extension and impenetrability may well seem the essence of matter; the builder, intent on the strains and dangers of position, will add degrees of cohesion and weight to his definition. At this stage metaphysicians and moralists will look down on matter as something gross and dead, and will imagine that motion and organization must be imposed on matter from without: not seeing that this external force, if it governed and moved matter, would be the soul of matter, and much nearer to its proper essence than the aesthetic aspects which its aggregates may wear to the human eye. Yet what could be more obviously material than thunder and lightning, sunshine and rain, from which the father of the gods borrowed his poetic substance? Weight and figure are not more characteristic of matter than are explosiveness, swiftness, fertility, and radiation. Planters and breeders of animals, or poets watching the passing generations of mankind, will feel that the heart and mystery of matter lie in the seeds of things, *semina rerum,* and in the customary cycles of their transformation. It is by its motion and energy, by its fidelity to measure and law, that matter has become the substance of our world, and the principle of life and of death in it. The earliest sages, no less than the latest moderns, identified matter with fire, aether, or fluids, rather than with stocks and stones; the latter are but temporary concretions, and always in the act of growing or crumbling. Even those who, partly for dialectical reasons, reduced matter to impenetrable atoms, attributed all its fertility to the play of collisions which swept perpetually through the void and drove those dead atoms into constellations and vortices and organisms. This endless propulsion and these fated complications were no less material, and far more terrible, than any monumental heap into which matter might sometimes be gathered, and which to a gaping mind might seem more substantial. If any poet ever felt the life of nature in its truth, irrepressible, many-sided, here flaming up savagely, there helplessly dying down, that poet was Lucretius, whose materialism was unqualified.[4]

It goes without saying that there are profound differences between Wordsworth and Santayana. The latter's vestigial Platonism has taken a form which renders his theory of art radically opposed to that of Wordsworth, for whom also Platonism has, as we shall see, suffered a sea-change. Nonetheless, for both men, "nature" is the matrix of life, mind, and value, as well as of "physical" existence; although Santayana's place

[4] George Santayana, *The Realm of Matter* (New York, 1930), pp. viii–x.

in the skeptical traditions of modern philosophy precludes his entertaining any very positive convictions concerning the nature of things.
Santayana reminds us of a Wordsworthian who has lost his way and
who, always honest with himself, sincerely regrets his bewilderment,
just as in other moods he regrets his lack of Christian faith.

> *The muffled syllables that Nature speaks*
> *Fill us with deeper longing for her word—*

a word which can be humanly spoken only by a supreme poet.

For many, if not for Santayana, Wordsworth is such a poet. His
approach to reality is not, of course, biological or scientific. Neither
should it be considered philosophical, if by that term we mean to imply
that his thinking is worked out in a system of discursive argument. His
thought is intuitive in its origins and is subject to no very strict discursive regimen. Wordsworth's vision belongs with those insights or
inspired guesses contributing, as Whitehead has recognized, to the formation of a world-view within which the arts and the sciences both may
develop. Whitehead speaks of "instinctive convictions" and "imaginative
backgrounds" upon which both science and philosophy depend.[5]

Indeed, Wordsworth came to believe that his view of things might
some day be accepted by the scientific student able to recognize and to
correct the limitations of his specialized investigations, and thus, to
reconcile science and poetry. Today it is not impossible to find students
of nature whom Wordsworth would have deeply admired. Let us consider the work of Albert Schweitzer, whose active interests, including
art, religion, experimental science, and philanthropy, have culminated
in a philosophy of life which, if we allow for differences in idiom and
for an historical background including Schopenhauer and Darwin, we
might almost describe as Wordsworthian. Like Wordsworth, Schweitzer
is critical of a narrow rationalism and he repudiates the Cartesian or
rationalist origins of modern academic philosophy. His alternative starting point reminds us of Jakob Boehme (d. 1624) whose obscure utterances indicate the presence at the very beginning of modern thought of
a philosophy wholly distinct from Cartesian rationalism. Schweitzer has
written:

> The unlearned man who, at the sight of a tree in flower, is over-
> powered by the mystery of the will-to-live which is stirring all round

[5] A. N. Whitehead, *Science and the Modern World* (New York, 1925), Chap.
I.

him, knows more than the scientist who studies under the microscope or in physical and chemical activity a thousand forms of the will-to-live, but, with all his knowledge of the life-course of these manifestations of the will-to-live, is unmoved by the mystery that everything which exists is will-to-live, while he is puffed up with vanity at being able to describe exactly a fragment of the course of life.

All true knowledge passes on into experience. The nature of the manifestations I do not know, but I form a conception of it in analogy to the will-to-live which is within myself. Thus, my knowledge of the world becomes experience of the world. The knowledge which is becoming experience does not allow me to remain in face of the world a man who merely knows, with reverence for the mysterious will-to-live which is in all things. By making me think and wonder, it leads me ever upward to the heights of reverence for life. There it lets my hand go. It cannot accompany me further. My will-to-live must now find its way about the world by itself.

It is not by informing me what this or that manifestation of life means in the sum total of the world that knowledge brings me into connection with the world. It goes about with me not in outer circles, but in the inner ones. From within outwards, it puts me in relation to the world by making my will-to-live feel everything around it as also will-to-live.

With Descartes, philosophy starts from the dogma: "I think, therefore I exist." With this paltry, arbitrarily chosen beginning, it is landed irretrievably on the road to the abstract. It never finds the right approach to ethics, and remains entangled in a dead world-and life-view. True philosophy must start from the most immediate and comprehensive fact of consciousness, which says: "I am life which wills to live, in the midst of life which wills to live." This is not an ingenious dogmatic formula. Day by day, hour by hour, I live and move in it. At every moment of reflection it stands fresh before me. There bursts forth from it again and again as from roots that can never dry up, a living world- and life-view which can deal with all the facts of Being. A mysticism of ethical union with Being grows out of it.[6]

Schweitzer's "most immediate and comprehensive fact of consciousness" described above is open to the untutored, who may in this sympathetic awareness surpass the *savant*. We are reminded throughout of Wordsworth's attitude in the lyrics of 1798. For both Wordsworth and Schweitzer, this sympathetic sense of life, often in its intensity a

---

[6] Albert Schweitzer, *The Philosophy of Civilization* (New York, 1949), pp. 308–9.

sort of spiritual intoxication, which haunts us "like a passion," must mature into a reflective philosophy. Schweitzer's notion of "reverence for life," with its consequent responsibility toward all living things, goes further than Wordsworth's explicit utterance but is not inconsistent with it. We can well imagine Schweitzer citing with approval Wordsworth's assurance that

> he who feels contempt
> For any living thing, hath faculties
> Which he has never used; that thought with him
> Is in its infancy.

Both Wordsworth and Schweitzer seem to feel that such sentiment must be matured in a reflective or philosophical consciousness. Perhaps Schweitzer's "reverence for life" is more closely related to the "primal sympathies" and less qualified by supranaturalism than is Wordsworth's later ethics of rational responsibility which reminds us of Kant and the Stoics. After the *Ode to Duty* there sometimes appears in Wordsworth's ethical thought a supranaturalism, which is magnificently expressed but is hardly consistent with the teaching of *The Prelude:*

> Her soul doth in itself stand fast,
> Sustained by memory of the past
> And strength of Reason, held above
> The infirmities of mortal love;
> Undaunted, lofty, calm, and stable,
> And awfully impenetrable.

In this mood, Wordsworth suspects the "tumult of the soul," forgetting his earlier faith in

> Emotions which best foresight need not fear,
> Most worthy then of trust when most intense.

But this is a problem of interpretation which we cannot pursue further.

Schweitzer and Wordsworth decline to separate consciousness from its world either in direct statement or by any form of implication. In other words, they repudiate all schemes of interpretation which center upon an initial awareness, or alleged awareness, of the conscious self as remote or isolated from its world. Mind is not a "looker-on," but a participant, sharing in the one life,

> the one interior life
> That lives in all things . . .

⁷ *The Prelude: MS.* See de Selincourt's edition, p. 512.

Consider also the attitude of the French ontologist, Merleau-Ponty, which is admirably summarized as follows: "The world is not what I think, but what I live; I am open to the world, I communicate with it, but I don't possess it, it is inexhaustible."

In opposition to this, as Schweitzer has noticed, the Cartesian *cogito* states the dominant theme of "classical" modern philosophy. It is a philosophical epitome, representative of the method and content of much subsequent thinking not usually considered as strictly Cartesian in spirit. "I think, therefore I am." Here, emphasis falls not upon feeling or even sensation, but upon intellectual judgment, the discrimination of the mathematician who frames his "clear and distinct" idea. My individual mind, whose existence I cannot consistently deny, is conceived as a substantial center of intelligence and decision sharply to be contrasted with my sensations and emotions, my body, and with the objects in the "external" world. This mind is more clearly aware of itself as a center of thought than it is of the many things in the world without. It enjoys an independence which isolates it from nature, a "reasoning, self-sufficing thing, / an intellectual All-in-all!" [8]

Thus, the Cartesian *cogito* indicates a movement toward an egocentric individualism, the very antithesis of Coleridge's "one life within us and abroad." Such a starting point makes possible as a sequel the more extreme forms of competitive individualism or social atomism which have often marred modern liberal thought. Consider Whitehead's comment.

The general conceptions introduced by science into modern thought cannot be separated from the philosophical situation as expressed by Descartes. I mean the assumption of *bodies and minds as independent individual substances,* each existing in its own right apart from any necessary reference to each other. Such a conception was very concordant with the individualism which had issued from the moral discipline of the Middle Ages. But, though the easy reception of the idea is thus explained, the derivation in itself rests upon a confusion, very natural but none the less unfortunate. The moral discipline had emphasized the intrinsic value of the individual entity. This emphasis had put the notions of the individual and of its experiences into the foreground of thought. At this point the confusion commences. *The emergent individual value of each entity is trans-*

[8] *The Poet's Epitaph.* These lines are   ones about the student botanizing on
more significant than the more famous   his mother's grave.

formed into the independent substantial existence of each entity, which is a very different notion.[9]

Now, Wordsworth presents a philosophy of individualism just as surely as Descartes. But it is an individualism to be realized in community. The individual, so conceived, is deeply rooted in nature and can complete himself only through participation in nature and the lives of his fellows. Everywhere individualism is tempered and enriched by an emphasis upon the community of men and things.

To be sure, Wordsworth does not directly challenge Cartesian logic nor does he hasten to construct a rival philosophical theory. Rather he insists that all theory by which we live must be nourished by experience, the experience not of a scientific observer but of the poet who approaches nature in "wise passiveness." Only thus can our sense of reality and value be awakened. Prolonged contemplation of abstraction may sharpen our wits but it leaves us surrounded by skeletal or formal patterns with which we are not at home and which offer us no compelling motivation. Such abstractions can satisfy only our intellectual curiosity. We cannot *experience* their reality or their importance. We cannot live among them. They are like silhouettes or, better, like maps veridical or useful if properly read, but drastically simplified and lacking in color, depth, and as John Crowe Ransom has put it, in "density." [10]

What we have, then, to learn from Wordsworth is not primarily a matter of theory. It is the practice of a certain kind of sensibility and of a certain awareness. From such awareness, new theories may arise and indeed the awareness is not quite complete until we have shaped a theory to perfect and interpret it—but the theory without the awareness is an empty verbalism, however elegant its syntax. Here, the thinker may learn from the poet and, if he is fortunate, share in that "sense of being" by which, transcending abstractions, we may step forth into the "light of things," beneath which the refinements of philosophical skepticism vanish as irrelevant and the abstractions of both science and philosophy are manifest as such. If Wordsworth is to be called the phi-

---

[9] Whitehead, *op. cit.*, p. 279. Italics mine. Compare Reinhold Niebuhr, *The Irony of American History* (New York, 1952), p. 13: "The Christian idea of the significance of each individual in God's sight becomes in bourgeois civilization, the concept of a discrete individual who makes himself the final end of his own existence. The Christian idea of provi-dence is rejected for the handy notion that man is the master of his fate and the captain of his soul."

[10] John Crowe Ransom, "William Wordsworth: Notes toward an Understanding of Poetry," *The Kenyon Review* (Summer, 1950), pp. 498–519. See especially page 503.

losopher's poet, it is because the philosopher, inclined by disposition and training to rigorous analysis, often finds in Wordsworth what he knows only too well is lacking in himself. Hence, the gratitude with which philosophers sometimes speak of the poet. The case of John Stuart Mill is too well known to require much comment. Wordsworth restored to Mill the sense of value, of importance, that the great utilitarian had, paradoxically enough, sacrificed to his analytic studies of human society and human well-being. But there are philosophers who find in Wordsworth even more than Mill was able to recognize: the beginnings of a comprehensive theory of knowledge, based on a sense of concrete reality and objective value. Thus, three of the outstanding philosophers of the English-speaking world have in recent years emphatically acknowledged a profound debt to Wordsworth. They are R. G. Collingwood, Samuel Alexander, and A. N. Whitehead. Let us quote from Collingwood:

> It was Wordsworth who wrote,
>
> > *The Child is father of the Man;*
> > *And I could wish my days to be*
> > *Bound each to each by natural piety.*
>
> It was Samuel Alexander, one of two or three men in our time, who have deserved to be called great philosophers, who took Wordsworth's lines as a kind of motto for his metaphysical work. When Alexander said that natural piety should be the clue to metaphysical thinking he meant to say, as many sound philosophers have said before him, that a metaphysician's business is not to argue but to recognize facts; and he meant to say also that these facts are not recondite or remote, to be recognized only after a long course of special training and specialized research, but simple and familiar, visible to the eyes of a child, and perhaps hidden from clever men because they are too clever. Certainly, he thought, they must remain hidden from those wise and prudent men who would accept nothing but what was 'proved'; and were revealed to any babe who would accept them as the child Wordsworth accepted the rainbow.
>
> There is, I suspect, far more of wisdom and truth in this than I could ever hope to expound.[11]

Alexander has outdone all philosophers of modern times in his insistence that we must respect the qualitied texture of things as they

---

[11] R. G. Collingwood, *An Essay on Metaphysics* (Oxford, 1940), p. 172. See Samuel Alexander, *Space, Time, and Deity* (London, 1920), II, 47, 392.

exist together in the concrete world. Our awareness of this world may
be interpreted in many ways but its content must never be identified
with or "reduced" to constellations of units qualitatively irrelevant to
the original objects. Alexander's stubbornness in this matter has often
rendered his philosophy perplexing and difficult but it has saved him
from oversimplification and false abstractions.

Much better known to students of literature is Whitehead's appreciation of Wordsworth in his *Science and the Modern World*. It may
be summarized by the following quotations:

> His theme is nature *in solido*, that is to say, he dwells on that
> mysterious presence of surrounding things, which imposes itself on
> any separate element that we set up as an individual for its own sake.
> He always grasps the whole of nature as involved in the tonality of
> the particular instance. That is why he laughs with the daffodils,
> and finds in the primrose thoughts "too deep for tears."
>
> Wordsworth, to the height of genius, expresses the concrete facts
> of our apprehension, facts which are distorted in the scientific anal-
> ysis.[12]

Wordsworth often called upon mountains, sky, and sea to bear
him witness. The concrete or concrescent universality of nature is in-
disputably present in the sublimity of open landscape. But it is equally
present in all things both great and small, as the poet must learn. Thus,
it is manifest in the quiet and composed intensity of a still-life, or in
any object that wholly possesses our attention: the swan and his image
in the lake, the face of a blind beggar, or even the bleak and dreary outline of an old stone wall. Here the unity of things appears, an inescapable and silent background, as in the concluding lines of a great
sonnet. I trust that the reader will pardon my presumption in attempting
to recall the quality of this awareness, even though I use words borrowed from Wordsworth. I am not sure that I shall be successful, or
always very intelligible but I can do no more than rely upon my own
experience of Wordsworth and of nature.[13]

Let us consider by way of comparison, the work of the painter
Cézanne whose effort to "realize" and record his own deeper imaginative
vision was desperately persistent. We may well hesitate to compare

[12] Whitehead, *op. cit.*, pp. 121, 122.

[13] In what follows, I am incorporating an English version of several paragraphs which appeared in French in an
essay contributed to a symposium. See
my "Scepticisme et Imagination," in
Deucalion, tome 3. La Baconniére,
Neuchatel (Suisse) 1950, pp. 34–44;
also my "On Poetry and Geometric
Truth," *The Kenyon Review* (Winter,
1956).

Cézanne's austere and silent landscapes and still-lifes, at first glance so awkward and incomplete with the "round ocean and the living air" of the English poet. But such obvious difference may be discounted. Cézanne and Wordsworth belong together. In Cézanne, the aloofness of the forms of nature is only superficial. We have to accustom ourselves to his passionate honesty which scorns all forms of pictorial "gaudy verse." Consider Elie Faure's comments upon Cézanne's rendering of concreteness:

> It is but of little importance that the object be exactly followed in all its contours and finished in all its details. That which is necessary is, that it be in its place in the depth of space as regards the other objects, that, at the same time, the gradations of its edges give it its own existence, and that the object, in relation to the world, and the world in relation to the object, possess complete solidarity.
>
> His still-lifes have the splendor of the heaps of fruit which concentrate into themselves the whole of surrounding life, and which seem to send forth their full and spherical form and their color in its saturation, from the innermost center of their matter.[14]

Cézanne has often recaptured or realized in his landscapes the voluminous omnipresence of our world, which fills our imagination and "broods like the day" over our consciousness. Once we are at home in his pictures they come strangely to life. Everywhere there is a world, or the worldliness of things pressing upon one another and engulfing our own awareness which is plunged deeply among them. Here, as our consciousness reverts toward its imaginative origins, lies the thickness, the very quality, of existence itself. The presence of the world is the compresence of things, each with its margin of influence. Here every center which can hold our attention begins to surrender its distinctness as an independent and recognizably isolated object. As commonplace objects relinquish their pragmatic hold upon us, the scene is characterized by certain pervasive features, often lost from notice. Multiplicity is prominent here, but it is a multiplicity without atomic components. There is an over-all unity, but it is a unity of interacting and reciprocating elements. The unity is sometimes ancillary and adjectival to the things within it; but it is for all that, inescapable, being sometimes as clear as the interplay of human features in a smile or frown. Within this unity, as Wordsworth noticed, each element may at times exercise

---

14 Elie Faure, *Modern Art* (New York, 1924), pp. 425, 426.

a "subtle reach" and "comprehensive sway" upon its neighbors. But this action is often reciprocal and there may be manifest a "mutual domination" and "interchangeable supremacy." Thus, we imagine or feel the togetherness of things and events before we *conceive* of space, time, and chains of causation. Indeed these conceptions owe their origin and their authority to our imaginative participation in the world.

Such imagination is not merely the character of our "stream of consciousness," which is after all, for anyone who has felt the compresence of things, in itself, an abstraction. As Whitehead has put it, "the primitive experience is emotional feeling, felt in its relevance to a world beyond." Nature, so perceived, includes our human responses within its scope, so that the face of nature may appear directly as threatening or attractive, "possessing the characters of danger or desire." Thus, Cézanne seems to feel the presence of a purely spatial challenge drawing us on or blocking our reach almost as sharply as less sensitive people feel the presence of danger itself. In Cézanne's work geometry is "realized" and space comes to life. But contrast Cézanne with Van Gogh, for whom sequence and power, rather than togetherness and solidity, are brought to full intensity. Here in Wordsworth's words there is "something evermore about to be." And,

> *The surface of the universal earth*
> *With triumph and delight, with hope and fear*
> *Work[s] like a sea.*

Such vision is perhaps more directly expressed by the painter and the musician than by the poet. To achieve this sense of immediacy is to maintain that "atmosphere of sensation" in which, according to Wordsworth, the poet may "move his wings" and which distinguishes art from analytic science. Cézanne, too, understood this. He knew that nature could not be *reproduced* pictorially; it must be interpreted, its rhythms and harmonies restated. But these rhythms and harmonies must be enjoyed in contact with nature, that is to say, through "sensation" whereby forms and colors are apprehended in togetherness or interpenetration.

In poetry, it is only through highly figurative, even tortured, language, as in Hopkins, that the primordial community of things, and of our place within it, can be brought even for a moment into full verbal consciousness. The primary justification of metaphor lies in the difficulty that we all encounter when we try to remain in the presence of the things we talk about. Metaphor in poetry, in painting distortion and non-representative composition, Cézanne's "plastic equivalents," that cannot be taken quite "literally" according to commonplace connotations, force us back upon imaginative perception. Sometimes when we pass from discursive toward imaginative consciousness, we seem almost to *recall* the primordial plenitude of nature as something with which we were once familiar. This is, I believe, the experience that Wordsworth has celebrated in his famous *Ode,* where he speaks of the "immortal sea that brought us hither." The world, as it lies open to imagination, resembles an ocean in more ways than one: its unity, the reciprocity of its elements, the urgency and power of its movements can often remind us of "mighty waters." And it is true that our adult consciousness, narrowed as it is by our theoretical interests and practical preoccupations, must be temporarily relaxed to allow imagination to regain something of its ancient predominance and clearly to reveal its world. Yet even our normal, adult consciousness is not wholly deprived of such vision, which often lingers as a marginal orientation. Thus, as we center our attention upon an area of concrescent objects, our sense of worldliness prevents us from considering the area as isolated. There is always our sense of the background to which the area belongs and upon which we ourselves depend. "In our experience," writes Whitehead, "there is always the dim background from which we derive and to which we return. We are not enjoying a limited dolls' house of clear and distinct things, secluded from all ambiguity. In the darkness beyond there ever looms the vague mass which is the universe begetting us." [15]

Perhaps the full import of such awareness does not clarify itself until we emphasize our sense of dependence upon this living background. Upon reflection, we feel certain that without such a background *we* would be—nothing at all. The "immortal sea" is *our* life and we are not creatures of a day.

Here we encounter an inversion of Platonism, or at least an inversion of the Platonic notion of reminiscence. We are not said to be "recalling" general truths, say, the principles of mathematics or of justice. It is rather the everlasting world of becoming, in its true char-

[15] A. N. Whitehead, "Analysis of Meaning" in *Essays in Science and Philosophy* (New York, 1947), p. 123. In this reference to the *Intimations* ode, I am trying to describe what I take to be its core of intuitive feeling. I cannot here discuss all the ideas which Wordsworth, Coleridge and others have at one time or another used to describe this feeling. See my *Strange Seas of Thought* (Durham, 1945), pp. 267 ff.

acter as a sea of concrescence, of which we are imperfectly reminiscent and in such reminiscence we are dimly aware of our own origins as thinking beings. The immutable ideas of the Platonist, the forms of mathematics, of science and philosophy, are still legitimate objects of our attention. Yet they do not, even when considered together as a a system, constitute our world, nor do they satisfy our demand for substantial value.

If we desired to express this doctrine in the shape of a myth, like that of Plato's reminiscence, we might invent a story running something as follows: When Prometheus, disobeying Zeus, shared with men the power of discursive reason and the intellectual instruments of analysis, the jealous gods exacted a penalty from the human soul. Although with an effort of detachment man may contemplate the eternal Ideas, his mind, fashioned now into a new form by the practice of dialectic, no longer delights in the immediate presence of his changeful world. So punished, man is often vaguely reminiscent of his past when he was really "in" nature and a part of it: not, as now, at a lonely distance from it, surrounded by his new discoveries, the eternal truths and the useful abstractions that he derives from them. And occasionally in privileged moments, he more clearly remembers his lost state and rejoices to recall it. Like Antaeus, man cannot long survive in health of spirit if he is deprived or deprives himself of such contact with nature.

Our imagination participates not only in the community of nature but in that of human life, without which nature herself is incomplete. Our human life, imaginatively conceived, as an object of "feeling intellect," is not a private matter or, as Wordsworth would say, a "punctual presence"—but is far diffused in space and time interpenetrating with the lives of many other human beings. Hence, we may become aware of a widespread unity of human nature, made possible by our sharing experience and judgment and by the growing sense of a common purpose, the unity of man.[16] The human community transcends the limitations of history and the "unimaginable touch of time" itself. We are reminded of Walter Pater's "essence of humanism," the belief that

> nothing which has ever interested living men and women can wholly lose its vitality—no language they have spoken, nor oracle beside which they have hushed their voices, no dream which has once been entertained by actual human minds, nothing about which they have ever been passionate or expended time and zeal.

[16] *The Prelude,* viii, 597–686; also xiv, 107 ff.

In contrast, consider the isolation of the spirit so awfully portrayed in Coleridge's *Ancient Mariner*. Here, it may be argued, Coleridge describes a negative individualism, an individualism of isolation. Here lies the true moral of the *Ancient Mariner*. For the mariner, the world has suddenly lost its living substance. The "sky and the sea, and the sea and the sky," which should have been the "round ocean and the living air" of *Tintern Abbey,* have become intolerable strangers to him. And he stands on a ship, manned by the dead who were once his fellow men. He finds himself loathing the sea now rotten with slime, and cursing the harmless water snakes upon it, and all the while hating himself for loathing and cursing. Somehow he feels responsible for the "dead" with whom he cannot communicate and he is burdened with a sense of guilt, for he knows that through some error of his own, his world has perished. And so he looks nothingness in the eye, a blazing and nauseating nothingness which consumes even the beauty of nature. Neither Wordsworth nor Coleridge have been able to rescue their posterity from such an experience of total frustration. We have only to think of the "nausea" of existentialist writers to come upon a contemporary illustration. Sartre's "nausea" and the Mariner's loathing of the rotting surface of the sea should be considered together.

Had I dreamed of this enormous presence? It was there, in the garden, toppled down into the trees, all soft, sticky, soiling everything, all thick, a jelly. And I was inside, I with the garden. I was frightened, furious, I thought it was so stupid, so out of place, I hated this ignoble mess. Mounting up, mounting up as high as the sky, spilling over, filling everything with its gelatinous slither, and I could see depths upon depths of it reaching far beyond the limits of the garden, the houses, and Bouville, as far as the eye could reach. I was no longer in Bouville, I was nowhere, I was floating. I was not surprised, I knew it was the World, the naked World suddenly revealing itself, and I choked with rage at this gross, absurd being. You couldn't even wonder where all that sprang from, or how it was that a world came into existence, rather than nothingness. It didn't make sense, the World was everywhere, in front, behind. There had never been a moment in which it could not have existed. That was what worried me: of course there was no *reason* for this flowing larva to exist. *But it was impossible* for it not to exist. It was unthinkable: to imagine nothingness you had to be there already, in the midst of the World, eyes wide open and alive; nothingness was only an idea in my head, an existing idea floating in this immensity: this nothingness had not come *before* existence, it was an existence like any other and appeared after many others. I shouted, "filth! what rotten filth!" and shook myself to get rid of this sticky filth, but it held fast and there was so much, tons and tons, of existence, endless: I stifled at the depths of this immense weariness. And then suddenly the park emptied as through a great hole, the World disappeared as it had come, or else I woke up—in any case, I saw no more of it; nothing was left but the yellow earth around me, out of which dead branches rose upward.[17]

Whether recent existentialism and the idealism of the romantics share the same heaven, it is difficult to say, but they agree heartily enough on the subject of hell.

Wordsworth's philosophy of imagination culminates in an ethics, the ethics of freedom. Imagination is the guide of life and it is through imagination that we apprehend the ideals that move us. The highest ideal is freedom, the "liberty" and "power" of autonomous selfhood, the high and enduring personality whose many interests are enlivened by compelling insights at once disinterested and inspired. Wordsworth makes no effort to "deduce" this ideal from a theory of human life, nor does he insist that *as a concept* it is a self-evident principle. What we mean by *freedom* is manifest as the finer essence and quality of those human lives we find most admirable and whose character we delight to contemplate. Here, imagination precedes understanding. The sympathetic imagination of the poet participates in the attitudes, purposes, and judgments of other individuals. In certain rare cases, the poet is thereby committed to an unqualified admiration and here imagination finds its ideal incarnate in human life. We may think of Michael and the Leech-gatherer, but especially of Beaupuy, Dorothy Wordsworth, the young Coleridge, and the poet's brother John (the Happy Warrior) who come to represent an ideal human nature in its several aspects. They afford the "factual" or experiential basis against which the ideal appears as unquestionably attractive and inspiring. Such admiration corresponds with what Bergson has described in the *Two Sources of Morality and Religion* as creative emotion, which enriches, even refashions, the life of the person who has felt it. Bergson's creative emotion is awakened

[17] Jean Paul Sartre, *Nausea* (Norfolk, Conn., 1949), pp. 180–81.

largely by our admiration for individual persons whose very presence before us evokes new ideals. Bergson speaks of Socrates, Jesus, and the mystics.

In his more cautious moments even the younger Wordsworth was ready to admit that such an unqualified idealism is not open to everyone: it is only the generous spirit that responds thus happily to the riches of life and nature and then perhaps only at privileged moments.

> Serene will be our days and bright
> And happy will our nature be,
> When love is an unerring light,
> And joy its own security.

Until such time, we stand in need of a sense of obligation based not solely on imaginative sympathy, but disciplined and rendered consistent by reason and qualified by a reasonable respect for tradition.

The free man participates by choice in many passages of activity which tend to sustain and strengthen one another. Just as in the emergence of consciousness subject to nature's harmonious workmanship several types of sensitivity come finally to support one another and unite in a unity of perception, furthering "the great ends of Liberty and Power," [18] so in the broader context of voluntary conduct many strands of activity may be drawn together into an autonomous concert of diverse energies which we recognize as fruitful and significant selfhood. Here, we recognize under the name or symbol of freedom the supreme manifestation of human value, a complete and unimpeded participation in the world, manifesting now the inner consistency of its organization as in a moment of conscientious decision, and now its "capacity," the far-flung scope of the energies in which it shares. In realizing such selfhood and freedom, the human being deserves, so Wordsworth believes, recognition as a "Power," a center of moral energy and of enlightening influence. Such power constitutes the true wealth of nations. It is the fulfillment of human life. With such a vision of human freedom, Wordsworth completes the argument of The Prelude.

Just as imagination orients us in the world and overcomes by fiat the isolationism of the rationalist, so it supports our sense of value. This can overwhelm the skepticism of the abstract thinker for whom any theory of value must be based upon a logically arbitrary assumption. For the rationalist, there is always the ultimate doubt: Is value,

[18] The Prelude. xii. 131 ff.. also i. 340 ff.

i.e., this or that standard of value, really important? And dialectic has no answer. It must "yield up moral questions in despair," as Wordsworth once did. It can call up "like culprits to the bar" all judgments, maxims, and creeds, but it will end by questioning its own authority to do so. But for imagination, there is always the aesthetic immediacy of concrete value, to be symbolized as freedom. Thus, somewhat as Schiller taught in his theory of the *schöne Seele*, moral value may be present to the pre-logical imagination through a non-reflective and uncritical sense of concrete importance, aesthetic in its immediacy. For most of us, freedom appears as an intrinsic value, concretely realized only in the work of the artist, where the integration of the powers centered in words and rhythms, or in lines and masses, stands as a final realization. In other fields, too often we demand "formal proof" before we have become acquainted with the values in question through participating in their realization. The imagination that has participated in the complex pressures and adjustments of a human undertaking is sensitive to the harmony that characterizes its fruition and the health of its influence. Just as a reader, whose imagination has participated in the development of a composition, may feel the apt significance of a phrase, so we may recognize the outcome of an enterprise in whose development we have shared, as an appropriate resolution of the themes involved. Here imagination is authoritative. Our discursive and deliberative understanding is, as Wordsworth and Blake insisted, a secondary power which can do little more than describe the broader reiterable features of those achievements in which imagination has found its fulfillment.

Thus, the human mind may make itself at home in nature, history, and the common world of every day, realizing here or nowhere that freedom in community which is the true quality of man. Thus

> *the mind of man becomes*
> *A thousand times more beautiful than the earth*
> *On which he dwells,*

as the perfection of that invisible or inscrutable workmanship of nature whereby man becomes worthy of himself.

Wordsworth's
6 Significance for Us

HELEN DARBISHIRE

UNLIKE MOST modern poets Wordsworth requires no commentary: his style is simple and lucid, his subject matter in no way exotic. Yet what he has to say is by no means obvious, by no means easily understood. Without presumption we may suggest that today when we are taught to look for surprise and excitement, not to say shock and violence in poetry, Wordsworth needs a guide to show his readers into the quiet world which his genius created.

His meaning has deep roots in spiritual experience, and for him the life of the spirit is vitally one with the life of the senses. This truth, not embraced by all moralists and religious teachers, is the first gift that he offers us.

Here is one of his lyrics:

> My heart leaps up when I behold
> A rainbow in the sky:
> So was it when my life began,
> So is it now I am a man:
> So be it when I shall grow old
> Or let me die!
> The Child is Father of the Man;
> And I could wish my days to be
> Bound each to each by natural piety.

Could anything be more simple? The language, except for the last line, is childlike, with a simplicity which distills itself in monosyllables. Yet the thought communicated has a span like the rainbow's. He leaves the image to do its work with no explanation. He simply tells us his experience: that images which have stirred his feelings vitally, continue to move through his mind with a lasting life. A rainbow awakened in him as a boy a sudden joy, a sense of wonder and admiration, so that all through the years its image has lived on, linking his days together with an undying radiance, a pledge of the life and power that is in the universe. There is no question that the life and power are spiritual, yet he penetrated to them through an image of the senses. The integrity and continuity of the experience are of one piece. Coleridge made a far-reaching reflection in an early number of *The Friend:* he says that there is an essential value even in the illusions of childhood, "if men were good and wise enough to contemplate the past in the present, and so to produce by a virtuous and thoughtful sensibility *that continuity in their self-consciousness* which Nature has made the law of their animal life." He then quotes Wordsworth's poem, *My Heart leaps up,* to set the seal upon his thought.

Wordsworth was a profound and subtle psychologist with an intense interest in growth and development. Like the leading psychologists of our own era he knew the outstanding importance of the experience of the child, and his analysis of his own early life in *The Prelude* should be of vital significance to readers of today. That simple dictum, "The Child is Father of the Man," to us a commonplace, was in Wordsworth's day a startling paradox. Each of his hard sayings has the true stamp of originality: their origin was in himself. The feeding source of what is most valuable in his poetry was his remembered life as a child; he had lived the physical life with intense enjoyment, delighting in boyish sports; yet, as an ardent nutter, he found "there was a Spirit in the woods," and a nocturnal expedition with a stolen boat on a mountain lake plunged him into "unknown modes of being." The world of sense was also a world of spirit; "the incumbent mystery of soul and sense" was for him as a child no puzzle, there was no disturbing division, no conflict: Nature offered him *one* world, *one* life. He had in childhood what he still retained in the best hours of his maturity a deep—we might say a physical sense of the order as well as the beauty of the universe. Nature was to him both law and impulse—another of his hard simple paradoxes. He had no desire to say anything brilliant or difficult. "I speak of what I know," he wrote, "and what we feel within." When Touchstone wished that the Gods had made Audrey poetical, Audrey rightly retorted: "I do not know what poetical is. Is it honest in deed and word? Is it a true thing?" We can answer for Wordsworth's poetry "Yes, it is a true thing: it *is* honest in deed and word." For what his poetry *does* is as sound as what it says. He himself trusted that its destiny would be "to console the afflicted, to make the happy happier, to teach the young and gracious of every age *to see, to think and feel,* and therefore to become more actively and securely virtuous." I believe this hope has been fulfilled. Leslie Stephen at a time of poignant grief and loss found Wordsworth the only poet he could read. John Stuart Mill found deliverance from sterile despondency in the sources of fresh and forceful feeling in Wordsworth's poetry. The miracle is that these sources lie all about us and are inexhaustible. Wordsworth found them as a boy in the beauty, power and mystery of the earth: in his manhood after his year of conflict and disillusionment in revolutionary France he returned to seek and find in man the same sources of mysterious power. He had reached down to something fundamental and perennial.

The hurry and noise of modern life, the mechanization which crushes out personal enterprise, leaving us with no time or stimulus to think, and see and feel, all this has shut us off from the simple resources that lie at hand. We have half forgotten that we belong to the earth as surely as to humanity. Wordsworth never forgets it. He reminds us that "the Sunshine is a glorious birth," that "waters on a starry night are beautiful and fair"; that Beauty is *a living presence* of the earth; recalls us to "the witchery of the soft blue sky," "the living air," "the lights and shades/ That march and countermarch about the hills/ In glorious apparition" on a day of sun and wind. And he takes us back to the fundamental things in human nature, "the unconquerable power of love," the elementary affections that bind family and friends together, the extraordinary force and tenacity of parental feeling, the stubborn, ineradicable devotion of a man to his homeland.

Wordsworth is often accused of being blind to the bitterness and hardship of our human lot. He knew it to its depth, even among his beautiful sheltered valleys.

Amid the groves, under the shadowy hills

(so the Solitary of *The Excursion* insists in haunting words)

The generations are prepared; the pangs,
The internal pangs are ready; the mad strife

Of poor humanity's afflicted will
Struggling in vain with ruthless destiny.

Wordsworth knew this; but he knew also of saving things in human nature: the passion for freedom which belongs to all healthy beings, "the native and naked dignity of man," the call of human brotherhood, and "the grand elementary principle of pleasure by which we know and feel and live and move." The shepherd Michael felt for his familiar fields and hills

> *A pleasurable feeling of blind love,*
> *The pleasure that there is in life itself.*

To this pleasure Wordsworth recalls us. He welcomed gaiety and enjoyment in human beings as the very spirit of life—setting aside moral issues, so it seems, with cheerful unconcern. The gay little liars, the Beggar-Boys, are as dear to his heart and to his poetic imagination as Benjamin the Waggoner in his drunken ecstasy. But then Wordsworth believed that feeling and imagination are essential to the moral life. Old Michael's intense power of feeling is what saves him when he loses his beloved son. He goes about his labors for his sheep with the same tranquil fortitude as before. Wordsworth simply says:

> *There is a comfort in the strength of love:*
> *'Twill make a thing endurable which else*
> *Would overset the brain or break the heart.*

Wordsworth's power of feeling stood a hard test. He lived through the French Revolution, and the Napoleonic wars that tore Europe to pieces—times as threatening and appalling as those we are living through now. He was one of those rare people who care intensely for humanity; he suffered much, and was sustained by heroic courage and by an unshakable belief in human nature.

Those readers who draw small comfort from his poetry of Nature may find inspiration in his Sonnets dedicated to National Independence and Liberty, where he shows himself the champion of freedom and of human brotherhood—our first great internationalist; acutely aware of the failings and errors of his own country yet confident in its rooted strength and independence, regarding it moreover as one of "the family of nations" (his own significant phrase). He was fundamentally Anglo-Saxon in his inveterate sense of fact and reality. He saw that in the relations between civilized nations, as between independent individuals, the requisites were decency, courtesy, recognition of a common moral basis, above all, respect for the independence and integrity of the other party. In these poems and in his great prose pamphlet, *The Convention of Cintra,* he reaches down to the physical roots of nationalism, and at the same time recognizes that its life can be sustained only by those qualities which we call moral. As with all men of genius, his thought and experience are of one tissue. His last word on nationalism and on internationalism is that

> *By the soul only*
> *The nations shall be great and free.*

His conception of poetry is closely knit with his own poetry and what it is and does. We make his thought sound commonplace when we say that it is as a humanitarian that he valued poetry. But we should let him speak for himself, remembering that poets see further into the past and future, feel more and *know* more than the rest of us.

"The Poet," he said, "is the rock of defence of human nature; an upholder and preserver, carrying everywhere with him relationship and love. In spite of difference of soil and climate, of language and manners, of laws and customs, in spite of things silently gone out of mind and things violently destroyed, the Poet binds together by passion and knowledge the vast empire of human society, as it is spread over the whole earth, and over all time."

We must end where we began. The life of the spirit was for Wordsworth the beginning and the end. He could draw nearest to the heart of it in the element of silence and solitude: "the silence that is in the starry sky, The sleep that is among the lonely hills." De Quincey records a saying of Wordsworth's: "so much solitude: so much power." To this truth, plain as daylight, yet too often ignored, Wordsworth's poetry bears witness. When he laid his ear to the earth he heard "authentic tidings of invisible things": he had a sure intuition of "the central peace, subsisting at the heart of endless agitation." Our noisy years seemed to him "moments in the being of the eternal silence." His deepest experience both of man and of nature, coming to him in rare moments, was the authentic experience of the mystic. One poetic rendering of it is in *Resolution and Independence* where the physical shape of the decrepit old leech-gatherer becomes the symbol of a well-nigh supernatural strength of spirit. Another is in his account in *The Prelude* of his crossing the Alps as a young man. Again the physical scene *leads into* the spiritual revelation:

Imagination . . . rose from the mind's abyss
Like an unfathered vapour that enwraps
At once some lonely traveller—I was lost.
                    . . . . in such strength
Of usurpation, when the light of sense
Goes out, but with a flash that has revealed
The invisible world, doth greatness make abode,
There harbours; whether we be young or old,
Our destiny, our being's heart and home
Is with infinitude, and only there;
With hope it is, hope that can never die,
Effort and expectation and desire,
And something evermore about to be.

We of our generation have witnessed the crumbling of creeds, the steadily loosening hold of the churches, yet we need desperately, as men have always needed, some abiding source of spiritual power. The experience of the mystic is not for most of us, but Wordsworth's poetry —and he thought the function of poetry was to *call forth and communicate power*—can meet our need. His greatest poetry owes nothing to theological dogma or to established creeds: it has its roots in an intimate knowledge of man and nature; it has the irresistible power to assure us of the spiritual basis of life.

iii: Coleridge

Coleridge as Artist

HERBERT MARSHALL McLUHAN

"AS I BENT my head," wrote Coleridge to Godwin, "there came a distinct, vivid spectrum upon my eyes; it was one little picture—a rock, with birches and ferns on it, a cottage backed by it, and a small stream." The peculiar combination of interests which in Coleridge has served for thirty years to make of him a figure of increasingly contemporary relevance appears in almost any excerpt from his writings or conversation. This note to Godwin is typical of his concern with the poetic vision as a process involved, even "as I bent my head," with ordinary experience. For it was Coleridge as much as anybody who hastened the recognition of the poetic process as linked with the modes of ordinary cognition, and with the methods of the sciences. The very great effort he made to thread the labyrinth of the arts and sciences compelled him to an encyclopedism unapproached since Francis Bacon. For Coleridge was convinced that in the heart of the poetic process was to be found not only the echo of human perception but the Filium Labyrinthi which Bacon sought in vain. Yet even the pursuit of that thread made Bacon's treatise as exciting for Shelley as the greatest poetry.

It is characteristic of Coleridge's encyclopedism, which so many find congenial today, that it locates the arts foremost among human interests as providing the material and the guide for every type of insight and pursuit. Not only the archaeologist but the anthropologist and sociologist, equally with the historians and reconstructors of the phases of human culture, repair today to the arts to acquire the disciplines and the techniques necessary for their creative analysis. It has taken a full century to move from the stage of artistic awareness of Edgar Poe to that of Siegfried Giedion. Poe put crime detection on a scientific basis by bringing into play the poetic process of retracing the stages of human apprehension. It is likewise the procedure of Wordsworth's *Prelude* and Sterne's *Tristram Shandy*. And this process of arrest and retracing, which has been consciously followed by poets since the end of the eighteenth century (when used by a cultural historian and analyst like Siegfried Giedion) provides the very technique of empathy which permits intimate insight into the processes and impulses behind products utterly alien to our own immediate experience. In fact, the Coleridgean awareness of the modes of the imagination as producer represents an enormous extension of the bonds of human sympathy and understanding, socially and historically. Coleridge wrote to Wordsworth *On the Night After His Recitation of a Poem On the Growth of An Individual Mind:*

> *The truly Great*
> *Have all one age, and from one visible space*
> *Shed influence!*

This has more than a neo-Platonic doctrinal interest at the present time when the instantaneity of communication between all parts of the world has brought into involuntary juxtaposition the whole diversity of human cultures. What century is it today in Peking or Jerusalem or Moscow? Yet the very speed of communication between these entities so discontinuous in space, time, and experience, makes for a simultaneity, in which lineal history is abolished by becoming present. Coleridge, a myriad-minded man living in a most tumultuous age, might not have enjoyed our time more than his own, but he was forced to invent a great deal of conceptual equipment which is indispensable to an intellectual of today. And more than any of his contemporaries or successors in the nineteenth century the modes of his apprehension and energizing compel the study and attention of the present generation.

The poetry of Coleridge has suffered from both doctrinaire approval and disfavor so that to avoid such pitfalls in approaching it there is much to be said for a genetic approach to the poetic problems and techniques which in the eighteenth century had preceded his own technical innovations. Writing in *Shelley and the Thought of His Time,* Joseph Barrell laments the split between Shelley's thought and expression: "For there is a vast difference in the manner with which the thought is expressed and in the logic, or way of thought, that the manner implies." So far as manner goes, he continues:

> The Greek way, which is Shelley's way and on the whole the Western way, is to take the reader, or listener, by the hand and lead him step by step from the old position to the new position. It seeks to explain and to demonstrate. Its logic might be described as linear and transitional . . . .
> The Oriental way is different. Its logic might be described not as linear but as radial. The recurring statements do not progress, but return to their center as the spokes of a wheel to their hub.

The dichotomy between linear and radial expression is not really as radical as might appear, but it has in such terms as "continuous" versus "discontinuous" or "statement" versus "suggestion" divided the allegiance of poets, critics, and readers from the time of Coleridge to the present. It certainly had much to do with the intellectual divergence between Coleridge and Wordsworth, between Browning and Tennyson, and between Pound and Eliot. In general, it seems to be felt that the Greek way of continuous transition in a poem makes for a habitable world of homely realities, whereas the Oriental way is inhuman in its austere demands of unflagging and unremitting intensity of contemplation and participation. In one case the poet leads us through the labyrinth of his work, and in the other we are left bewildered to multiply variety in an illusory world of mirrors.

In actual fact the quarrel is pointless so far as art goes since both kinds are inevitably dynamic, following the stages of cognition, which are equally the base of religious ritual and human creation. Francis Bacon knew this very well when he divided the modes of human communication into "magistral" and "probative" or popular and esoteric. The Ciceronian delivers knowledge in a concatenated form having regard to its direct reception and retention. The Senecan, on the other hand, is less concerned with the reception and retention of any given body of data than with having the learner experience the actual process by which the data were achieved. The one is concerned with preserving and transmitting an achieved body of truth, the other with maintaining the process by which truth is achieved. This division embroiled the ancient world. In the twelfth century it recurred as the quarrel between St. Bernard and Abelard, between the historical method of the patristic humanists and systematic or scholastic procedure. In the sixteenth and seventeenth centuries it continues as the quarrel between the Ciceronians and the Senecans, the ancients and the moderns. With Newton, however, the balance is upset in favor of the modern or scientific party. And despite the rise of the Hellenists the arts in the main have followed Newton ever since Thomson's *Seasons*.

That is to say that Newton's *Optics* established a correspondence between inner and outer worlds, between the forms and textures of the world and the faculties of perception and intellection, which has affected the practice of every poet and painter since his time. This correspondence once ascertained, it was possible for a Hartley to derive our inner world from the outer or for a Berkeley to indicate that the outer world was the fiat of our perception and creative imagination. This split between "the physics of the Self and the Not-Self," as it is called by Wyndham Lewis in *The Enemy of the Stars,* helps to explain the differences between the early and later Wordsworth and Coleridge as well as the aesthetic quarrel which grew up between them. And it tells much of the story of the impressionists versus the expressionists or symbolists. At the theological level the Hellenic dualist finds the quarrel insoluble on the assumption of the eternity of matter. The Oriental and the Romantic monist simply fuse inner and outer, matter and spirit, seeking an H-bomb formula of annihilation for ego and existence alike. For the Christian there is no problem since he accepts the revelation that the world was made from nothing as well as the dogma of the resurrection of the body. But for the practising artist there is no point in the quarrel since works of art are not made from ideas or doctrines but, like ourselves, must come into existence by a process which is indifferent to the winds of doctrine. Yet if the artistic process must always be the same the conditions of art and the artist are always changing. Certainly Newton helped to change the circumstances and the matter employed by the artist. The problems faced by Coleridge were of Newton's making.

Until Newton the Senecans had dominated the literary scene from Montaigne to Pascal and from Donne to Pope. Their preoccupation was with the literary techniques for arresting and projecting some phase of the human mind: to arrest in order to project, and to project in order to contemplate. Like the inventors of cinema at the beginning of this century they hit upon the technique of stylistic discontinuity as a means of analyzing or arresting a moment of consciousness. The movie camera takes a thousand still shots in order to capture the aspects of a brief movement. The *style coupé* and the "cutted period" attempted something comparable in the essay and the poem. But to have carried this art further than Pope was probably impossible. At any rate the advent of Newton's *Optics* diverted artistic effort from poetic statement to the use of external landscape as a means of projecting and controlling states of mind under the guidance of two major concepts. The first of these was derived from the study of the visual harmonics of the spectrum which led to a revival of the classic images of the harps of Aeolus and Memnon. If the surfaces of matter were varied prisms for revealing the qualities of light, then the entire visible and audible world could be conceived as a species of visual music. The second concept is related to the first. For, if the external world is attuned to the mind of man then the whole of Nature is a language and the poet is a pontifex or bridger between the two worlds. He conducts the symphony of mind and nature.

The harp and language themes are fused in *Frost at Midnight:*

> . . . *so shall thou see and hear*
> *The lovely shapes and sounds intelligible*
> *Of that eternal language, which thy God*
> *Utters . . . .*

And in *France: An Ode* the pontifex theme is linked to the harp.

> . . . *on that sea-cliff's verge,*
> *Whose pines, scarce travelled by the breeze above,*
> *Had made one murmur with the distant surge!*
> *Yes, while I stood and gazed, my temples bare,*
> *And shot my being through earth, sea, and air,*
> *Possessing all things with intensest love . . . .*

The poet here is exercising his priestly powers of purifying the wells of existence, exerting his primary imagination which is the agent of all perception, not the secondary imagination which brings art into existence as an echo of the functions of perception.

The world felt as Aeolian harp and as an apocalyptic language, on one hand, and the poet as pontifex or magus, on the other, pretty well sets the stage for all the problems of aesthetics from Thomson, Collins, and Akenside to Coleridge, Keats, and Shelley. These problems, moreover, remain our own. For the work of Yeats, Joyce, and Eliot represents a continuous development of poetic theory and practice along these lines. The artist becomes scientist, hierophant, and sage, as well as the unacknowledged legislator of the world.

Naturally enough, accompanying this hypertrophy of the artistic role in society has come a good deal of bewildered dissent, and it has centered around Matthew Arnold's claim that the business of poetry is in the middle realm of culture or the region of ethical and political teaching. The poet may be pontifex between this world and the next, but our business is to live well in this world. This dilemma is a crux for Coleridge and Wordsworth and helps perhaps to explain their gradual cessation of poetic activity as well as their turning to social and ethical speculation. That this was the way in which the disciples of Coleridge interpreted him is perfectly plain from the activities of John Sterling, Thomas Arnold, and F. D. Maurice. But it is significant that it is not this side of Coleridge which interests the modern student of poetry. When Voltaire approached Congreve as a celebrated poet and was told that the dramatist wished to be considered "only as an English gentleman," he replied that had he thought of Congreve that way he should never have troubled to seek him out. Were Coleridge to tell a young intellectual today that he wished to be considered only as the author of *The Statesman's Manual* he would get the same reply as that given by Voltaire. Mr. Basil Willey's discussion of Coleridge in *Nineteenth Century Studies* sets him in his proper Victorian perspective as the alternative to Bentham. Coleridge represented the movement to reconcile neo-Platonism and Christianity as a means of envisaging social and political institutions *sub specie aeternitatis,* as opposed to the utilitarian functionalists and mechanists for whom the entire fabric of society was unpenetrated by the divine. In this regard, the prose of Mr. Eliot since *The Use of Poetry and the Use of Criticism* (1933) has for the most part been concerned to promote the same point of view. Whereas Mr. Richards, in accord with the work of Lord Russell, has attempted to retain and to assimilate Coleridge's post-Hartleian speculations on aesthetics within Bentham's scheme.

To approach Coleridge's art, however, it is necessary to see him at work amidst the technical developments of the poetry of his time. For poetry being concerned with obtaining specific effects must always be seeking new means for these effects amidst the constantly changing conditions of culture. For young Coleridge the most immediate and intense poetic experience was obtained from the sonnets of Bowles. For Mr. Eliot the same awakening occurred when reading FitzGerald's

Omar Khayyám. In each instance there was a very striking technical innovation which, in the particular circumstances of each of these poets, released a chain of consequences. FitzGerald held up to Mr. Eliot the technique of discontinuous vignettes with their endless power of comment and revelation of one another by the mere fact of their harmonic or ironic juxtaposition. Subsequently Mr. Eliot found this paratactic principle embodied in varying modes in all the great art of the world from Homer to Pope. But it was revealed to him by the unlikely Fitz-Gerald. In the same way Coleridge found in the sentimental flaccidities of William Bowles the technique of exploring an arrested moment of emotion by fixing it spatially in a particularized landscape. This technique had already been elaborated in painting, music, and poetry since the later seventeenth century. But by Bowles it was revealed to Coleridge for the first time. Just as the tone of FitzGerald was perhaps an antidote to certain strenuous banalities of the Victorians, so the languid sentiment of Bowles struck Coleridge as tender, natural, and bracing amidst the rhetorical posturings of the later eighteenth century. And what pleased him in Bowles he was soon to find more fully in the old ballads and in Wordsworth's *Evening Walk* and *Descriptive Sketches.* What is evident at once from a glance at *An Evening Walk* and *Descriptive Sketches* is the extreme artiness of young Wordsworth. He is a master of every visual and auditory nuance dear to the picturesque school:

> *Where falls the purple morning far and wide*
> *In flakes of light upon the mountain side;*
> *Where with loud voice the power of water shakes*
> *The leafy wood, or sleeps in quiet lakes.*

Those "flakes of light" were not to be discovered by painters until much later. But already in a poem "written in very early youth" there is the opening line which fixes amidst the picturesque techniques the mature vision:

> *Calm is all nature as a resting wheel.*

That is the master vision of all those "spots of time" for which Wordsworth painfully sought the precise objective correlative in carefully wrought landscapes. It is the key to all his lyrics and even to *The Prelude,* which in order to follow his process of enlightenment has to arrest for contemplation the entire movement of his mind from youth to age:

> . . . *we have traced the stream*
> *From the blind cavern whence is faintly heard*
> *Its natal murmur . . . .*
> *Imagination having been our theme.*

Moments of insight in Wordsworth's poetry are explicitly associated with an experience of an arrest in time:

> *And, on the shape of that unmoving man,*
> *His steadfast face and sightless eyes, I gazed,*
> *As if admonished from another world.*
> *Though reared upon the base of outward things,*
> *Structures like these the excited spirit mainly*
> *Builds for herself; scenes different there are,*
> *Full-formed, that take, with small internal help,*
> *Possession of the faculties,—the peace*
> *That comes with night; the deep solemnity*
> *Of nature's intermediate hours of rest,*
> *When the great tide of human life stands still:*
> *The business of the day to come, unborn,*
> *Of that gone by, locked up, as in the grave . . . .*

Wordsworth was an artist with an intensely educated and sophisticated eye. Coleridge by comparison has an illiterate eye but shows a cultivation of the auditory powers greatly superior to Wordsworth. It is a distinction which also separates Joyce and Eliot from Pound. Wordsworth is the indefatigable watcher thrilling to the dramatic minutiae and nuances of vision:

> *Once again I see*
> *These hedge-rows, hardly hedge-rows, little lines*
> *Of sportive wood run wild: these pastoral forms*
> *Green to the very doors; and wreaths of smoke*
> *Sent up, in silence, from among the trees!*

In his management of external landscape Coleridge is by comparison a botcher but usually he redeems his landscapes with some auditory touch of magic:

> *And watch the clouds, that late were rich with light,*
> *Slow saddening round, and mark the star of eve*
> *Serenely brilliant (Such should Wisdom be)*
> *Shine opposite! How exquisite the scents*
> *Snatch'd from yon bean-field! and the world so hush'd!*

The stilly murmur of the distant Sea
Tells us of silence.

Coleridge gave a good deal of deliberate attention to the forms of the external world, but it is significant that as with Eliot external forms exerted their greatest power upon him through the medium of books. So filtered, the external world became for Coleridge an internal moon-haunted landscape which he could manipulate with the utmost effect. Seen this way, the division of labor which Coleridge and Wordsworth proposed in their project of *Lyrical Ballads* corresponded to the diversity of their native powers. But the aesthetic theory which they largely shared awarded the bays to the poet of the eye and daylight. So that Coleridge could hardly fail to take a desponding view of his own poetry. Since Rimbaud, Mallarmé, Eliot, and Joyce the enormous advantages in scope, learning, and precision of the interior landscape over external landscape have become evident, and the poems of Coleridge have accordingly gained in interest. But it may well have been that for Coleridge his own acceptance of the theory of imagination and perception exemplified in the poetry of Wordsworth was a detriment to the continuance of poetic activity. The theory of language and communication shared by Mallarmé, Valéry, Joyce, and Eliot would have proved as unwelcome to Wordsworth as it might have been inspiring to Coleridge. In *The Use of Poetry and The Use of Criticism* (p. 111) Eliot gives this account of the matter:

> What I call this 'auditory imagination' is the feeling for syllable and rhythm, penetrating far below the conscious levels of thought and feeling, invigorating every word; sinking to the most primitive and forgotten, returning to the origin and bringing something back, seeking the beginning and the end. It works through meanings, certainly, or not without meanings in the ordinary sense, and fuses the old and obliterated and the trite, the current, and the new and surprising, the most ancient and the most civilised mentality.

That passage makes a better critical account of *The Ancient Mariner* than perhaps Coleridge or Wordsworth knew how to give as critics. It explains what they were up to in bringing the old ballad rituals and verbal simplicities into juxtaposition with the lyric impulse generated by their study of the aesthetic moment and its attendant landscape.

But Wordsworth the seer had little sense of the auditory dimensions of language which could control great vistas of erudition and collective experience. For the auditory labyrinth is charged with the experience of the past of the race and unites the poet with history in a continuous present. Whereas the poet of the eye is more solitary than social, finding his satisfactions in stylized patterns rather than in the acoustic accumulations of learning and collective insight. It is thus perfectly natural for Coleridge to justify the mode of his poetic activity by an auditory image which Wordsworth would have avoided: "The reader should be carried forward . . . by the pleasurable activity of the mind excited by the attractions of the journey itself. Like the motion of a serpent, which the Egyptians made the emblem of intellectual power; or like the path of sound through the air;—at every step he pauses and half recedes, and from the retrogressive movement collects the force which again carries him onward." The latter comment seems to set the gloss subsequently added to *The Ancient Mariner* in a sufficiently luminous light while retorting to Wordsworth's critique about the discontinuity of the poem.

As poetic practitioners Wordsworth and Coleridge were in agreement about two things—that poetry was concerned with the rendering of an instant of arrested awareness which freed the mind from the clogs of habitual perception, and that a landscape with human figures was the necessary means of achieving this end. The aim was to dislocate the reader into attention not so much by rhythmic or verbal novelty such as Eliot or Auden rely on, as by some startling visual fact which did not distort but reveal nature:

> During the first year that Mr. Wordsworth and I were neighbors, our conversations turned frequently on the two cardinal points of poetry, the power of exciting the sympathy of the reader by a faithful adherence to the truth of nature, and the power of giving the interest of novelty by the modifying colours of the imagination. The sudden charm, which accidents of light and shade, which moonlight or sunset diffused over a known and familiar landscape, appeared to represent the practicability of combining both.

As for the human figures in these landscapes, "it was agreed that my endeavours should be directed to persons and characters supernatural, or at least romantic; yet so far as to transfer from our inward nature a human interest and a semblance of truth sufficient to procure for these shadows of imagination that willing suspension of disbelief for the moment, which constitutes poetic faith."

Scattered up and down in *The Prelude* and *The Excursion* Wordsworth has a good deal to say about the aesthetic program enunciated by Coleridge, leaving no doubt concerning the reasons for their divergent theories of communication and the poetic process. But because the landscape techniques of neither Coleridge nor Wordsworth have been much studied the point of Wordsworth's polemic seems to have been missed. Although Coleridge had no difficulty in locating the excellence of Wordsworth's poetry, Wordsworth could not but attribute the very virtues of Coleridge's poems to disease:

> *I have thought*
> *Of thee, thy learning, gorgeous eloquence,*
> *And all the strength and plumage of thy youth,*
> *Thy subtle speculations, toils abstruse*
> *Among the schoolmen, and Platonic forms*
> *Of wild ideal pageantry, shaped out*
> *From things well-matched or ill, and words for things,*
> *The self-created sustenance of a mind*
> *Debarred from Nature's living images,*
> *Compelled to be a life unto herself . . .*
> *   . . . had we met,*
> *Even at that early time, needs must I trust*
> *In the belief, that my maturer age,*
> *My calmer habits, and more steady voice,*
> *Would with an influence benign have soothed,*
> *Or chased away, the airy wretchedness*
> *That battened on thy youth.*

The patronage aside, Wordsworth is here making a technical critique of Coleridge which he knew Coleridge was gloomily disposed to accept. For if the imagination is the very agent of perception, the means of communication between persons and objects in nature, and if the poetic process is an echo of this imagination, then the poet deprived from earliest years of intimate communion with natural objects (poor Coleridge left only to commune with the stars on the slates of Christ's Hospital) is necessarily in an "airy" and undernourished state.

The *Prelude* is a full-dress reconstruction of the rich and glorious stages of sensuous apprehension by which Wordsworth escaped the "airy" fate of Coleridge. Coleridge and the auditory imagination provide the subplot of that portrait of the artist as a great river, the image which recurs when Wordsworth thinks of himself in poetic act. Wordsworth would seem to elect himself to play St. Michael to Coleridge's Lucifer.

Confronted with the corrupt and artificial labyrinth of the city, Wordsworth slips into the language of Coleridge and the inner landscape of "fancy":

> *With deep devotion, Nature, did I feel,*
> *In that enormous City's turbulent world*
> *On men and things, what benefit I owed*
> * To thee . . .*
>   *. . . more exquisitely fair*
> *Than that famed paradise of ten thousand trees,*
> *.   .   .   .   .*
> *A sumptuous dream of flowery lawns, with domes*
> *Of pleasure sprinkled over, shady dells*
> *For eastern monasteries, sunny mounts*
> *With temples crested, bridges, gondolas,*
> *Rocks, dens, and groves of foliage taught to melt*
> *Into each other their obsequious hues,*
> *Vanished and vanishing in subtle chase,*
> *Too fine to be pursued.*

"Too fine to be pursued" would seem to be an echo of Milton's demonic disputants "in wandering mazes lost." Some lines further in the same book Wordsworth explains how though he, too, could indulge an oriental fancy, unlike Coleridge, he was blessed with a redemptive grace:

> *   . . . 'mid the fervent swarm*
> *Of these vagaries, with an eye so rich*
> *As mine was through the bounty of a grand*
> *And lovely region, I had forms distinct*
> *To steady me: each airy thought revolved*
> *Round a substantial centre, which at once*
> *Incited it to motion, and controlled.*
> *I did not pine like one in cities bred,*
> *As was thy melancholy lot, dear Friend!*
> *Great Spirit as thou art, in endless dreams*
> *Of sickliness, disjoining, joining, things*
> *Without the light of knowledge.*

Within the intellectual scheme of the late eighteenth century Wordsworth could give himself the airs of a modern working-class intellectual condescending to a millionaire Marxist. As a poet reared in the city Coleridge could have fancy but not imagination. So that exercising his own genius for the interior landscape Coleridge was as one born out of due time. And gratuitously he seems to have accepted his fate as a hopeless barrier to major poetic activity. At least it is worth suggesting this line for further study, that there is something doctrinaire rather than spontaneous and necessary about the stages leading to the decline of his poetic activity. For the future of poetry lay on the path which Wordsworth avoided and that Coleridge was prompted to discontinue even after having discovered the way of the interior landscape in his great poems.

The exterior landscape serves very well for certain states of mind and some areas of experience. But it is necessarily a cumbersome apparatus ill-suited to the variety and compression of the modern city:

> *Au cœur d'un vieux faubourg, labyrinthe fangeux*
> *Où l'humanité grouille en ferments orageux,*

> *On voit un chiffonnier qui vient, hochant la tête,*
> *Buttant, et se cognant aux murs comme un poëte.*

Inspired by Edgar Poe, as Poe was by Coleridge, Baudelaire developed the technique of the interior landscape as a means of revealing the intensities generated by the harsh dissonances, overlayerings and discontinuities of city life. The picturesque world of Wordsworth, on the other hand, has not proved capable of carrying the complex freight of modern experience nor of assimilating the riches of the collective human past which the modern poet needs to evoke in the midst of city landscapes.

Wordsworth and Coleridge were agreed that the poetic process coincided with the learning process, but Coleridge saw that the formal learning of philology and philosophy was not incompatible with the poetic process. And in this he pointed the way to restoring erudition to the scheme of poetic communication. Writing to Cottle, he said:

> I should not think of devoting less than twenty years to an epic poem. Ten years to collect materials and warm my mind with universal science. I would be a tolerable Mathematician. I would thoroughly understand Mechanics; hydrostatics; optics and Astronomy; Botany; Metallurgy; Fossilism; Chemistry; Geology; Anatomy; Medicine; then the mind of man; then the minds of men, in all. Travels, Voyages and Histories.

This is the full classical program of studies, the *eguklios paideia*, pursued by Virgil, Dante, Chaucer, Spenser, and Milton. In intention, at least, it is recognized as necessary by modern poets like Valéry, Joyce, Pound, and Eliot. And there is the work of Lowes to show how much of this kind of learning went to the making of *The Ancient Mariner,* which is at least a little epic.

Despite the fact that the epyllion or little epic is a classical form which has been used continuously in classical, medieval, and modern times, it has been given little scholarly or critical attention. Most readers might scarcely recognize *The Waste Land* or *Four Quartets* as epyllia. But such is also the form of Hemingway's *The Old Man and the Sea,* a work which readily associates itself with *The Ancient Mariner.* Eliot's intimate mastery of this compact and learned form enables him to point out the debt of Byron to Coleridge in working up a poem like *The Giaour:*

> As a tale-teller we must rate Byron very high indeed: I can think of none other since Chaucer who has an equal readability, with the exception of Coleridge whom Byron abused and from whom Byron learned a great deal . . . . Byron's plots, if they deserve that name, are extremely simple. What makes the tales interesting is first a torrential fluency of verse and a skill in varying it from time to time to avoid monotony; and second a genius for divagation. Digression, indeed, is one of the most valuable arts of the story-teller. The effect of Byron's digressions is to keep us interested in the story-teller himself, and through this to interest us more in the story.[1]

If Byron's plots are so simple as scarcely to deserve the name it is because his tales are nature rituals like *The Ancient Mariner.* *The Giaour* (jour-day) follows the east-west movement of the sun, through the hours of the day and the signs of the zodiac, celebrating the fire principle. Such is presumably the larger pattern of the *Iliad,* whereas the *Odyssey,* like the *Ulysses* of James Joyce, the *Cantos* of Pound, and *The Ancient Mariner* involves the ritual of both sun and moon. As Lowes has shown, Coleridge's great plans for hymns to the sun, moon, and the four elements are reduced to, or realized in, the *Mariner.* This clears up at once the problem of the "motiveless malignancy" of the old navigator in killing the albatross. For the action of the poem is not on the ethical plane of social or political existence, but, like *The Giaour,* concerns a spiritual adventure of ascent. This appears plainly in the commentary of Thomas Taylor, one of Coleridge's

[1] *From Anne to Victoria,* ed. Bonamy Dobree (1937).

favorite writers, on "The Wanderings of Ulysses," as well as in Porphyry's *Cave of the Nymphs*. Porphyry says of the episode of the blinding of the Cyclops who is the natal daemon of Ulysses:

> For it will not be simply, and in a concise way, possible for any
> one to be liberated from this sensible life, who blinds this daemon,
> and renders his energies inefficacious, but he who dares to do this,
> will be pursued by the anger of the marine and material Gods,
> whom it is first requisite to appease by sacrifices, labours, and pa-
> tient endurance. . . . Nor will he even then be liberated from
> labours; but this will be effected when he has entirely passed over
> the raging sea, and, though still living, becomes so ignorant of
> marine and material works as to mistake an oar for a corn-van.[2]

Taylor also comments that whereas in superior souls the natal and
essential daemons are one, it is not so in imperfect souls whose natural
lot, like that of Ulysses, is cast on the plane of ethical and political
striving: "As he is, however, departing from a sensible to an intellectual
life, though circuitously and slowly, he is represented in so doing as
blinding and irritating his natal daemon. For he who blinds the eye
of sense, and extinguishes its light, after his will has profoundly assented
to its use, must expect punishment for the deed; as necessary ulti-
mately to his own peculiar good, and the general order of the universe."

The Mariner's natal daemon is the albatross, as is the white whale
the daemon of Captain Ahab; and Coleridge was right in saying that
the poem had, if anything, too much of the moral in it.

What is relevant here to the art of Coleridge concerns the confessional and digressive character of *The Ancient Mariner*. For it is
this confessional and circuitous character which has penetrated not
only Byron's tales but the art of *The Ring and the Book,* the novels of
Henry James, of Ford Madox Ford, and of Joseph Conrad. It is the
pattern of Pound's *Mauberley* and the *Cantos,* and provides the thread
to the labyrinth of Eliot's poems from *Prufrock* to *The Cocktail Party.*
Seen as movements of ascent or descent, of abstraction or concretion,
these works follow the stages of human apprehension and cognition,
of purgation and fruition. So that in linking the primary and secondary
imaginations as analogous, and as providing the key to the poetic process and pattern, Coleridge would appear as the master of the literary
art of our time.

The dislocation of the simple chronology of events is not a whim

[2] Taylor's translation.

directed to obscurity, but, as in the wanderings of Ulysses, a fidelity
to a higher order of intelligibility. As Conrad put it, it is *that you may
see:* the endless circuits and digressions follow the path not of raw
events but of the extraction of the significance from events in the order
of learning and experience. This is the course of Tiresias, the narrator
of *The Waste Land.* And Edward Chamberlayne in *The Cocktail Party*
(in which there are three cyclopean guardians) having made a decision,
sets in motion a machinery that he is as powerless to arrest as the old
navigator in *The Ancient Mariner.*

Since many modern readers have complained about the illogical
order of symbolist art it is worth stressing the fact that the order of
learning and insight is not the order of rational concatenation but of
analogical perception. And it is much owing to Coleridge that since
Poe and Baudelaire poetry and fiction have largely employed the pattern
of the spiritual and intellectual quest rather than that of realistic narrative. Thus, Eliot notes that "Byron developed the verse *conte* con-
siderably beyond Moore and Scott . . . . Byron's verse tales represent a more mature stage of this transient form than Scott's . . . . Scott
perfected a straightforward story with the type of plot which he was
to employ in his novels. Byron combined exoticism with actuality, and
developed most effectively the use of *suspense.*" Only suspense is not
for thrill but for arrest of movement for contemplation, and to create
one of those "spots in time" which permit a flash of intuitive wisdom.

It is plain, in the light of Eliot's remarks, that not only the nineteenth-century verse tale but the short story as handled by Flaubert,
Henry James, Joyce, and Hemingway is in debt to nature ritual, of
which *The Ancient Mariner* is the great exemplar.

If the development of medieval art was from ritual to romance,
the process of art since Coleridge has been from romance to ritual, and
The Ancient Mariner like its precursor *The Wanderings of Cain* fore-
shadows *The Waste Land.* In this perspective Eliot's further remarks
on *The Giaour* become luminous:

> *The Giaour* is a long poem, and the plot is very simple, though
> not easy to follow . . . . We subsequently discover that the story
> of this vendetta—or part of it—is being told by the Giaour himself
> to an elderly priest, by way of making his confession. It is a singu-
> lar kind of confession because the Giaour seems anything but peni-
> tent, and makes quite clear that although he has sinned, it is not
> really by his own fault. He seems impelled rather by the same motive

as the Ancient Mariner, than by any desire for absolution—which could hardly have been given: but the device has its use in providing a small complication to the story.

The complications and interruptions are necessary artistically (witness those which impede the narrative of Sweeney in *Sweeney Agonistes*) in order that not just the understanding but the whole man may become involved in response to the developing situation. The few interruptions which Coleridge at first provided for the narrative of the old navigator may well have seemed insufficient for this artistic purpose, and so he may have been led to add the gloss to the poem years later to provide a kind of cosmic chorus. So completed, the poem achieves a kind of continuous parallel between two levels of action, as does Joyce's *Ulysses* in moving simultaneously in modern Dublin and ancient Ithaca. And it is in this same way that Tiresias in *The Waste Land* moves "between two lives."

A great deal more needs to be said and done about the poetic art of Coleridge in relation to his contemporaries and to ourselves. His own development from a poet of rhetorical statement to a master of symbolic ritual prophetically enacts the history of art and poetry of the century which followed him. Seen, moreover, in its full light this development was impossible without the great intellectual labor which is too often supposed to have sterilized his poetic gifts. But it may well have been that, as with Rimbaud, the very magnitude of the change he experienced in his own modes of thought and feeling discouraged further experiment along lines that made such exhausting demands on mind and heart.

8 The Thought of Coleridge

D. G. JAMES

1

IT IS CLEAR that Coleridge's attempts at philosophy have been more seriously and sympathetically considered in our time than ever before. We must indeed allow for John Stuart Mill's excellent essay; and there are the pages in F. D. Maurice's *Moral and Metaphysical Philosophy* and in other books by him. Mill was indeed a model of fair-mindedness in what he wrote; but as the years passed, his own influence told heavily and increasingly against Coleridge's. Maurice was no doubt Coleridge's most distinguished disciple; but his pages in *Moral and Metaphysical Philosophy* contain little enough substance; he hardly knows, we feel, quite what to say: there seemed, after all, so little of a philosophy to expound; and Maurice was, as the years passed, to become not a little disillusioned and exasperated with the master's writings: Coleridge stood for so much that was important, but it came, somehow, to so little; it evaporated in the effort to bring it to order, to make it signify something quite clearly. In the meantime, there was no doubt about Coleridge's reputation as a poet and as a critic; and there has been no hint of a decline. But the twentieth century was well under way when Miss Alice Snyder's labors on the unpublished philosophical manuscripts marked a new epoch in the study of Coleridge's philosophy. In 1930 Mr. Muirhead published his work *Coleridge as Philosopher;* in 1931 Mr. Wellek's *Kant in England* appeared, and in 1934 Mr. Richards' *Coleridge on Imagination,* which sought specially to see Coleridge's philosophy in relation to his criticism; in 1949 Miss Coburn published her excellent edition of the *Philosophical Lectures* of 1818–1819; and we have recently read of the generosity which will make possible the publication of all the unpublished writings. It is true that Sir Edmund Chambers, in his biography of Coleridge published in 1938, said that when Coleridge died, he left "a handful of golden poems, an emptiness in the heart of a few friends, and a will-o'-the-wisp light for bemused thinkers"; but to speak like this was no longer in accordance with the temper of the time; there was more to it than this; and what more there is, many are deeply anxious to discover.

2

IF WE HAVE regard to the prevailing spirit of Coleridge's thought, and to his place in a broad classification of thinkers, we shall not do better than read John Stuart Mill's essay on him. Mill there places Coleridge alongside one of the leading representatives, in that time, of the tradition of eighteenth-century thought; what he says is an aid to comprehension of Coleridge's place in the history of European philosophy: it enables us to see Coleridge as taking his station in a series of thinkers who, in their different ways, have opposed themselves to the great stream of influence which has flowed out of eighteenth-century "rationalism": Burke, Wordsworth, de Maistre, Newman, Arnold, Kierkegaard, to name only some of the celebrated. It is true that these writers opposed the stream unavailingly; and the great stream has become a flood. Still, it is natural to think that our present great interest in Coleridge's thought arises from the alarm we feel in the face of our present situation. The interest in and the influence of Kierkegaard on the continent of Europe is one of the most notable spiritual phenomena of our time. In England, and, I imagine, in America, we feel a certain natural and right-minded distrust of anything so extreme and one-sided. All the same, I think it probable that we look in our time and in our circumstances with special interest to Coleridge as one out of temper with the "rationalistic" and "mechanical" abstractions so strong in his age, and, after years of alliance with "scientific" naturalism, still stronger in ours; and we hope that he may, in spite of all the obvious discouragement his writings provide, have a saving power for us. It is therefore a matter of some moment to find out whether this is so, and whether the generations which lie between Coleridge and us have not done ill in disregarding what Mill called a "seminal" mind in his time.

If Coleridge's mind was indeed "seminal," and if he has been wrongly disregarded, he may now perhaps come into his own; and it becomes our duty to bring about this result.

3

IT IS NOT necessary for my purpose to recount the way in which Coleridge's thought changed and developed in his early years. At the beginning of his adult life he was naturally deeply affected by eighteenth-century ways of thought: he was radical in his politics, unitarian in his religion, associationist in his theory of knowledge. I shall say only that in the first year of the new century he finally rejected associationism; and at this time also the influence of Kant broke upon him. It is true that he said, in *Biographia Literaria,* that something of the fundamental thesis of the *Critique of Pure Reason* had dawned on him, like a "guiding light," before he read the book; and we must allow for the influence on him of neo-Platonism, and of Cudworth [1] before he read Kant. Still, his study of Kant was climacteric. Again, it is no concern of mine to narrate the history of Kant's influence on Coleridge. But it is certainly not possible to ignore either the influence or its history. We are free no doubt to agree with the view implied in the remark of Sir Edmund Chambers which I quoted; it is perhaps natural to feel a lively sympathy with it; but it is not really possible to fail to take seriously the way in which Kant told on Coleridge's mind and the quite momentous consequences it had for him.

We must remember that by the time Kant set, or at least largely determined, the course of Coleridge's mind and thought, Coleridge had written his greatest poetry. The golden years were past. No doubt, during them, his mind had been in a philosophical ferment; and his experience of poetic creation must have caused him to look for philosophical principles more able to deal with the material provided by his and Wordsworth's excitement. But however that may be, we remark that January, 1800, saw the publication of Wordsworth's Preface to the second edition of the *Lyrical Ballads;* and in the Preface Wordsworth said that poetry is "the breath and finer spirit of all knowledge; it is the impassioned expression which is in the countenance of all Science." Now this claim is a large one. Wordsworth was no philosopher, and Cole-

[1] See R. L. Brett, "Coleridge's Theory of the Imagination," *Essays and Studies,* New Series, II (1949).

ridge never succeeded in making him one; but here was, in effect, a sweeping philosophical pronouncement. It is not surprising if Coleridge, more speculative and less prophetic than Wordsworth, felt the need of a more elaborate philosophical statement; and no doubt he was quick, in reading the *Critique of Pure Reason,* to seize what Kant said about the imagination. Years later, in *Biographia Literaria,* he was to write his often-quoted sentences about the imagination; and it is little more (with "imagination" substituted for "poetry") than a restatement of Wordsworth's declaration in his Preface: he said that the imagination is the living power and prime agent in all human perception, and that the imagination of the poet is of a piece with this power and identical with it in kind.

4

NOW IT IS important to see what Wordsworth and Coleridge said about the imagination (and indeed all that certain other Romantic writers said about it) against the background of two centuries of earlier reflection on human knowledge. For what Descartes and Spinoza had to say about imagination was that it is the living power and prime agent in all human error; if, they said, the human mind is to come by truth, it is by discarding, in the greatest possible degree, the images of sense and by seeking out clear and distinct ideas; and to come by these, the exercise of thought in its greatest purity was necessary. They sharply set the power of imagination over against the power of thought: senseperception and the images of poetry confused and deceived; we needed, they said, to achieve, in all our thought, the perspicuity of mathematics; and certainly the ideal of mathematical reasoning mastered their own philosophizing. Spinoza might call perception a kind of "thought"; but if it was "thought," it was at best obscure thought and must be resolved into the clarity of intellectual idea.

In England, as on the continent, the ideals of the intellect were far outweighing the ideals of perception and art. Hobbes began his career as a typical Renaissance humanist and translated Thucydides; but a time came when he read Euclid, and his doing so determined and controlled the rest of his life: here was the image and model of all true knowledge. But in this "Euclidean" world, history and art could find little standing ground; their existence might be excused, they might even serve some useful purposes, they might conduce to virtue; but, said

Hobbes, "the Light of humane minds is Perspicuous Words, but by exact definitions first snuffed, and purged from ambiguity; *Reason* is the *pace;* Encrease of *Science,* the *way;* and the Benefit of man-kind the *end."* In this world, history and poetry could lay no claim to Reason and Science; they could only claim to be of some little benefit to mankind.

Still, it was not Descartes or Spinoza or Hobbes who was to be the master of the eighteenth century: Locke was to be the master of those that knew in that time. When the *Essay concerning Human Understanding* was published in 1690, the systems of Descartes, Hobbes, and Spinoza took a shattering blow. Locke's temper was cool, modest, sober; he was not possessed by the soaring intellectual ambitions of his predecessors, and he was profoundly antirationalist: he had a way of appealing quietly to obvious fact, and unassumingly won the confidence of his contemporaries and of the century which he inaugurated. In the jargon of philosophy, Locke was empiricist; but even in his empiricism he was restrained; and in his analysis of sense-perception, he was at no great pains to hide his stumblings and uncertainties. In the strict philosophical sense of the word, Locke was certainly no rationalist, as Descartes, Spinoza, and Hobbes had been; but in the vaguer and looser sense of the word, his temper was "rationalistic." For all his sweetness and light, his mind was eminently cautious; and he declared that to believe any proposition except by "the irresistible light of self-evidence, or by the force of demonstration," is to act on our inclinations and is so far "a derogation from the love of truth as such"; the love of truth, he said, can "receive no evidence from our passions or interests" and "should receive no tincture from them." These sentences appear in his chapter *On Enthusiasm* which he added in the fourth edition of the *Essay;* they are not, I think, true to the prevailing temper and deepest insights of the *Essay* as a whole; but they helped to make easy the paths of the Tolands, the Collinses, and the Bolingbrokes, and to initiate an age (despite Bishop Butler and the many unlettered souls whom John Wesley touched) which was unaware of the adventures and ardors of religious faith.

It is not then surprising that Locke, like Descartes and Spinoza, did not think the arts important or able to manifest what is real. He does not even allow that they bring even extrinsic advantages: "Poetry and gaming," he said, "which usually go together, are alike in this too, that they seldom bring any advantage, but to those who have nothing else to live on." No mines of gold or silver may be discovered in Parnassus:

Parnassus may have a pleasant air; but it has a barren soil. So he said in his *Thoughts on Education*. In the *Essay* he had said that if "we would speak of things as they are, we must allow that all the art of rhetorick, besides order and clearness, all the artificial and figurative application of words eloquence hath invented, are for nothing else but to insinuate wrong ideas, move the passions and thereby mislead the judgement and so indeed are perfect cheats . . . ." These words were written well within the century which saw the first performances of *Hamlet* and *King Lear*.

5

THERE WAS bound to be a reaction from all this. In England Blake was the first reactionary, full of power, violence, and excess. But the road of his excesses did not lead him to any obvious wisdom; and he was too little of a philosopher to combat, with even the rudiments of system, the spirit of the later seventeenth and the eighteenth century. Coleridge was both a great poet and a professed philosopher; and he was the only English philosopher of the nineteenth century who set himself, with any show of method, to provide a philosophical justification of both art and Christianity. Up to 1817, the year of the publication of *Biographia Literaria,* he was preoccupied, in his philosophical thinking, with the philosophy of art; from that time onwards he was preoccupied with the philosophy of religion. The year 1817 is a fairly clear dividing line; and we are left to regret that he never set himself to integrate, at least in any considerable measure, his reflections on the nature of poetry with his reflections on religion and Christianity.

I shall, at a later stage in this essay, speak in turn of these two periods in Coleridge's intellectual history. Before doing so, I remark on the prevailing antirationalism of all his reflection. He was certainly no rationalist in the sense in which that word may be applied to Spinoza; the chief purpose of Kant's writings had been to set drastic limits to the power and scope of the human intellect; and Coleridge himself, early in his career, before he knew that the Sage of Koenigsberg had already performed the feat, had seen the need to do so. But he opposed himself also to rationalism in that wider sense, which is well illustrated in the quotations I have given from Locke, which consists in a certain temper of the personality more than in any set of formulated doctrines, and which may be shared by minds whose precise beliefs by no means coincide: it is the prevailing temper of the later seventeenth century, the eighteenth, the nineteenth, and the twentieth century. It shows itself as a disposition to believe that the intelligence is capable of acting in all matters in more or less complete freedom from "prejudice," faith, or again, tradition; that thought is truly trustworthy only when it issues out of the greatest possible abstraction from the life and commerce of the personality in its entirety; that philosophy is trustworthy only when, in a state of such abstraction, it may partake of the "impersonality" of scientific or mathematical procedure; that human personality may rightly be required to bow to the deliverances of the abstracted intelligence or, when such deliverances (through a necessary lack of demonstration and evidence) are not possible, may rightly be required to undergo, as far as is possible, a corresponding suspense or arrest. Now such a rationalistic disposition cannot be wholly satisfied; the thought and the being of a personality cannot thus be sundered: a man's thought images what he is; and scientific and mathematical procedures do not provide to philosophy its norms and standards: if they do so, the philosophy which results will be shallow enough to show clearly the unacknowledged bottom of prejudice upon which it rests; and its effect can only be, in the last resort, to weaken or destroy the freedom and responsibility of what is properly human. Rationalism is an attempt, necessarily vain, to become emancipated from time and space, history and tradition, the particularity of the finite; it is to decline the humility which may fairly be expected of something both finite and thoughtful.

Now Coleridge saw that this is so, as Burke had seen before him and Newman was to see after him. He speaks indeed on these matters in an ebullient and even grandiose way which is distasteful to us, as the manner of Burke and of Newman is not. In the ninth chapter of the *Biographia Literaria* he says that "the term, Philosophy, defines itself as an affectionate seeking after the truth; but Truth is the correlative of Being." He goes on to say that anyone acquainted with "the history of philosophy, during the two or three last centuries, cannot but admit that there appears to have existed a sort of secret and tacit compact among the learned, not to pass beyond a certain limit in speculative science . . . . The few men of genius . . . who actually did overstep this boundary, anxiously avoided the appearance of having so done." He speaks of the mystics, George Fox, Jacob Behmen, William Law, as men to whom he owes a special gratitude; for, he says, "the writings of these mystics acted in no slight degree to prevent my mind from being imprisoned within the outline of any single dogmatic system. They contributed to keep alive the *heart* in the *head;* gave me an indistinct yet stirring and working presentiment, that all the products of the mere *reflective* faculty partook of DEATH, and were as the rattling twigs and sprays in winter, into which a sap was yet to be propelled from some root to which I had not penetrated, if they were to afford my soul either food or shelter. If they were too often a moving cloud of smoke to me by day, yet they were always a pillar of fire throughout the night, during my wanderings through the wilderness of doubt, and enabled me to skirt, without crossing, the sandy deserts of utter unbelief." Sentences of Burke and of Newman occur to the mind in reading these lines. Newman, for example, spoke of "the all-corroding, all-dissolving scepticism of the intellect in religious enquiries"; "no truth" he said, "can stand against it, in the long run." This is what Coleridge also is saying in the words I have quoted. He was to have much to say of imagination, reason, faith; by each of these names he meant no partial faculty, no abstracted power, but the total personality, in which intelligence, will, passion are integrated; in this unified being of the mind he beheld the only agency of what he liked to call vital truth, of what are properly *ideas;* by contrast the abstracted intelligence was capable, he said, only of "lifeless and sightless notions." This thought is fundamental in all Coleridge's writings, both on poetry and the imagination, and on religion, reason, and faith. This is his antirationalism. It is not indeed a doctrine without grave dangers, and some of Coleridge's writings illustrate the dangers. But like Burke and Newman in their different ways, he provided, or sought to provide, the necessary safeguards against their action.

6

I TURN NOW to say something, and briefly, about the substance of Coleridge's reflections up to 1817. At about the beginning of the century he broke with the associationism of which, up to then, he had made the best he could. He would have done better, in the earlier years, if he had read Locke as closely as he read Hartley; he was always unfair to Locke whose doctrine was, however, more wise and catholic than Hartley's. In any case, the *Critique of Pure Reason* amply confirmed him in rejecting associationism, and he seized on what Kant had to say

about the role of imagination in knowledge. I shall not here try to
expound Kant's doctrine of the part imagination, as he believed, plays
in perception, nor indeed Coleridge's statement of it: this has been sufficiently done. I shall only emphasize the importance Coleridge attached
to the difference between "fancy" and "imagination." "Fancy" was the
word ordinarily employed by the Augustans to denote the power which
they opposed to "judgment." Hobbes said (in his *Answer to the Preface
to Gondibert*) that "judgment begets the strength and structure, and
fancy begets the ornaments of a poem"; he says in *Leviathan* that in
writing history "Fancy has no place, but onely in adorning the stile";
but in poetry fancy should be pre-eminent over judgment, because there
we look for and are pleased by "Extravagancy." Now it is precisely this
doctrine which Coleridge must attack. Hobbes had defined "fancy" as
quickness in perceiving similitudes unperceived by others, but it is also,
he said, a power which provides only "ornament" or "Extravagancy."
But if, Coleridge replies in effect, the power of simile and metaphor,
which is the central poetic power, provides only "ornament" and
"Extravagancy," Hobbes cannot be speaking of what may rightly be
called imagination; for the perception of similitude which shows itself
in simile and metaphor is, to judge by Shakespeare, no decorative or
extravagant agency but the very heart of poetic genius; and is the
genius of Shakespeare a genius for ornament merely and extravagance?
Therefore, Coleridge will indeed allow what Hobbes calls the "fancy";
but it is *not* the perception of similitudes; for if the perception be of
a real similitude, is it ornamental and extravagant merely? Surely not.
But if so, "fancy" does not perceive previously unknown features of
things; it can only reshuffle things perceived and held in the memory;
it may by doing so achieve striking, quaint, and ingenious effects
(Otway's "lutes, lobsters, seas of milk, and ships of amber"); but it
is not a power which discloses real features of things.

Still, Coleridge will not suffer us to speak of the imagination as an
agency which perceives similitudes merely; in the creation of metaphor
we do not discern similitudes; instead, we see an image "modified"
by, or "fused with," another and so transformed. Metaphor is therefore
not an act of comparison, but an operation of symbol: it *changes* its
object which thus comes to be for us only in this "modified" form.
Besides, what is true of the individual metaphor is true of the work
of art, the play or novel, as a whole: it is symbol, in terms of which
the poet's world is at once created and manifested by the poet: it is

the poet's world as it has come to exist for him; what lies outside it is no "world" but the mere raw material of experience; as symbol, it "partakes of the reality which it renders intelligible." The imagination is therefore a beholdment of the real in the only form in which, in its concreteness, it can be beheld, namely as symbol.

This is Coleridge's argument. It is not a Romantic theory of art, as opposed to a Classicist; it is a theory of art, simply; it may not be opposed to the Augustan theory, for the Augustans, whatever their practice, did not allow, in doctrine, for the prime requisite for artistic creation. The Augustans rightly emphasized the need for judgment, the sense of the whole and structure of the work (as, for that matter, did Coleridge also); what they did not acknowledge is the central symbol-making power which must be called "imagination." It is not indeed surprising that they did not; their rationalism (of whatever kind) disposed them to be interested not in symbol but in illustration, not in the refinement of perception but in the containing concept.[2]

We must regret that Coleridge did not think more, and more methodically, about the imagination and the nature of symbolism. But he wrote at some length in *Biographia Literaria* about the ways in which imaginative power shows itself. Of these ways I have not now the space to speak. But it is clear that the consequences of Coleridge's doctrine for the practice of criticism were sweeping. It required criticism to be, in the first place, a re-enactment of the poet's creation, as that, in turn, Coleridge liked to say, is a "dim analogue" of God's creation; it must remake the work of art in its unity of imagination and judgment, that is, as formed symbol; and the final judgment must come upon it as true or as false. The work of art has its *philosophical* claims on us; and to criticize it is not to treat its abstracted "literary" qualities, but to understand and then judge its exhibition of reality in the form of symbol. The work of art is living *idea,* "partaking of the reality which it renders intelligible"; and as idea, not as something "emotional" merely, it must be judged. For the imagination of which Coleridge speaks is, as I have said, no mere "faculty": it is the whole person, with passion, intelligence, will, united in the act of perception or vision of the world. The quality of the writer's emotions, the delicacy of his con-

[2] I am not now generalizing about Augustan poetry. But it is easy to observe, for example, that the comparative absence of metaphor from Milton's poetry is one of its major differences from Shakespeare's; and we remember Dryden's sullen and half-hearted defenses of metaphor in his Prefaces.

science, his power of judgment, all show themselves in the act which in its complexity and unity is called imaginative.

7

A F T E R 1816, the year of the publication of *Biographia Literaria,* Coleridge came chiefly to reflect on what he called the Reason; he became less concerned with imagination. But the transition, though apparently drastic, is seen, on inspection, to be not so. For reason, like imagination, is direct and immediate in its action; it also, like imagination, is a unity of the spirit. What the imagination is in art, the reason is in morality and religion: it gathers up the varied life of the mind into a single organ of spiritual perception: the mind perceives and knows.

Coleridge certainly owes as much to his reading of Kant for his doctrine of the reason as for his doctrine of the imagination. But it is also in his doctrine of the reason that he most signally declined to follow his master. Kant had declined to give an absolute validity to the ideas of the reason; he had given them a practical necessity only; we could not know and declare them for true. Coleridge will not have this; the reason, he said, is "a source of *actual* truth"; the soul beholds, it does not hypothesize. Here, Coleridge claimed, and rightly, that he was doing no more than returning to a primary tradition in European thought, only declaring again a doctrine asserted by Plato, Aristotle, the Schoolmen. He liked to quote Milton where he speaks of the soul receiving reason from God:

> . . . *and reason is her being,*
> *Discursive or intuitive.*

Coleridge never undervalued discursive reason. He only deplored a civilization which gave itself up to the labors of the "understanding" and declined, in its pride, the deliverances to it by the reason of the ultimate and saving truths. It may achieve power; it cannot come to wisdom. It may achieve "understanding"; it cannot come to vision.

I said that the transition from Coleridge's doctrine of the imagination to his doctrine of the reason is not as discontinuous as it seems. He could, in all conscience, have helped us, more than he did, to see the unity of the thought which can contain them both. But the unity is there for the seeking. In art the integrated mind perceives and orders its finite world and exhibits it in the symbol of the created work. But the life of art is incomplete and must lead beyond itself; it is not self-contained, and its symbols exhibit an incompleteness. Then the mind must move to perceive what transcends the sensuous; and here the imagination gives way to the reason. But if it gives way, it is not dispensed with; the reason in its operations remains, so far as may be, imaginative and sensuous; and the role of symbolism, though different now, is indispensable. "A symbol," he said, "is characterized by a translucence of the special in the individual, or of the general in the especial, or of the universal in the general. Above all, by the translucence of the eternal through and in the temporal." In this last "translucency" the role of symbolism in religion is realized. In the highest reaches of the reason in perceiving spiritual reality, the sensuous retains its place, and the reason remains imaginative. We may speak therefore indifferently of the spiritual imagination or of the imaginative reason. In an appendix to the first Lay Sermon, Coleridge says that "the completing power which unites clearness with depth, the plenitude of the sense with the comprehensibility of the understanding, is the imagination, impregnated with which the understanding itself becomes intuitive, and a living power." He goes on to say that "the reason (not the abstract reason . . .) . . . without being either the sense, the understanding or the imagination, contains all three within itself, even as the mind contains its thoughts and is present in and through them all." This, Coleridge declared, is the true rationalism affirmed by the main European tradition of thought, and from which the "rationalism" of the seventeenth and eighteenth centuries is an aberration.

Religion therefore does not shed the sensuous and imaginative; it does not despise, it gladly accepts, the role of imagery in all its apprehension. "Rationalism" must despise the imagination and cast it off, as well as it can; the reason, as Coleridge sees it, keeps it as integral to its perceptions. It is only the pride and power of the intellect which would slip the yoke of sense; for Coleridge, the symbol, partaking of the reality which it renders intelligible, comes, in religion, to a place of more abundant honor.

8

I HAVE TRIED, in what I have written, to set out those things in Coleridge's doctrine which I have judged to be most important: most important then, and most important now. Of many aspects of his teaching, I have been able to say nothing: of his political teaching for example, where his master was not Kant, but Burke ("in Mr. Burke's writings indeed the germs of almost all political truths may be found," he said in *Biographia Literaria*). Again, I have not been able to point out those parts of his thought where he is most assailable by fair criticism: he never, I think, wholly and certainly detached himself from the "subjectivism" of Kant's theory of perception; he too readily used his doctrine of the reason uncritically to establish doubtful protestant doctrines; he did not acknowledge the rightful and important role of natural theology in religious thought; he sometimes fell a victim to a deplorable voluntarism and attached excessive value to the thought of William of Ockham; and there are other things we must regret. But I have concentrated on the vital, crucial things in which, in all essentials, Coleridge seems, to me at least, to have said things profoundly true and important. He was little enough listened to in his own time. No doubt he had himself, in large measure, to thank: he rarely thought things out, and he composed prose which could hardly be worse. Had his mind had more order and resolution he might have had an influence comparable to the greatness J. S. Mill discerned in him. He had indeed a notable influence on John Henry Newman, though the movement and conclusion of Newman's thought would have dismayed him; but he might also have impressed Mill more even than he did and rescued him (as a half of Mill's mind wished to be rescued) from a pernicious tradition; and he might have prevented English thought from succumbing so widely to the influence of Hegel. But this was not to be. As it is, we, even at this late hour, are well advised to listen, out of the ever-deepening ditch of rationalism and naturalism which civilization has been digging for itself during these last centuries, to the passionate, profound, and inchoate pleadings which Coleridge addressed to his fellow-men.

9 Coleridge Redivivus

KATHLEEN COBURN

THERE ARE some claims that no longer need be made for Coleridge and others I should not wish to make. The multifariousness of his interests and the extent of his influence are recognized even if they are not yet fully known and understood. One need only think of certain names: Wordsworth, Davy, Allston, Peel, Sterling, Newman, Maurice, John Stuart Mill, John Morley, Emerson, Marsh and the New England transcendentalists, Saintsbury, Lowes, Muirhead; if we think of more recent writers who have found in him something congenial, or—as he said of Kant—something "cathartic, tonic and directly nutritional" we have a remarkable panel: Ivor Richards, Basil Willey, Herbert Read, Humphry House, Geoffrey Grigson, Maud Bodkin, Wilson Knight; Allen Tate, Robert Penn Warren, Kenneth Burke, W. Jackson Bate, R. P. Blackmur, C. D. Thorpe, Myer Abrams, Elisabeth Schneider, not to mention many others, and many tangentially or indirectly or unconsciously affected by him. T. S. Eliot's *The Idea of a Christian Society* is full of a part of Coleridge, and in a recent critical symposium from Chicago, edited by R. S. Crane, *Critics and Criticism* (1952), Coleridge appears to be a point of reference more frequently than anyone, except, perhaps, Aristotle.[1] And I cannot help thinking that but for a fatal accident, Coleridge's views might have found their most penetrating exposition in the work of a surrealist painter, poet, critic and film director, the late Humphrey Jennings.

[1] Had this handsome and otherwise very useful book an index I should be able to state the facts with more confidence.

113

Coleridge has been looked upon as the founder or forerunner of enough antipodal theories, or used for the grinding of enough axes, to make one suspicious of attempts to assign him to any school or any school to him, and indeed the best modern criticism has made guarded qualifications as to his niche. It is no longer considered wise to throw him to the German transcendentalist lions. The various attempts to claim him as a patron cannot be held against him as indicating vagueness or a careless eclecticism; I believe they are a sign rather of vitality, and of the fundamentally educing function of his thought. "Its merit is that it is an enquiry, that it shows us what we have to seek for, and that it puts us into a way of seeking," F. D. Maurice wrote of *The Friend*— and in the same essay,[2] describing the effects of the other prose works on him, he said of the *Biographia Literaria:*

> I learnt from him, by practical illustrations, how one may enter into the spirit of á living or a departed author, without assuming to be his judge; how one may come to know what he means without imputing to him our meanings.

Or again:

> I rejoice to think that those who have most profited by what he has taught them do not and cannot form a school . . . my feeling towards him though not founded upon any personal acquaintance . . . is . . . strictly and vividly personal.

Maurice suggests that what Coleridge offers is not a creed but a method rooted in his own personal experience and the struggle to understand it, and that it is capable of rich philosophical, religious, literary and practical implementation; in other words, that it is an integrating method.

Coleridge moreover does not stand today by virtue of his particular opinions, philosophical, theological, social, or even literary. We cannot consult him as an authority to settle our disputes in any of these fields. His opinions were formed on less information and with a more limited relevance than our more complicated twentieth-century world demands. What Coleridge thought of the theory of evolution, or the relation between property and government does not affect our views on these questions. He is not an oracle, even to his most admiring admirers. Even in that gradually broadening domain of literary criticism where

---

[2] The Dedication to Derwent Coleridge of the second edition of *The Kingdom of Christ,* 1842; it comprises thirty-two pages of expression of indebtedness to S. T. C.

as one of the most acute self-observers among poets and critics he speaks with very exceptional authority, there are some respects in which we have gone beyond him. He would be the first to recognize that modern psychology has greatly extended the data, and modern scholarship the techniques.

Nor is he where he is in our thinking today because of mere priority—or the priority in England at any rate, of many of his opinions. His indebtedness to the Germans has been both exaggerated and minimized, and the emotions behind both attitudes probably render them untrustworthy. The facts, as Sara Coleridge saw, are impossible to untangle, at any rate until much more work is done on the unpublished manuscripts, especially the philosophical marginalia. In the intellectual climate, personal and contemporary, in which Coleridge lived, the question is anyhow irrelevant and unimportant except for its historical interest; overstressing it distracts us from the real nature of the movements of thought in his time, and in his own works. Even some of the originalities most prominently and frequently connected with his name I should hesitate to attribute wholly and solely to him. Contribution was, I suspect, drawn from nearer rills, as well as the German, and I could wish for time and space here to develop the possible additions of the two other triumvirs of English criticism in the period, Lamb and Hazlitt. His debt to Plato, the Schoolmen, and the Cambridge Platonists, particularly Cudworth, has not been fully explored, and perhaps can never be known. He found, he said, that he had read Plato by anticipation, and so he had—in Plotinus, Lessing, Jeremy Taylor, Jacob Behmen, as well as in his own head. No one can be more roundly condemned out of his own mouth as no originator; yet one of his real contributions is to teach us how to borrow with originality. In this connexion a study of his marginalia would make an important addition to scholarship and criticism. He reads without the slightest trace of condescension or servility. Several times on Law's *Behmen* he refers sympathetically to Behmen's struggle against lack of education and a philosophical language, yet he can also write against an early adverse comment of his own: "The above note was written while I was but in the dim dawn of Knowledge—and wholly in the *subjective* Thinking— of course incapable of coming near Behmen. S. T. C." [3] At his best he

---

[3] His profusely annotated copy of William Law's quarto edition of *The Works of Jacob Behmen* (4 vols., 1764–81), is now in the British Museum.

There is another copy in California with some of Coleridge's annotations transcribed by another hand.

enters with his full powers as poet and philosopher into a writer's mind, and often, in the same breath, startles us with an insight prophetic of things to come.

> Imagine a Poet intensely watching a Tree in a Storm of Wind, unconsciously imitating its motions with his body, and then transferring to the Tree those sensations and emotions that accompanied his own gestures: and then you may understand Behmen, and his mode of describing the acts of Nature by ante-dating the passions, of which yet those Acts may be, perhaps, the nascent state and fluxional quantities.

The marginalia, next to the notebooks which share some of their character, are to my mind among his most delightful prose writings. As in this example and description of empathy he tends to show us new aperçus rather than massive original discoveries, a mind at work and an invitation to participate rather than a final answer.

A third claim that cannot be made is that his position depends on a system, using the word in the sense of something formal and complete. There is no doubt he loved system, and longed to create a great complicated structure, his *Opus Maximum,* which would embrace all knowledges seen in their relations. Goethe, as he had more gift for system, more drive, health, continuous energy, felt no need of it. Coleridge knew the curse of "power without strength"; the inability to drive and complete were his torture. He was at his best when the compulsion was least pressing, when the diagrams and the Platonic architectonics could be forgotten, when he was free to inquire, to criticize, to discriminate, and to imagine, to share in talk or on margins, or "to dare to commune" with his own "very self" in notebooks.

I am not interested then in resting Coleridge's high claims to attention on his authority, priority, or system. I do think he has more to say to us today than any other departed modern critic, and that it is not true to suggest that his "main theoretical ideas are derivative and secondhand" or that "these derivative principles are those which are most admired." [4] He offers us something more congenial to our age than a closed system, and something more productive. In making this affirmation I should like to contend against what strikes me as the commonest and least comprehensible fallacy of the commentators,

[4] T. M. Raysor (ed.), *The English Romantic Poets* (New York, 1950), pp. 116–17.

explicit in many statements and implicit in the common division of interest in him, that his poetry and his philosophy have no relation to each other in content or attitude. The fallacy has two chief forms, (a) that the philosopher destroyed the poet in him after 1798, or (b) that his philosophical views are not expressed in his poetry and did not influence it.[5]

Such bifurcation of Coleridge's thought becomes impossible on a reading of almost any of his prose works, but it is gainsaid with special definiteness by the *Treatise on Method,* later incorporated in *The Friend.* He himself said it was the basis of all his philosophical writings and late in life he included it among those passages by which he wished especially to be understood and remembered. Though editors have valued it,[6] the literary critics, with rare exceptions, have tended to overlook it.

Beginning characteristically with the word "Method," in Greek "a way, or path of transit," he explains how he means to apply it.

Hence the first idea of Method is a *progressive transition* from one step in any course to another; and where the word Method is applied with reference to many such transitions in continuity, it necessarily implies a Principle of UNITY WITH PROGRESSION. But that which unites, and makes many things *one* in the Mind of Man, must be an act of the Mind itself, a manifestation of intellect, and not a spontaneous and uncertain production of circumstances. This act of the Mind, then, this leading thought, this "key note" of the harmony, this "subtile, cementing, subterraneous" power, borrowing a phrase from the nomenclature of legislation, we may not inaptly call the INITIATIVE of all Method. It is manifest, that the wider the sphere of transition is, the more comprehensive and commanding must be the initiative; and if we would discover an *universal Method,* by which every step in our progress through the whole circle of Art and Science should be directed, it is absolutely necessary that we should seek it in the very interior and central essence of the Human intellect.[7]

[5] E.g. "Though Coleridge played the philosopher all through his life, his finest poetry owes little to his philosophical views and exists almost in defiance of them."—C. W. Bowra, *The Romantic Imagination* (Cambridge, 1950), p. 288. Such statements are legion.

[6] I should like to pay tribute to the acumen of the late Dr. Alice Snyder in editing it as a separate work and pointing out differences between *The Friend* version and the *Preliminary Treatise.* Her pioneer work in calling attention to the philosophical materials has been inadequately recognized.

[7] A. D. Snyder, *Treatise on Method* (London, 1934), pp. 2-3.

Here is one of the several assertions of the core of the dynamic philosophy, that voluntarism which was his qualification of Plato and Kant and by which he thought his position was to be distinguished. But in addition to the emphasis on the subject, its active principle, its individuation, and self-determination, there is also an insistence on the reality of the object. The initiative (the conscious ego function?) lies with the mind—but "the *relations* of things form the prime objects of Method"; we must try to know our own knowledge, experience our own experiences, by seeing things in their unity and simultaneously in their development; whole, yet becoming; actual, yet potential; a process of integration in a unity and a recreation in a vital progression. It is central for him to state the activity and unity of the subject and the reality of the object, and that neither can exist without the other. He is, perhaps, among other things, a phenomenologist before Husserl.[8] Hartley and Berkeley were the schools in which he learned the inadequacy of monistic positions.

> The great principles of all Method we have shown to be two, *viz,*
> *Union* and *Progression* . . . . The state of Mind adapted to such
> progress holds a due mean between a passiveness under external
> impression, and an excessive activity of mere reflection; and the
> progress itself follows the path of the Idea from which it sets out;
> requiring, however, a constant wakefulness of Mind, to keep it
> within the due limits of its course. Hence the orbits of Thought, so
> to speak, must differ among themselves as the initiative Ideas differ;
> and of these latter, the great distinctions are into Physical and
> Metaphysical. Such, briefly, are the views by which we have been
> guided in our present attempt to Methodize the great mass of Hu-
> man Knowledge.[9]

Such passages remind us that the basis of his thought is epistemological rather than ontological.

As one application of the principle of Method is the extension or acquisition of scientific knowledge, he compares the history of magnetism and electricity. With the new insight into the principle of polarity, electricity was set on its path of unending discoveries. Similarly, zoology, botany, and chemistry stagnate until the "initiative" that is capable of directing progress is found. Chemistry pursues this "unity of principle

---

[8] According to Herbert Read he is, with Schelling, an existentialist before Kierkegaard.—*Coleridge as Critic,* p. 29. No label, in any complete or exclusive sense, fits him.

[9] *Treatise on Method,* ed. cit., p. 11.

through a diversity of forms," and the pleasure and excitement of chemistry lie in finding "the ONE FORM" by which "water and flame, the diamond, charcoal and the mantling champagne, with its ebullient sparkles, are convoked and fraternized by the theory of the Chemist . . . . It is the sense of a principle of connection given by the mind, and sanctioned by the correspondency of Nature." [10] Coleridge had seen Davy's mind in action; and he himself asked some penetrating scientific questions by the mental process which he was later to analyze as "Method." "It is strange," he wrote Poole in May, 1799, "that we do not adopt some means to render our artificial lights more white." After seeing some smelting houses near Goslar, he realized that the central fact of light is brightness or whiteness and from that unifying fact of all light, moved on to speculate about practical applications. One could make from his writings a considerable collection of such imaginative observations.

In education the principle of Method means an emphasis on the unity of the child's personality, and the problem is the educing of it progressively outwards into an enlarging universe. It is in relating itself to ends and means that the growing mind will discover the appropriate and necessary disciplines, not in submission to arbitrary external and irrelevant authority.

In medicine, the application of Method means emphasis on the unity of the personality of the patient. Coleridge makes more than once the radical suggestion that treating the disease is not enough. The patient's "initiative" must be sought, many disorders not ordinarily considered illness are such, and medicine must extend itself in both subjective and objective realms.

Of society he was to write later in *Church and State* that "the two opposite interests of the State under which all other State interests are comprised, are those of *permanence* and *progression*." [11] And similarly of the English constitution: there is the ideal, permanent, unified entity, and there are the flexible laws that are to be changed at need, out of considerations of growth and expediency. The constitution of a country has its centre in the human situation, part of which is permanent and universal and part of which is in flux, and conditioned by circumstances. The church as an institution he tried to recall to its historic rôle as an intellectual centre as well as a spiritual force in society. Christianity must find its strength in and go out to meet the multiple human situation.

[10] *Ibid.,* pp. 24–25.
[11] *On the Constitution of the Church and State* (London, 1830), pp. 23–4.

It is the distinction of Coleridge [Tulloch said in a review of Traill's *Life of Coleridge* in 1885] to have once more in his age made Christian doctrine alive to the reason as well as the conscience—tenable as a philosophy as well as an evangel. And this he did by interpreting Christianity in the light of our moral and spiritual life . . . . There was nothing absolutely new in this luminous conception, but it marked a revolution of religious thought in the earlier part of our century.[12]

In its attitude to the Bible, for instance, he recommends that the church should differentiate between the spiritual truths at its core and its fallible human agents and interpreters. To quote Tulloch once more (after he has referred to other men who also helped to initiate the "higher criticism"):

. . . still to him belongs the honour of having first plainly and boldly announced that the Scriptures were to be read and studied, like any other literature, in the light of their continuous growth, and the adaptation of their parts to one another.

Similarly the principles of Method are the principles of literary criticism. One form of Method is Imagination—that synthesizing power which reconciles opposites into a unity—the internal and the external, the particular and the universal, man and nature. Either the poet in some degree becomes all things in the manner of Shakespeare, or all things become him in the manner of Milton. He tames the chaos, progressively, into a unified whole by an act in which he himself achieves, at least for the moment, a kind of personal integration. The making of poems "calls the whole soul into activity," reconciling the insights of reason with sense impressions, conceptual knowledge, and all levels of consciousness.

The principle of Method determines the criteria of criticism. First of all it establishes that there are criteria, since it is possible to distinguish the objectively real "unity" and "progression" from their opposites. They will be criteria for poetry as poetry and not as some other thing, plural criteria based on the variety of initiatives, and on different sorts of unification, and the unlimited possibilities of progression. Criticism can be multilateral since something dynamic is in question which rises out of and addresses many different levels of conscious and unconscious activity. Much of our language about poetry falsifies the

---

[12] John Tulloch, "Coleridge as a Spiritual Thinker," *Fortnightly Review*, XLIII (January, 1885), 11–25.

meaning of the word "poem." [13] For a poem is not an object at all. It is a twofold, two-way operation between subject and object, i.e., between the poet and the potential poem, and between the reader and the words; criticism is similarly an affair between critic and poem, and between critic and audience. The dynamic interrelations of the unity and activity of both polarities create works of imagination on the one hand and "genial criticism" on the other. A poem is an act and an experience, and cannot be completely or finally understood as a structure, or a texture, or a collection of devices. No word, nor any group of words, will sufficiently describe poetry any more than it will define *life*. "Imagination" itself is merely a word pointing to something untrapped in any definition of it, something directly recognized in a poem, a painting, a piece of music, a man, when they exhibit characteristics of integration, and have power to make the participating intelligence comprehend or respond anew. As the meanings of a poem are inexhaustible, so are the criticisms, and must be renewed in every age.

> Not only Chaucer and Spenser; but even Shakespeare and Milton have as yet received only the earnest, and scanty first gatherings of their Fame. This indeed it is which gives its full dignity and more than mental grandeur to Fame . . . . it becomes wider and deeper, as their country (and all mankind are the countrymen of the man of true and adequately exerted Genius) becomes better and wiser.[14]

The basic principles of criticism as of poetry are those laid down in the eighteenth chapter of the *Biographia:* the principles of grammar (the developing and progressive unity of language), of logic (the developing unity of thought), and of psychology (the developing unity of the poet, critic, or the human material of the poem); the end is to maintain the progressive vitality of the poem. Coleridge was already fighting the tendency to make poetry a function of criticism.[15]

One of the links between his theory as philosopher and critic and his practice as poet is found in those well known passages in the *Treatise on Method* in which Shakespeare and Plato and Bacon are taken as examples of minds working methodically, i.e., minds showing strong initiative in their power to see relations among things and to establish

---

[13] His clear distinction between "poetry" and "poem" is important and critically useful.

[14] MS Notebook.

[15] Randall Jarrell, "The Age of Criticism," *Partisan Review*, XIX (March–April, 1952), 185–201.

them in a work of art or science, in the freedom to move out into and incorporate experience. All are in a sense poets. It is clear to anyone who knows Coleridge that his analysis of their virtues is developed out of his sense of his own defects. It is not necessary to know that many of the phrases he uses here occur in more private contexts in the notebooks. The actuality of his sense of the importance of the initiating Method and of the paralysis from its loss is plain everywhere in his writings, including the poems.

Dejection states the theme explicitly and personally, some of the other poems state it more broadly and generally; for the sense of the recurring frustration of the initiative, its distortion or misdirection resulting in a consequent disintegration and improgression, lies at the heart of his sense of the tragedy of human life. The philosophical principle of Method is the systematization of what was expressed earlier in intuitive form in the poems of the *annus mirabilis:* the joy and power of the creative drive, and the fatality of its blocking and numbing by emotional conflict, illness, drugs (daemonic possession) and poverty, by restrictions on personal freedom by tyranny of any sort, social, political, religious or domestic. However variously the interpretations of *The Ancient Mariner, Kubla Khan,* and *Christabel* may be worked out in detail, is it not true to say that they are all based on the tragic loss of the "initiative"? The Mariner, by an aggressive act which is disintegrating to him personally, setting up guilty conflict within himself and disrupting his relations with his shipmates and the natural world, is derelict until he regains some of that vital mental and moral power. Increasing self-awareness and a spontaneous moment of empathy restore, imperfectly but with accessions of wisdom, a more creative imaginative spirit with him. Christabel, too, has lost the direction of her own life, under some threat to love and hope, some daemonic domination that again is disintegrating to personality, that separates her from her natural human relations, i.e., to the father, the mother's spirit, and the absent lover, and clearly violates the creative life principle. *Christabel* again introduces the theme of loneliness and isolation of spirit—the third canto was to have been "The Song of her Desolation" [16]—and whatever the ending, the pathos lies in the old conflict between life, pure and innocent, and death-in-life, in various forms. In

[16] MS Notebook. This is discussed more fully in my article "Coleridge and Wordsworth and 'the Supernatural,' " in the *University of Toronto Quarterly,* XXV (January, 1956), 121–30.

Kubla Khan, too, the frustration of creative purposes, the destruction of the pleasure dome of poetry (unity), and the disappearance of the sacred river (progression) "in tumult to a lifeless ocean" is described in a symbolic language, charged even in the tenses of its verbs with the sense of tragic loss. Something dark, submerged, violent, has destroyed Paradise and broken up the ordered symphony and song.[17]

So it is in many of the other poems. In the Preface to *The Three Graves* the theme of mental disruption is specifically stated to be the point of the poem. In *The Wanderings of Cain* it is present in another form. In *Frost at Midnight,* the drive is positive and not frustrated, the child in the cradle representing that Hope [18] in which the poet finds a compensating integration and self-extension. In this connexion it may be too obvious to be worth mentioning that the similarly serene ending of *Dejection,* with its midnight stars hanging bright above one dwelling as the moon quietly shines on the other, comes from a similar progression—love for Sara Hutchinson and hope for her happiness in her own life; the poem thus exhibits the imaginative process at work, the creative power of the outward-moving love for the object (S. H.) making for the harmony and serenity of the subject (S. T. C.), at the same time that it describes, painfully, the tragic negations of the paralyzing death-in-life recession.

The poet and the philosopher are one, as he himself knew; [19] and neither his poetry nor his philosophy would be what they are without the other, nor without his awareness in his own personal life of the need of a dynamic, and the conditions, inner and outer, for a free operation of the "initiative," at once stabilizing the present and reach-

[17] After this article was written, the late Humphry House expressed a contrary view of the meaning of *Kubla Khan* in *Coleridge* (London, 1953), pp. 114–22. With the greatest respect for his criticism, I must nevertheless leave this statement as it stands. The most adequate treatment *Kubla Khan* has received, according to my view, is in the final chapter of Elisabeth Schneider's *Coleridge, Opium and Kubla Khan* (Chicago, 1953).

[18] The stress on Hope in Coleridge's poems is a subject for an article in itself. It is in fact the mental initiative on the moral level and, like Joy, a principle of "unity with progression." See the poems *passim,* from the earliest one on Easter holidays to the last.

[19] The lines in *Dejection,*

*And haply by abstruse research to steal
From my own nature all the natural
man,*

are often interpreted to the contrary. Yet "abstruse" is not 'abstract' or philosophical research, but research into the recondite, hidden, off the main march, and "the natural man" is the man in love with Sara Hutchinson. The lines have nothing to do with metaphysics killing poetry, though they do potently portray that flight from himself which gave him so abject a sense of failure.

ing out towards the future. Nor did the philosopher kill the poet, in spite of Coleridge's own avowed sense of their conflict within him. The poet did not die, for one thing, but went on writing poems that would make a lesser poet important. The loss of vitality of the special sort that releases emotions and images which without it tend to be suppressed with the years, especially in conditions of guilt and conflict such as Coleridge increasingly endured, deprived us of the *Ancient Mariners, Christabels* and *Kubla Khans* we suspect we might have had. The unification of experience no longer took place at the freely imaginative level; the attempts became more intellectual in a narrower sense, more guarded, more self-conscious; they called less of the "whole soul into activity," though the temperament of the man and the poet, and the realism of his point of view, prevented them from becoming merely cerebral.

I hope I shall not be understood as saying that Coleridge taught his philosophy in his poems. I am trying to say that the poet and the philosopher were one man with one face, and that from the very beginning of his writings, through years of wavering and testing and never finding any one philosophy or church, or political party or aesthetic theory to satisfy him, he did work out a way of looking at the various kinds of thought and experience that illuminates them and also gives them, whether in prose or poetry, a certain integrated unity. The process, though informal, was far from haphazard. It is surely a magnificent human irony that anything so impersonal as a *method* (which, as compared with a system or a creed lays so light a hand on those who come after), should be wrenched as intimately as Coleridge's was, out of personal experience. This is, I think, what Maurice meant by saying his feeling towards Coleridge was "vividly personal." The fact that it is a *method* Coleridge conveyed, accounts, too, for the persistent value and vitality of his thinking. This is why the conclusions and opinions are often unimportant and why the claims and disclaimers of priority are irrelevant. The starting point is clearly defined and the process described and exemplified everywhere we turn in his work. The combination of an essentially empirical willingness to apply a method together with the affirmation of positive values has been one source of the conflicting interpretations of Coleridge's position, emphasis being placed now on the empirical, relative, psychological, critical side, now on the ideal, transcendental, moral side; the inconclusiveness of the one annoys some critics, the *a priori* assertions annoy others. The fact is, Coleridge's method is open to free use and varying emphases. The method is, as I have tried to show, not a dead hand, and the often vehement and contradictory revival of interest in him in our time is a sign of the creative nisus in his thought.

Gerard Manly Hopkins once said, "When I took in any inscape of the sky or sea, I thought of Scotus." When we take in any inscape of man's mental and emotional horizons—or any inscape of sky or sea either, for that matter—we may easily think of Coleridge, not because he described them first, but because by precept and by example "he puts us into a way of seeking." This is his unity, and this is his progression. After a dozen decades, he is himself recognizable as a method.

IV: Byron

10 Irony and Image in Byron's Don Juan

ERNEST J. LOVELL, JR.

1

IT IS CLEAR that much of Byron's poetry must be judged to be imperfect, for reasons well known and generally accepted. Much of his work is flawed because, for the achievement of many poetic effects, he lacked the necessary delicately tuned ear. We must, I believe, agree with the general sense of Eliot's judgment (although its *ex cathedra* tone and the absence of essential qualification may well annoy us) that Byron's ear was "imperfect, and capable only of crude effects." He lacked the indispensable gift necessary 'for writing consistently excellent lyric poetry, a heightened sensitivity to the subtleties of sound combination. The degree to which this deficiency could betray him is fairly illustrated by "Fare Thee Well," a stock anthology piece. The defect is less fatal in the early verse tales, and they will still hold the excited attention of undergraduates. Yet the melodramatic heroes of *The Giaour* or *The Bride of Abydos* are without interest for most of us, except for their historical and autobiographical importance. Their minds and characters are immature, their stories without moral significance. We cannot take them seriously: Byron's life is more interesting.

The last two cantos of *Childe Harold* represent an advance, of course (although there are passages in the tales of keen psychological insight and effective picturesque description). But these two cantos suffer from qualities whose presence is clearly implied by the success with which most of Byron's romantic poetry may be translated into a foreign language. As Samuel C. Chew has noted, such poetry bears translation "with little loss of effect." The reasons are clear. The diction of *Childe Harold* is essentially the diction of good prose and frequently the language of summary, abstraction, or generalization, often expressing a call to action and hence rhetorical or persuasive. Both diction and imagery, therefore, are often curiously limited in their power to evoke rich and complex overtones of meaning, although the poem at its worst fails even to achieve the precision of good prose. To summarize these well-known difficulties—and there are others—is not to imply, however, that *Childe Harold* is without all value for our time. It is merely to say that its chief value lies in its substance, not its form, which today has little to teach us.

Manfred, on the other hand, is a work of near perfection in the sense that it accomplishes nearly perfectly what it sets out to do— embody the essence of the romantic Byronic spirit, not omitting its theatrical or melodramatic aspects. The blank verse is unusually firm, sure, and certain of itself and sets off to advantage the intervening lyrics. The chief flaw I find is that the several characters are sometimes insufficiently distinguished one from another in the tone of their speeches. Their accents are too similar (reflecting Byron's limited power to create characters other than Byronic), almost as if the poem were an expressionistic debate between opposing aspects of the poet's mind. From the successive failures of the hero's quest, however, the structure of the poem derives both unity and balanced symmetry, qualities present to a much less impressive degree in *Childe Harold,* which is improved by editorial selection. But the style of *Manfred* depends so completely on the personality of the poet and our knowledge of him that it defies instructive formal analysis: the impassioned words derive their passion and power, as the best of Byron's romantic poetry normally does, from the strength of the poet's feelings. Few works so well illustrate the cliché that the style is the man. The miracle is that the man, or one half of him, shines so brightly through the simple, occasionally commonplace diction, a fact which illustrates again that poetry may be written without excessive concern for the problems of surface texture—provided the poet has something to say and feels strongly enough about it.

Both the chief difficulties already mentioned, Byron's relative insensitivity to the sounds of words and his rather consistent reliance upon direct statement and the diction of prose, also reduce the quality of the plays, although to a lesser extent than in most of the nondramatic work. The dramas, however, suffer in a way *Childe Harold* does not from Byron's inability, shared with many of the Romantic poets, to create a host of richly diverse characters. He seems to have lacked that capacity for empathy which is essential to the writing of great drama. Although he wrote more good plays, probably, than any of his contemporaries (G. Wilson Knight has compared his dramatic achievement favorably with that of Shakespeare), the clear fact is that Byron is not of the first rank in the drama. The judgment of Paul Elmer More still holds true: "He lacked the dramatic art."

What, then, apart from the derivative Popean poems, are we left with? The three great satires, obviously, *Beppo, The Vision of Judgment,* and *Don Juan,* in that order of ascending excellence. Believing that every poet is to be judged finally by his best work and assuming that the virtues of *Beppo* and *The Vision* are frequently those of Byron's greatest masterpiece, I have limited the remainder of these remarks to *Don Juan,* and more particularly to the elements of unity, irony, and imagery in *Don Juan,* a work of great originality and undeniable excellence, essentially unlike anything before it. It has much to say to the mid-twentieth century, an age which, distrusting the grandiose, sentimental, and otherwise oversimplified quite as much as Byron did, has sought the poetic means of expressing its characteristic emotional complexity, as Byron also did, in the oblique, liberating forces of irony and ambiguity. *Don Juan* is, in fact, one of the most pertinent of all poems for us today, reminding us, at a time when we are in particular need of reminder, that a poem is made for people other than its creator, and so first must entertain them, with an artistic recreation of the stuff of their own life, and finally must heal them, with a revelation of its essential meaning, that the community may know itself and so avoid deceiving itself. These are among the primary assumptions of *Don Juan.*

2

THE PREREQUISITE to any consideration of the art of *Don Juan* is an analysis of its unity, denied or overlooked often enough to make its explication at this time a task of prime critical importance. Unity denied, the poem is reduced at once to a picaresque series of loosely jointed fragments, however brilliant. It must be clearly demonstrated, therefore, that there is a controlling, unifying principle at work throughout and, more particularly, that each main narrative episode, without exception, is somehow integral to a larger structure.

That unifying principle, I suggest, is the principle of thematic unity —here, the basically ironic theme of appearance versus reality, the difference between what things seem to be (or are said or thought to be) and what they actually are. Thematic unity established, it can then be seen readily that the most significant structure is a complex and carefully considered organization of ironically qualified attitudes and that manner and matter, consequently, are flawlessly fused; for irony is here integral to both theme and mode. It is inherent in the theme, hence it functions also as a necessary principle of narrative structure; and it is, at the same time, the primary device for manipulating manner or mode, to achieve a variety of richly mixed, fully orchestrated tonal qualities, which are themselves reconciled by and subordinated to the dominant theme. In terms of substance, this means that the diverse materials and the clash of emotions gathered together in the poem are harmonized finally by Byron's insight into the difference between life's appearance and its actuality, into the highly mixed motives which ordinarily control men and women, and into their genius for self-deception and rationalization.

A summary, then, of the consistently organic relation between episode and theme is the essential prelude to any purely stylistic discussion of *Don Juan*. Such a summary of the narrative or dramatic expression of theme will make clear, in the course of it, that Byron's irony is neither shallow, cynical, insincere, incidental, nor typically romantic, whether the latter type be understood as self-irony, self-pitying disillusion, or the willful destruction of the dramatic illusion. It is, instead, ordinarily the precise, necessary, fully orchestrated, and artistically functional expression of his own hard-won point of view, almost never a mere attitude adopted for its own sake, the tone of it almost never that of the simple irony of a reversed meaning.

At the risk of grossly oversimplifying the rich complexity of a great poem, then, one may begin by recalling the original hypocrisy of Juan's education, incomplete and thus false to the actual facts of life. Indeed, the entire poem may be read as a richly humorous investigation of the results stemming from a canting, maternal education which attempted to deny the very physical foundations of life. Because Juan has been so ill-educated, he is correspondingly ill-equipped to deal with

Julia, understanding neither his own emotional state nor hers, until too late, and so is sent ironically on his travels, "to mend his former morals," while Inez, undaunted, takes to teaching Sunday school. Before this, however, in a passage of far-reaching irony, Juan, transformed temporarily into a nympholeptic nature poet, has engaged in obscure Wordsworthian communings with nature, ludicrously deceiving himself and overspiritualizing the natural world. This self-delusion neatly balances and underlines that of Julia, who, overspiritualizing her passion, engages in the deliberately engendered hypocrisy of Platonic love. Here, as well as elsewhere, the appearance-versus-reality theme focuses on the moral danger of denying the physical basis of life and love, although Byron does not overlook the ideal end of either. The tone of all this comic but quite meaningful irony is deepened, finally, by the criminal hypocrisy of Inez in using her own son, unknown to him, to break up Julia's marriage. Indeed, one form taken by the philosophic irony underlying the first canto suggests that cant and hypocrisy may endanger the very continuity of civilized tradition. But the crowning stroke, after the irony of Julia's tirade while her husband searches her bedroom, is that she who has so viciously deceived herself with so much talk about spiritual love should be sent to live in a convent, where presumably she may contemplate the spiritual forever.

Byron points again at the wrongheadedness of such ill-founded love, hypocritically denying its own physical basis, when he allows Juan to become seasick in the midst of protesting his eternal devotion to Julia while rereading her pathetic letter. One may profitably compare Auden's dramatization of the tension between an asserted life-long fidelity in love and the mutabilities of physical experience, in "As I Walked Out One Evening." But if life and love must be viewed "really as they are," so also must death. When the ship's company would resort self-deceptively to prayers and "spirits" for identical reasons, to enable them to face the reality of drowning, Juan keeps them from the "spirit room," symbolically, at pistol point, while Byron without preaching attacks an easy crisis religion. The sentimental illusion of Julia's spiritual love, however, is dissipated for good with the appropriate final disposition of her famous letter. Its disposition is quite equal to that accorded Damian's note to May, in *The Merchant's Tale,* and it has much the same function—to strip the tinsel savagely and finally from false sentiment and reveal it for what it is. It is also at once grimly, ironically appropriate that the loser in the drawing of lots should be

Juan's tutor, representative of that hypocritical race, instruments of
Inez, who are responsible finally for Juan's being where he is. The
chief satire of the shipwreck episode, however, is not directed against
either the sentimental falsification of the great traditions or of the
experience of love, but against the overspiritualization of nature, against
"this cant about nature" preached gravely by those who, concerned
too exclusively with the "beauties of nature," would overlook its de-
structive aspects.

Byron's use of ironic qualification within a lyric context, to achieve
the illusion of increased comprehensiveness and complexity, is especially
noteworthy in his treatment of Haidée's romantic paradise, which could
no more exist on half-truths than Milton's Garden of Innocence. It is
also a significant paradox that Juan and Haidée, lacking a common
language, communicate nevertheless more precisely than if they shared
the same tongue. But the tone of the Haidée episode is much more nearly
similar to that of *Romeo and Juliet,* qualified and enriched as it is by
such discordant elements as those supplied by the witty Mercutio and
the bawdy Nurse, than it is to that of *Paradise Lost.* Byron has qualified
the lyricism of the episode explicitly with the character of Zoe, who
cooked eggs and "made a most superior mess of broth" while Haidée's
world turned back its clock to paradise (II, 139, 144–45, 148, 153).
Zoe, a graduate of "Nature's good old college," the perfect complement
to the innocence of Haidée, pure "child of Nature," is thus an important
ally in enabling Byron to avoid overspiritualizing the romantic love
of Juan and Haidée and abstracting one element of the experience to
imply that it is the whole.

> *I'll tell you who they were, this female pair,*
> *Lest they should seem princesses in disguise;*
> *Besides, I hate all mystery, and that air*
> *Of clap-trap, which your recent poets prize;*
> *And so, in short, the girls they really were*
> *They shall appear before your curious eyes,*
> *Mistress and maid; the first was only daughter*
> *Of an old man, who lived upon the water.*

Space allowing, one might pursue here the full thematic and tonal
implications of such ambiguities as those resulting from Byron's skillful
fusion of tragedy, comedy, and satire in the character of Lambro (which
permits, among other far-reaching effects, a subtle divorce of the Rous-
seauistic union of virtue and taste). Or one could explore Lambro's

resemblance to the old Byronic hero as well as to Byron himself (see III, 18, 51–57) and hence his implied kinship to Juan. The boy or child imagery descriptive of Juan and the mother imagery descriptive of Haidée (see II, 143, 148) add another element of richness to the characterization. And the ironic frame, audaciously suspended and unnoticed over eighty-five stanzas (III, 61–IV, 35), which results from Lambro's unknown presence, encloses with telling effect the famous lyric on the isles of Greece (ironically enframed a second time by the Southeyan poet who sings it), the equally famous Ave Maria stanzas, and the stanzas to Hesperus. Here Byron achieves an effect quite as complex as that resulting in *The Waste Land* from Eliot's use of the same lines from Sappho, for more directly satiric purposes. Although it is impossible to discuss here these subtle, significant variations of tone and theme, or the consequent added dimensions, it may be said that nowhere else, perhaps, as in the third canto has Byron so skillfully manipulated the knife-edge dividing comedy and tragedy, or suggested more fully, within a successfully maintained romantic frame and setting, the ambiguities and rich complexities of actual existence.

Having successfully established and developed the central theme of appearance versus reality, Byron presumably felt free to permit himself a farcial variation on it: Juan disguised as a woman in a Turkish harem. But the harem episode also lays bare the romanticized Turkish travel book, the Oriental tale, and, perhaps, the romantic submissiveness of Byron's own early Oriental heroines. For Juan is literally a "slave to the passions." Who but Byron could have taken the old cliché, read it literally, and so have turned its seamy side inside out—to reveal the ridiculous nature and self-defeating characteristics of purely sensual love, allowing us, notwithstanding—by means of the magnificently mixed tone—to pity its symbol as a woman! But Gulbeyaz, the enslaved specialist in love who should have known better, also represents the final self-deception of one who thinks that love, the free gift of self-surrender, may be bought and commanded. And to the extent that love, Juan's chief interest and most serious occupation, is equated in the poem with all of life, Byron is saying, without heroics, that life itself is impossible without freedom, however attractive a loving or benevolent despot may seem to be, or whatever luxuries may seem to surround the "escape from freedom."

Byron prepared for his ironic demolition of modern war, "Glory's dream unriddled," in his portrait of the Sultan, disguised as lord of all he surveys except his latest favorite wife and the Empress Catherine, whose boudoir he so well might have graced, as Byron points out, to the furtherance of both "their own true interests." The two courts of the opposing rulers, each so seriously concerned with "love," form of course an ironic frame for the bloody siege of Ismael, the narrative vehicle of Byron's attack on the false heroics of war. Although the irony is too pervasive to describe, it may be recalled that the immediate theme is not an unqualified pacifism but the hypocrisy and cant of war ("the crying sin of this double-dealing and false-speaking time"), with especial attention to the unsavory paradox of a Christian war of conquest and the attendant Christian mercies of the invading Russians, shortly to become members of the Holy Alliance. But Byron's satire does not depend on a simple reversal of the hypocrisy of war; his tone is carefully qualified, as it ordinarily is, with the result that the satire is never thin or one-dimensional. Successfully avoiding the easy resolution of a comment on the general meaninglessness of war, he can thus frankly recognize its excitement, the intense loyalties and the heroism it evokes, and the paradoxical acts of generosity it calls forth.

Juan at the court of Catherine completes the ironic frame of the war cantos and allows Byron to play his own variation on the old theme of "to the brave the fair"—the sickening lust of the gentle sex to possess a uniform and see "Love turn'd a lieutenant of artillery"— only to show that such generous reward of the returning hero will debilitate him and that such a surrender of arms (to other arms) may well bring him nearer death, even, than his wars did. Meanwhile the relations between Catherine and Juan are without hypocrisy, and are known to all. Juan even has an official title. Gross as Catherine's appetites are, they are not so reprehensible as the hypocrisy of Inez's letter (X, 31–34), which serves the further purpose of recalling, without naming, Julia's hypocrisy of Platonic love and Byron's insistence on the necessity of recognizing the physical basis of love. The Catherine episode qualifies the latter insight by making the obvious point that the merely physical, lacking spiritual warmth, will sicken even the greatest lover and force him to more temperate climates.

As Juan moves on across the Continent, Byron ironically deflates the tradition of the picturesque tour (XI, 58–64), chiefly by rhyming a roll call of famous cities and a list of natural resources. When Juan reaches England, where hypocrisy and cant achieve a dazzling multiplicity of aspects, Byron's satiric exposition of the difference between appearance and reality rises, without shrillness, to its greatest heights. He reveals pretense to be the pervading rottenness of an entire culture—beginning with the irony of the attempted highway robbery, shortly after Juan arrives in the land of freedom, law, and order, and closing with the magnificent final irony of the Duchess of Fitz-Fulke disguised as the ghost of the Black Friar, emblematic of a land where the sensual comes draped in the robes of the spiritual, while a country girl in a red cape is brought before the lord of the manor charged with immorality. It is a land where the wealthy, to escape the press of the city, crowd together in the country. Assembled in all their boredom and frivolity at Norman Abbey, weighty with the great traditions of the past, they may well remind us of Eliot's similarly ironic juxtaposition of richly traditional setting and spiritual poverty in *The Waste Land*. In Juan's England, even the food masquerades in foreign dress, fit nourishment for a hypocritical people. Things in *Don Juan*, then, are never what they seem, not even the title character, the "natural" man at home in every "artificial" society, the exile and wanderer never haunted by a sense of quest. He finds equilibrium in the "changeable" sex and his moments of eternity in the symbol of the physical here and now. He is the world's most famous lover, yet he never seduces a woman. Although he treads a rake's progress, he does so without becoming cynical or worldly minded. He is a man famous in love and war, yet a child in search of a mother (who will also be mistress and goddess), and he finds her, repeatedly, in woman after woman!

3

A N E F F O R T , however inadequate, has already been made to indicate that the functional irony of *Don Juan* is seldom the simple irony of a reversed meaning. To abstract the meaning of the narrative in an attempt to suggest the pervasive unity of the main theme and establish the organic relation of each of the chief episodes to it, may suggest that some oversimplification has taken place. As a corrective, therefore, it may be well to say again that Byron repeatedly used irony as a qualifying device within the larger frame of his satire, and so saved it regularly from oversimplification, thinness, and monotony of tone. The point, which deserves to be emphasized, may be illustrated by a brief analysis of the richly mixed tone characteristic of Byron's feminine portraits. It is significant that *Don Juan* combines and reconciles within itself the extremes of the love poem and of the satire, mingling and fusing attitudes of almost pure approval and almost complete disapproval—at once a great hymn to love and a satire on women, and frequently concerned with the comedy of love. Thus the satire may merge so successfully with comedy or at other times with tragedy that it is often hardly recognizable as "serious" satire: seldom or never is it narrowly satiric or expressive of unqualified disapproval. The tone, in other words, is almost never "pure."

.Consider Julia, for example. Is she a hypocritical self-deceiver viciously leading herself and Juan on with the cant of Platonic love, or is she a woman betrayed originally into marriage with an old man, led deliberately into a trap by Inez, and sentenced finally by society to a convent, to pay for a single indiscretion? Is she a tragically pathetic figure or a comically shrew-tongued termagant? Byron, it seems, can have it several ways at once, as he does also (though in different wise and reconciling other extremes) with Haidée, the island goddess who is also Juan's mistress, mother, and nurse, attended by the earthy figure of Zoe. There is also the richly ambiguous Lambro, at once an affectionately comic parody of the Byronic hero and the unwitting agent of tragedy, who sheds his own ambiguous light over the entire episode. Byron, of course, was quite aware of the romantic character of the Haidée episode, and so repeatedly qualified and enriched its tone with heterogeneous materials, creating an atmosphere of lyrical tenderness, but at the same time intellectually awake to the physical actualities. In the final tragedy he asserts the validity of the romantic vision, but he is aware too (as the violent shift in tone at IV, 74, indicates) that life must go on, as dangerous, as ludicrous, or as humiliating as ever, despite tragedy or the death of romance. Thus Bryon was able to explore fully the experience of ideal, romantic love without ever forcing his romanticism. Although he bases the dream squarely on a physical foundation, supporting and guarding the lyrical motif with numerous discordant elements, his is not in any sense the self-contradictory attitude of romantic irony. The romance is not canceled out but intensified.

Byron's treatment of Gulbeyaz offers an instructive contrast to that of Haidée and illustrates how skillfully he can qualify and develop a tone which is basically comic. The Sultana, who loses the game of love by reason of the very device which made it possible for her to win, Juan's disguise, is the woman comically scorned by Juan in petticoats. But she is at the same time genuinely pathetic in her frustrated tears, which turn, note, metaphysically and murderously, into a tempest that nearly drowns Juan finally, sewed up in a sack. (Byron develops a tear-tempest figure over several stanzas, V, 135–37.)

In the portrait of Adeline, however, neither predominantly romantic as Haidée nor comic as Gulbeyaz, but present for purposes of pure satire, Byron uses ironic qualification with perhaps even greater skill. Here his chief concern was social satire, focusing on English hypocrisy, and Adeline, clearly, was to be one of its chief exponents. We see her entertaining her country guests in a bid for their votes, then ridiculing them when they have left. We see her indeed as acquiescent hostess to all the hypocrisy and pretense assembled at Norman Abbey; and we see her inevitably deceiving herself, with the subtle deceit of an ill-understood friendship for Juan. But in ironic qualification of all this deception, she has most of the solid virtues and all the charm of the polished society which she reflects and symbolizes at its best. And, paradoxically, it is this very quality of polished smoothness which gives rise, simultaneously, to Byron's satire and to his sympathetic approval. The coldly polished manners of these frozen Englishmen, with their philosophy of *nil admirari,* reduce them to a comically bored, colorless sameness; but it is the same quality of self-discipline which accounts for the achievements and virtues of Adeline, making her a perfectly gracious hostess, a musician, and a poetess, able to admire Pope without being a bluestocking. Despite the effort required and the vacancy in her heart, she can love her lord, nevertheless, "conjugal, but cold." And although she is falling in love with Juan, she refuses to admit it even to herself. But such restraint and self-discipline, Byron knew, is won at the price of bottling up and suppressing the emotions beneath a layer of ice, thus doubly distilling them and ironically intensifying their explosive qualities, enabling them the more effectively to break down the cold and icy walls of polished restraint (XIII, 36–39). Even Adeline's hypocrisy with her country guests arises out of a kind of sincerity, her *mobilité.* Thus recognizing the complex origins of hypocritical social conduct at the very time that he is attacking hypocrisy, achieving a triumph of mixed tone, Byron can acknowledge the attractiveness of Adeline, one of his most subtle projections of the appearance-versus-reality theme. He elevates her to something like a symbol of one aspect of the English character, and allows her, "the fair most fatal Juan ever met," his richly endowed and highly ambiguous "Dian of the Ephesians" (XIV, 46), to merge finally, with his other goddesses of love, into the complex and all-embracing figure of "Alma Venus Genetrix" (XVI, 109).

Don Juan does therefore show a significant thematic unity. Its most significant structure is a considered organization of attitudes expressed by means of a rich variety of ironically qualified tones, and each of the chief narrative episodes bears an organic relation, clear but subtly varied, to the larger theme. There remains to be considered the instrument which Byron forged to render it, "style" in the limited sense.

4

I T I S S U R E L Y one of the monstrous ironies of our time, the present critical Age of Irony and Ambiguity, the Period of the Poetic Paradox, that Byron, the master of these, should have been so neglected by the new critics. For *Don Juan* shows remarkably detailed affinities (excepting one important quality) with the recent poetry of our century and with the "respectable" forebears which its critics point to with pride. One might easily show, for example, how consistently *Don Juan* meets the tests of "modernity" formulated and applied by Selden Rodman as a guide in selecting poems for his *New Anthology of Modern Poetry* (1946):

> imagery patterned increasingly on everyday speech
>
> absence of inversions, stilted apostrophes, conventional end-rhymes, "poetic" language generally . . .
>
> freedom from the ordinary logic of sequence, jumping from one image to the next by "association" [evident in the digressions of *Don Juan*] . . .
>
> emphasis on the ordinary, in reaction against the traditional poetic emphasis on the cosmic . . .
>
> concern with the common man, almost to the exclusion of the "hero" or extraordinary man [see *Don Juan,* I, i]
>
> concern . . . with the social order as against "heaven" and "nature"

Or consider the point by point correspondence between the commonly recognized qualities of Byron's "medley" style and those described in the following discussion from C. Day Lewis' *A Hope for Poetry:*

Both Eliot and Edmund Wilson have called attention to the kinship between the French Symbolists and the English metaphysicals. Wilson outlines the similarities: 'The medley of images; the deliberately mixed metaphors; the combination of passion and wit —of the grand and the prosaic manners; the bold amalgamation of material with spiritual.' And again, speaking of Corbière's poetry, he calls it 'a poetry of the outcast: often colloquial and homely, yet with a rhetoric of fantastic slang; often with the manner of slapdash doggerel, yet sure of its own morose artistic effects.' Exclude the word 'morose,' and the passage gives an exact description of Auden's work. That combination 'of the grand and the prosaic manners,' a constant alternation of the magniloquent and the colloquial, is a quality shared by Donne, Wilfred Owen and Auden . . . .

Or, one might add, by Byron.

This "constant alternation of lyricism and flatness . . . , the salient characteristic of post-war technique" (making deliberate use of slang, prosaic words, commonplace images, and bathos to produce verse of an "uneven, conversational surface"), Day Lewis traces to "the emotional complexity to which the modern poet is so often subject." Byron again might have been mentioned, for the trait is fundamental in him. Rooted in his essentially modern sensibility, it made sustained lyrical writing and absolute purity of tone as difficult for him as they now are for many of his poetic descendants. It has now become a critical cliché that Auden shows important similarities to Byron (Auden's long "Letter to Lord Byron" made the comparison inevitable; Byron's continuing influence is evident in *Nones*). Yvor Winters, however, significantly unsympathetic with much in contemporary poetry, is the only critic, I believe, who has ever suggested, and he briefly and unflatteringly, that Byron stands at the head of that long line of masters of the double mood and the conversational-ironic manner which comes down through Laforgue, Pound, and Eliot to the most recent poetaster of ironic discord. It is a significant and little-known fact, too, that Byron was one of the favorite poets of Joyce.[1]

[1] See also the tributes paid to *Don Juan* by Yeats, writing to H. J. C. Grierson, February 21, 1926 (*Letters of W. B. Yeats*), and by Virginia Woolf in her *Diary*, August 8, 1918. Yeats wrote, "I am particularly indebted to you for your essay on Byron [in *The Background of English Literature*]. My own verse has more and more adopted . . . the syntax and vocabulary of common personal speech. The passages you quote [which included *Don Juan*, II, 177, 181, 183–85, 188] are perfect personal speech. The overchildish or over pretty or feminine element in some good Wordsworth and in much poetry up to

Why, then, the pronounced critical disfavor from a quarter which so obviously might offer its homage? The new critics have insisted rightly enough on the importance of a richly qualified tone, on the complexity and comprehensiveness which may result in a poetry of synthesis or inclusion, invulnerable itself to irony because incorporating the principle of irony within itself, and avoiding oversimplification and sentimentality by uniting or reconciling impulses ordinarily opposed. With all this Byron would have been in sympathy. Like many of the poets in present favor, he frequently juxtaposed discordant elements in a deliberate effort to crash through the cant of his day ("the mart/ For what is sometimes called poetic diction,/ And that outrageous appetite for lies"), awaken his etherized reader, and shock him out of his complacency into some new perception or fresh insight. But the new critics, in large number, have gone on to insist that the chief or sole instrument of the irony must be the metaphor or simile and that the synthesis must take place within the single image, which, as Pound's influential definition noted, will present "an intellectual and emotional complex in an *instant* of time" (italics mine). Thus Eliot writes: "We have come to expect poetry to be something very concentrated, something distilled; but if Byron had distilled his verse, there would have been nothing whatever left." It becomes a matter of some importance, therefore, to inquire into the spatial limits of the area of fusion. How great an area may be allowed, how small a one is actually demanded before the fusion or reconciliation is achieved successfully, before it will produce, in Pound's words, "that sense of sudden liberation; that sense of freedom from time limits and space limits; that sense of sudden growth, which we experience in the presence of the greatest works of

---

our date comes from the lack of natural momentum in the syntax." Yeats concluded that Byron was "the one great English poet" who constantly sought this quality, although he did not always achieve it.

Virginia Woolf saw in the style of Byron's poem "a method [which] is a discovery by itself. It's what one has looked for in vain—an elastic shape which will hold whatever you choose to put into it. Thus he could write out his mood as it came to him; he could say whatever came into his head. He wasn't committed to be poetical; and thus escaped his evil genius of the false romantic and imaginative. When he is serious he is sincere: and he can impinge upon any subject he likes. He writes 16 cantos without once flogging his flanks. He had, evidently, the able witty mind of what my father Sir Leslie would have called a thoroughly masculine nature. . . . Still, it doesn't seem an easy example to follow; and indeed like all free and easy things, only the skilled and mature really bring them off successfully. But Byron was full of ideas—a quality that gives his verse a toughness and drives me to little excursions over the surrounding landscape or room in the middle of my reading."

art"? Byron's successful practice, attested for over a century by critic and general reader alike, although in the present terms unanalyzed, would seem to offer an answer. For Byron's peculiar distinction was to achieve a style which, within the self-imposed limits of a conversational metric and manner, could not only express the author's many-sided awareness of the world, in all its immense complexity, but also speak clearly to the common reader. Byron successfully reconciles within his verse quite discordant elements, yet does so without excessive verbal density or compression and the consequent obscurity, without forcing the image to bear an unbearable weight of meaning, which in fact many a modern poem buckles beneath. He achieved, in other words, almost all the virtues of ambiguity and comprehensiveness which may accompany a poetry of synthesis (proving himself, incidentally, to possess "a mechanism of sensibility which could devour any kind of experience," as Eliot said of the metaphysicals), yet achieved them without benefit of the metaphysical image and certainly without screwing up the tension of the poem to a painful degree. The careless ease of *Don Juan,* often remarked, is the necessary counterweight or safety valve to the audacity of the ironic juxtapositions and is the mark of the balanced point of view, recently enshrined by the new critics, and of the poetic voice under easy control (and *in* control of its materials), explosive as its effects typically are. In short, the comprehensiveness of vision, chief justification of the metaphysical image, is achieved without the use of violently compressed or telescoped imagery and without sacrificing the sense of wholeness, the clear subordination of imagistic detail, itself a form of reconciliation, to theme and larger purpose.

It is important to remember, furthermore, that Byron's compositional unit is not the single line or succinctly phrased image, but the stanza, within which he frequently brings together the same elements of ironic incongruity so much in present favor. It may be objected, perhaps, that so to assemble them is to dilute them or relieve them of their electrifying tension. But, obviously, the typical stanza does possess its charge, characteristically an ironic demolition which produces its own shock and has its own characteristic voltage, much more appropriate to the long conversational poem than the image of high intellectual tension which may be well enough suited to the typical short poem of our day. Indeed, prevailing taste and present critical theory are often inimical to and inadequately prepared to deal with the long poem of conversational tone. The critical tools are still to be developed, or rediscovered. Overintensity, of course, would have paralyzed Byron's satiric purpose, impeded the flow of his thought, and been incongruous within his conversational manner. When his imagery functions ironically to qualify an idea or thrust it under a clear comic light, the irony is under conscious *control,* and the imagery is necessarily so ordered as to cut off any associations, ironical extensions, or ambiguities except those deliberately sought. His imagery is usually thinner, less allusive, with a slighter degree of intensity or extension, and without the depth or density of much twentieth-century verse. It nonetheless accomplishes its purpose perfectly and does so, in its larger context, without oversimplifying.

It is not characteristic of *Don Juan,* of course, to see a world in a grain of sand, an infinity of suggestiveness in the particular image or symbol extending to embrace simultaneously several different levels of thought, to end with a fusion, or blurring, of the actual and the ideal. Such a use of the image would frequently have produced a fundamental contradiction in the very purpose of the poem, which rests on the clear difference between appearance and reality and makes that difference its main theme, the principle of its stanzaic structure (typically a microcosm and image of the whole poem), and the *raison d'être* for its ironic manner. Thus Byron often refrained from reconciling discordant elements even within the single stanza (achieving unity within a larger structure of attitudes), choosing instead to use the image to illustrate or qualify the idea, linking image and idea, not divorcing them in an effort to make the image substitute for the idea. The method, to be sure, is that of Pope, whom Auden calls his master; and, as Louis MacNeice has pointed out, it is also the method of ordinary conversation, which uses images "to drive home a meaning, to make a point, to *outline* a picture (for an outline is distinct from a suggestion)." But the method is not that which uses imagery as mere decoration.

It is perhaps finally a matter of congruity. Byron's satiric purpose was first to portray his world, still disconcertingly ours, as he saw it in all its complexity and then to attack the element of pretense or deception in it. Seriously concerned with this larger purpose, he knew that to give undue regard to the parts, fusing imagery at white (and unapproachable) heat, spotting little island nodes of "pure" poetry in the great ebb and flow of his conversational epic, would detract attention from his main theme, obscure his meaning, and magnify the subordinate elements of imagery out of their proper focus. So Byron used the humorous figure, the extended or multiple simile, the conversational metaphor, accumulating images instead of compressing them, much as certain neoclassical poets did: to draw the mind back a little from the main action or idea, place it in clearer focus, qualify, and so light it up in proper perspective, "to show things really as they are." To illustrate more specifically, we can see him using imagery drawn from classical mythology in order to suggest the godlike eternity in time at the otherwise very human heart of his heroines and so indicate the element of strangeness at the center of the physical or the sexual, and the mystery at the heart of the comedy of love (V, 96; XVI, 49, 109). Conversely, he can use simple, almost commonplace garden imagery to establish a tone of lyric tenderness and suggest the fragility and transience of his heroines (VI, 65), or, as with Dudù, to suggest natural innocence in the midst of artificiality (VI, 53). He can describe the sea in Canto II in terms of the treacherously human and so personalize a great and otherwise impersonal natural force (42, 49), pointing by the same means at the human causes contributing to the tragedy and at the mistaken pantheistic creed of some of his contemporaries (34, 52). In the midst of a satiric attack on hypocritical social convention he can use traditional imagery of various kinds, frequently drawing upon ancient or modern history, and so suggest that although a rebel, even a "revolutionary" reformer, he is not a man adrift in time, cut off from a sterile and meaningless past, but one who values the continuity of the great traditions, desiring not their destruction but their modification (XII, 78; XIII, 11). Byron had not heard that a poem must be disjointed if it is adequately to express an age out of joint, but he can, nevertheless, ironically juxtapose images suggestive of both classical and nineteenth-century civilization and so give to the satire of the contemporary scene increased depth, order, and perspective (IV, 75–79; XI, 7). Or he can use imagery drawn from his personal life and so leaven the "objective" narrative of Juan, the public myth of himself allowing him to use imagery which is personal but seldom private or cryptic. We see him using deliberately discordant images to qualify the tragedy of the shipwreck episode (II, 92), the romance of the Haidée episode, or the comedy of the harem scene (V, 92), thus establishing a state of tension between image and dramatic situation. He can explore a figure at length in order to set forth the ambiguities in such a character as

Adeline's (XIII, 36–38) or the subconscious urges of Dudù (VI, 75–77), accumulate figures as an aid to securing suspense (I, 102–4), or use an image for purposes of greater concentration or precision. He is master of the purely derogatory image (III, 94–95), but he can also use imagery playfully so as to avoid confusing the satirical and the hysterical tones, referring to the lust of Catherine, for example, as follows:

> *She could repay each amatory look you lent*
> *With interest, and in turn was wont with rigour*
> *To exact of Cupid's bills the full amount*
> *At sight, nor would permit you to discount.*

On the other hand, he is quite able to use imagery which allows a mingling of the approbative and the satirical attitudes and permits him to disassociate himself from both parties, as in the famous Daniel Boone stanzas (VIII, 60–67).

The style of *Don Juan* thus provides an answer to several problems which still confront the modern poet: offering first of all a means of accommodation within a single form, without oversimplification and yet without obscurity, of a wealth of material drawn from all levels of existence. It is a style which has solved the problem of communication, and solved it moreover, in important part, even by means of a number of devices needlessly out of present favor and lacking which poetry is the poorer—such devices as narrative, comedy, rhetoric, and invective, which allowed Byron not only to speak out in full voice or whisper subtly and devastatingly but also to canvass the whole range of tones between. A completely uninhibited style, flexible beyond anything before it, it is able at once to give the impression of dramatic conversation, using rhythms close to the movement of modern speech, and also to allow the nearly complete lyric, humorous, or meditative expression of the whole man behind it. To paraphrase Eliot's recent appeal for a new poetic drama, it is a style which not having lost touch with colloquial speech can bring poetry into the world in which the reader lives and to which he returns when he puts down his book. By means of it, Byron was able to explore many levels of his personal experience and complex sensibility, giving full expression to his own personality, but able, in addition, always to place the personal reference or image in perspective, inserting flat, colloquial statements, deliberately banal or flashy, and so to achieve not only a release from the merely personal but also a simultaneous extension of his field of reference.

All this he achieved, furthermore, without ever sacrificing common humanity or passion or attempting to purify his poetry of its human associations. He would not have understood the current neoformalism, nor sympathized much with it if he had. If we may believe Louise Bogan, writing in *The New Yorker* (June 9, 1951), "Glances at life, as a matter of fact, are now thought to be vulgar and naive, and emotion becomes increasingly suspect as problems of surface texture receive primary emphasis." Now Byron had as much reason as any man to suspect emotion, but he did not therefore squeeze it out of his poetry. What we receive finally from *Don Juan* is the many-faceted image of Byron himself, looking freely and with intelligent interest *outward* on the human situation as he saw it and remembering always that the first concern of any writer is to entertain, to make his work interesting. He was quite incapable of that cold vanity which leads a poet, having convinced himself that "the question of communication, of what the reader will get from it, is not paramount," to sing for himself alone; and the example of Byron's vigorous satire, necessarily looking outward, but never neglecting the inner man, could be a healthy counterinfluence upon the inward lookers and private singers of our day, as well as upon those who so scrupulously erase the living author in order to build a "flawless" structure. The felt and serious present need for the return of intelligible personality to poetry is well illustrated by the recent work of the English neo-Romantics.

The peculiar appropriateness, for our time, of a flexible style such as that of *Don Juan,* with its strong colloquial element, may be indicated in the words of C. Day Lewis, although he gave only passing reference to Byron. Concluding a lecture delivered in 1947 in praise of *The Colloquial Element in English Poetry,* exemplified by certain poems of Donne, Browning, Hardy, Frost, and MacNeice, he said,

> There is a time for pure poetry, and a place for the undiluted grand manner, but I doubt if they are here and now, when the press of events, the crowding novelties, the so rapidly changing features of the world in which we live seem to demand of the poet that he should more than ever be responsive, fluid, adaptable; that his utterance should be human rather than hierophantic; that he should study to make his technique as supple and elastic as he may, to mould it to the intricate contours of modern experience.

The example of *Don Juan,* finally, may well provide another service, less purely stylistic, to modern poetry: teach it how to put irony, neither self-defeating, static, sterile, nor depressive of the will to action, back into the service of propaganda, that the main stream of poetry may become again a poetry of action, helping man to take confidence again in himself and his society without being at all blinded to the defects or limitations of either. *Don Juan* offers an example of a poetry which allows an indignant exposure of the world's folly and the hypocritical deceptiveness of man, whose failure to see or act upon the difference between appearance and reality is at once comic and tragic. But it is also a poetry which is of the world and free of despair, avoiding the extreme position of the congenital disillusioned idealist. It counsels man to live in his world and be reconciled with it, if only the more effectively to correct it. It is a poetry of satirical attack upon the world which is at the same time, miraculously, a poetry of acceptance, not rejection. It is a poetry of clear present use.

Byron and Some Current Patterns of Thought

1 1

WILLIS W. PRATT

NO ONE WHO writes on Byron's thought in relation to our own day can ignore the disconcerting fact that many recent critics—among them several whose opinions have carried much weight in the past twenty years or so—have had little interest in his poetry, and in some quarters at least have been particularly contemptuous of his thought. T. S. Eliot, for example, following Matthew Arnold's dictum that Byron was "empty of matter," describes him as not very well informed, and calls his mind an uninteresting one. Such a verdict fails to recognize, first, the variety, the scope, above all the intense seriousness of the subject matter in Byron's later poetry, and second, the wealth of literary and topical allusions that reflects an agile intelligence which, for all its surface brilliance, probes deeply into the underlying implications of the social scene. Admittedly, Byron's was not a mind that worked with the careful precision of a great machine: as Leslie Stephen said of Pope, anything like sustained reasoning was beyond his grasp; but Byron's was an equipped mind, one that could make its point with accuracy and driving power. Like Pope, too, he "felt and thought by shocks and electric flashes," a phrase which calls to mind Byron's own description of himself as leaping out like the tiger upon his prey or growling back into his den when he has missed the mark. Thus, feeling in Byron is often so intensively directed that in precision of observation and mordant wit it becomes the equivalent of thought.

In searching for an explanation of the adverse judgments of Eliot and others, I have been able to find several fairly clear-cut reasons for

149

them; but, paradoxically (and paradox somehow creeps into all writing on Byronic subjects), of the five which will be my main topics of discussion, four contain elements that link Byron quite clearly with patterns of thought often found in modern poetry.

The first, and it seems to me the only, persuasive reason for the contemporary indifference to Byron's thought is simply this: many of the most traditionally Byronic of his poems strike us now as shoddy and adolescent, sentimental, or cheaply rhetorical. We have seldom returned to them since our first dutiful reading in anthologies and courses in literature. We are, for example, offended by the callow self-pity in Cantos I and II of *Childe Harold;* we are suspicious of the grandiose expressions of romantic defiance in *Manfred* and *The Prisoner of Chillon;* we find little penetration into character in the historical dramas *Marino Faliero* and *The Two Foscari;* and we are no longer deeply moved by the subjective sentimentalities of "Fare Thee Well," "There's not a joy the world contains," the "Stanzas to Augusta," or a dozen others of Byron's personal lyrics. It should be admitted at the outset, then, that much of the best known, the anthologized Byron seems to us neither cogent in thought nor profound in emotional expression. It takes a long time for a poet to be remembered, as every poet finally is, by what is best in him—much longer than the years which separate Byron's day from ours—so that only now are we discarding the superficial and tawdry. In such a winnowing process, however, it sometimes happens that the whole of a poet's work suffers from the indifference that results from the right condemnation of a part. We are beginning to think of Byron in terms of the best—the final cantos of *Childe Harold's Pilgrimage, Beppo, The Vision of Judgment,* and the immense canvas of *Don Juan,* works which are penetrating in thought, the reflections of a mind as kindling and fresh as it was when it was first heard. That we have discarded so much—the bulk of it poetry written before Byron was thirty—is, it seems to me, a healthy sign. At the same time, this helps to explain why Byron has attracted so little serious criticism in recent years. It should perhaps be noted, too, that as interest in Byron's poetry has diminished, preoccupation with the complexities of his personality has increased; so that for one reader familiar with the rich *Ubi sunt* stanzas of *Don Juan,* Canto XI, there are a hundred who know all the ins and outs of the chatter about Augusta.

Among the less valid reasons for the neglect of Byron, the first of four that I have been able to define more or less clearly arises from a seeming duality in his character. For many critics Byron seems to be a kind of Janus figure, with one face shouting defiance at the stars for man's unkind fate and asserting his own will to power, the other looking at a far from satisfactory world with humorous skepticism and classical detachment, and the two seem to be irreconcilable. Hence the charge of insincerity that so many writers, especially his British critics, have leveled against him. But when we look at the third canto of *Childe Harold,* one of the clearest expressions of the romantic side of Byron, we see not simply the disenchanted sentimentalist with his heart on his sleeve, but also a sensitive and chastened idealist, immature but thoughtful, trying sincerely to find in Wordsworthian pantheism as expounded by his friend Shelley, a philosophy that would give him spiritual equilibrium, and finding that philosophy wanting. With all the will in the world to live not in himself but to become a portion of that around him, to "mingle" and become "absorbed" in spirit with the "mountains, waves, and skies," Byron was quite unable to give up the grasp upon physical reality that such a belief demanded. At the end of the canto, as the strength of his personality reasserts itself, he moves into a position more compatible with his temperament and experience, towards the firmer ground, for him, of intellectual skepticism:

> to steel
> *The heart against itself; and to conceal,*
> *With a proud caution, love, or hate, or aught,—*
> *Passion or feeling, purpose, grief, or zeal,—*
> *Which is the tyrant spirit of our thought,*
> *Is a stern task of soul;—no matter—it is taught.*

Canto III of *Childe Harold* is, then, a kind of halfway point in Byron's search for that poise of spirit which every thoughtful man must struggle after, a search in which the odds are admittedly against him, but which he continues to carry on with unremitting energy and courage. In the face of his own inner conflicts and the disillusionments of the post-Napoleonic world, fully as discouraging as those we face today, Byron did not withdraw into "a padded cell of metaphysical self-analysis" which has been the unhappy retreat of many gifted writers of our own day. As he moved into Italy in the final canto of his poem, written a year later, he saw with somber clarity the inadequacy of his early dreams:

> *for waking Reason deems*
> *Such over-weening phantasies unsound,*
> *And other voices speak and other sights surround.*

As this fledgling realist leads us in stanzas of impressive descriptive power through the dying grandeurs of Venice and Florence, to Rome, symbol of political tyranny and the mutability of human ambition, we are aware of being in company with a mind which is becoming increasingly "at one with itself," to which "no changes bring surprise," which sees the world clearly, and will in its own time sketch that world "exactly as it goes." The point I would make, then, is that the dichotomy between the romantic and the classical Byron is not as final as it is usually accepted as being, nor does it imply at all any insincerity from either point of view. From the mature romanticism of Byron in 1818, it is a short and logical step to the classical satirist of the later poems—those which are the most meaningful for this century. When we look carefully, the Janus figure merges into one complex and vital entity, the creator of *Don Juan* and *The Vision of Judgment*.

Even in the most patently romantic and grandiose of Byron's poems, the oriental tales, there is discernible in the portrayal of the Byronic hero an admixture of classical objectivity. This hero, who stands "among them but not of them," living his experiences actively and intensively, at the same time stands off and appraises himself and his conflicts with pitiless frankness and accuracy. It is this same "doubleness" of character that Malcolm Cowley sees in a modern writer like F. Scott Fitzgerald, and he might easily have been describing Byron when he wrote of Fitzgerald recently: "He stood on the corner and jeered at himself while himself was leading the parade. He was at the same time the hero and his worshippers, the prodigal son and his father, the criminal and his judge. . . . He was the observer as well as the participant, and in both roles he was simultaneously enchanted and repelled." With minor deviations the same thing might be urged of William Faulkner and his unhappy but defiant heroes in their lost paradises never to be regained. They, too, shake a Byronic fist at heaven and yet laugh sardonically at their own inadequacy and the futility of resolving their conflicts into any sort of equilibrium.[1] To go back to Byron, then, is to go back to the archetype of characters

[1] See Vincent C. Hopper's perceptive article, "Faulkner's Paradise," *The Virginia Quarterly Review*, Vol. XXIII (1947), for the fuller expression of this idea.

found in some of the most powerful writing of our own day, an archetype not depicted with the intricate and fine-spun subtleties of the in-
heritors of Freudian psychology perhaps, but with the bold and
unmistakable strokes of an artist who understood, as T. S. Eliot says,
his own creation perfectly. To read again such a masterpiece of self-
analysis as Byron's description of his hero, Lara (sections xvii–xviii),
is to find oneself in the familiar psychological realm of Earwicker's
remorseful conscience in *Finnegans Wake* and the harried victims in
the novels of Kafka:

> *He stood a stranger in this breathing world,*
> *An erring spirit from another hurl'd;*
> *A thing of dark imaginings, that shaped*
> *By choice the perils he by chance escaped:*
> *But 'scaped in vain, for in their memory yet*
> *His mind would half exult and half regret.*
> *With more capacity for love than earth*
> *Bestows on most of mortal mould and birth,*
> *His early dreams of good outstripp'd the truth,*
> *And troubled manhood follow'd baffled youth;* . . .
> *Till he at last confounded good and ill,*
> *And half mistook for fate the acts of will.*
> *Too high for common selfishness, he could*
> *At times resign his own for others' good,*
> *But not in pity, not because he ought,*
> *But in some strange perversity of thought,*
> *That sway'd him onward with a secret pride*
> *To do what few or none would do beside;* . . .
> *So much he soar'd beyond, or sunk beneath,*
> *The men with whom he felt condemn'd to breathe.*
> *And long'd by good or ill to separate*
> *Himself from all who shared his mortal state.*

Here, we are able to see with surprising clarity the beginning of the
disenchanted era in which we live, to recognize the same accelerating
confusions and attendant moral uncertainties that we are familiar with
in W. H. Auden, in Hart Crane, and in the distorted world of the
Pisan Cantos of Ezra Pound.

Three further critical objections have been responsible for the
general indifference to what Byron has to say. Some critics find that
the clarity with which Byron expresses his thought makes it too obvious
to be taken seriously; others resent his scorn of metaphysical specula-

tion; still others complain that they cannot find in his work a consistent point of view. In *The Trembling of the Veil*, Yeats provides us with a vantage point from which to examine these criticisms in the light of the mature satirical poetry of Byron: "We should satirise rather than praise . . . original virtue arises from the discovery of evil." It is doubtful if there was ever a time when English-speaking peoples were more willing to submit themselves to conscientious self-analysis in order to find out their own weaknesses and follies than they are now. This is particularly evident in the honest self-criticism and sincere self-satire in much of our poetry written since 1930. The subject matter of this poetry has, however, been generally channeled into the relatively short, compressed, explosive lyric which derives so much of its inspiration from the highly intellectualized poetry of the seventeenth century. In following this aesthetic, it has been the experience of many fine modern poets that in expressing their ideas so subtly and metaphysically—especially those who have cast their thought in a kind of private imagery—they have not been understood. By the same token, readers have been warned to suspect the immediately intelligible and have been led to believe that clarity implies the superficial, that expansiveness betrays an inability to achieve effective communication. Thus satirists like Byron and Chaucer, who express themselves discursively and colloquially, who never sacrifice lucidity to verbal conceit, are suspect. There are signs, however, that the latest generation of poets—Karl Shapiro, Peter Viereck, Richard Eberhart, for example—is attempting to communicate again with an almost vanished public; there are portents that to be modern, "that curious word which devours its own meaning with every tick of the clock," is to be understood. It is in a sense to come closer to a state of mind which is receptive to what a broadly ranging satirist like Byron has to say. It may be that what is needed is a special classification such as "colloquial" or "vernacular" to describe the kind of poetry we find in Byron, in some of Chaucer, or in Alexander Pushkin's *Eugene Onegin*. Such a pigeon-holing might give Byron the prestige that belonging to a special category almost always brings. At any rate, the accessibility of his ideas, which leaves the modern technical critic with so little to do, and which has, therefore, frequently excluded him from serious consideration, may now perhaps be counted as a generally desirable characteristic for a poet to have.

As Byron shunned obscurity in the expression of his thought, so too he avoided metaphysics. Again and again in his later satire he expresses the idea that systems of thought, more especially metaphysical speculations, are futile and misleading. Byron leveled his skeptical sights at the abstract philosophizing of the leading poets of his age with their "systems to perplex the sages," contending that not one of them, from Platonists to Wordsworthian pantheists, could submit his speculative system to the light of common experience and survive intact. Although he did not use the word ideology, he would have been as skeptical of the implications of this word as was Napoleon when he used it to describe the visionary theorizing of "hot-brained boys and enthusiasts." Certainly he would have been in agreement with Lionel Trilling's conviction that ideologies are masks assumed when a movement has despaired of having ideas and is turning to dogma to enforce its point of view. Byron knew how quickly ideologies subside into mere systems of gains and losses, and he would have none of them.

Thus Shelley's dream worlds, however beautiful and desirable, were so much "mystifying metaphysics" for Byron; Wordsworthian pantheism, which he tried sincerely but vainly to embrace in 1816, was for him a narrow and exclusive doctrine. Byron believed, along with David Hume, that we have no logical right to pass from our sporadic and evanescent sense-data, which yield evidence only as to the here and now, to belief in a stable system of permanent things governed by law. Thus Byron, ranging about "with reckless raffish honesty" in the world of sense-data, reflects quite perfectly that desideratum of Yeats—the poet's right to explore—especially what has been long forbidden—not only with high moral purpose but "gaily out of sheer mischief or sheer delight in that play of the mind." Hence it comes that in Byron we seldom feel the sense of disappointment that we sometimes recognize in Milton, or in Wordsworth and Shelley when they failed to realize their ideals by direct political actions and revolutions. Byron never for a moment thought that successful revolution against tyranny would lead to a perfect society, even in a remote future. In a mood familiar to modern poets, he even had some doubts about the essential dignity of man; but he never lost his sense of outrage at indignities to the individual; he was always ready to fight against his own detractors and against the detractors of others. As a champion of free inquiry he was especially angered by any attempt at thought control; as he says in *Don Juan* (Canto IX):

> *And I will war, at least in words (and—should*
> *My chance so happen—deeds), with all who war*
> *With Thought.*

Thus political demagoguery got short shrift from Byron:

> *I wish men to be free*
> *As much from mobs as kings—from you as me.*

As a moralist also, Byron is skeptical of codes and conventions; in his plea for naturalness and frankness he is akin to D. H. Lawrence —though he would have abjured the mysticism with which Lawrence surrounded sex. For Byron is, as Oscar Williams declares the poet to be, "always on the side of life. . . . When a poet," Williams insists, "promulgates the sensuous pleasures he is no less moral than when he paints the hope of heaven, or reveals the truth of tragedy. To be on the side of life is to be moral."

Byron's greatest hatred, perhaps, is directed against war, that systematic despoiler of whole societies and nations:

> *"Let there be Light!" said God, "and there was Light!"*
> *"Let there be Blood!" says man, and there's a sea!*

Nowhere in the literature of our time has the stupidity and futility of war been laid before us with more graphic power than in Cantos VII and VIII of *Don Juan*. In the shocking and dramatic mingling of mockery and blood in the account of the siege of Ismail, in the sardonic picture of the Russian Souvaroff, "who loved blood as an alderman loves marrow," Byron is speaking for our time as well as for his own. In this respect he is one of the few poets of the past who does not have to answer the charge of the English war poet, Roy Fuller:

> *Not one of them has had to bear such shame,*
> *Been tortured so constantly by government,*
> *Has had to draw his life out when the age*
> *Made happiness a revolution, fame*
> *Exile, and death the whimsy of a sergeant.—*

Although we may feel that Byron's motives in going to Greece were mixed, we hold in memory the picture of the poet drilling troops, writing war songs, paying the army, settling disputes among intransigeant and incompetent Greek patriots—carrying out with immense energy his conviction that men should fulfill the promise of their words in deeds, that individually at least men are worth saving, that the only world worth living in is a free one. And here we are brought sharply into the range of thought of such a poet as Stephen Spender whose ringing challenge, "Not Palaces, an Era's Crown" is an invitation to action that Byron had fulfilled a hundred and thirty years before:

> *Drink from here energy and only energy,*
> *As from the electric charge of a battery,*
> *To will this time's change.*
> *. . . Drive of a ruining purpose,*
> *Destroying all but its age-long exploiters.*
> *Our program like this, yet opposite:*
> *Death to the killers, bringing light to life.*

To apprehend Byron's dislike of systems, however, is to realize that here is a mind that refused to align itself with any doctrinaire group, for such a group, he thought, will inevitably seek to impose its ideas upon the individual through the force of numbers. Thus he became, as he was proud to assert, "a citizen of the world," belonging to no party, and in consequence, he says bitterly, "I shall offend all." But this is the Byron whose intellectual independence has a most apposite meaning for us today. As Peter Viereck points out, "there is no vitiating discreetness in his defence of liberty," but an "unrespectable detestation of every despotism in every nation." The writer of *Don Juan* would have been quick to see the moral significance in the action of a youthful believer in world federation who gave up his citizenship to become a symbol of protest against the prejudice and systematic greed behind the nationalism which reasserted itself so quickly after World War II. He would have admitted the hopelessness, even the ridiculousness of such a position, but it would never have brought forth from him the laugh behind the hand, for

> *if I laugh at any mortal thing,*
> *'T is that I may not weep.*

Thus Byron enters the company of those whose lips, as Spender says, are "touched with fire":

> *who in their lives fought for life,*
> *Who wore at their hearts the fire's center.*
> *Born of the sun they traveled a short while towards the sun,*
> *And left the vivid air signed with their honor.*

The last of the invalid charges to be brought against Byron's thought is directed at a trait corollary to his hatred of systems. Since he could never embrace any philosophical system without reservations, he remained in a position of never making up his mind about what he believed, and that is always distressing, especially to the critic who feels that one should be able to state of a poet "what he thought." A distinguished modern writer, for example, recently lectured George Santayana severely for not making up his mind whether he was a materialist or a Platonist. But, to demand this "irritable reaching after fact and reason" is to miss the very strength of Byron's restless and widely ranging mind. It is to set a higher value upon the simplicity and clarity of the half-truth, than upon the complex, eclectic state of doubt and uncertainty from which emerges that quality of "Negative Capability," which Keats ascribed to the man of real achievement in literature. As Shelley observed in his droll Preface to *Julian and Maddalo* in 1818: "What Maddalo [i.e., Byron] thinks on these matters is not exactly known," but he certainly did not mean to imply that Byron had no serious thoughts about a matter so vital to Shelley as the origin of good and evil. At most, there is in Shelley's remark a touch of light irony and disappointment that Byron could not see what was perfectly plain to Shelley—that man can be good if he wills to be good—and so get on with the task of putting to rout the evils of the world. Byron could not then and never did make up his mind about the possibility of abolishing evil, but in this failure lies perhaps the strongest link between his thought and that of our own day. For we have in Byron a mind playing with facility and grace upon a great many subjects, forming them into a contrapuntal pattern that has much of the modern temper about it.

In the sweeping plan of *Don Juan*—and I am convinced, in spite of Byron's light-hearted denials, that he did have a plan above and beyond presenting a panoramic and incisive picture of hypocrisy and cant in

> that Microcosm on stilts,
> Yclept the Great World

—the large theme of the self-delusion of his historical and fictional characters is played off in dramatic tension against his own increasingly clear understanding of the limitations of human knowledge. Thus, after unfolding with devastating sarcasm the self-delusion of Donna Inez in her mishandling of Juan's education, and Julia's self-delusion in the overspiritualizing of love, and the Wordsworthian overspiritualizing of the natural world by Don Juan himself, Byron broadens his satirical canvas in the shipwreck scene of Canto II to include the delusive notion of all mankind that they are far removed from brutes, particularly in times of stress when the instinct for self-preservation so easily breaks through the thin veneer of human and social values. In the later cantos, as the poem increases in subjectivity, Byron becomes more and more self-assertive and insistent that in the face of the irreconcilable complexities of life, to be honest is to admit how little we know of ultimate values, especially in relation to the ever-expanding truths of physical science; in fact, we know no more than that

> *we live and die,*
> *But which is best,* you *know no more than I.*

In the somber cantos beginning with the ninth, and ending with the fragmentary seventeenth (cantos neither talked about nor often read), Byron reveals an increasing awareness of how much of what we believe depends upon (to use a word not yet in common use in his own day) our metabolism. As early in the poem as Canto V, he inquires:

> *Who*
> *Would pique himself on intellects, whose use*
> *Depends so much upon the gastric juice?*

In Canto IX he asks who would trade a sound digestion for all of Buonaparte's fame: "Without a stomach what were a good name?" And in Canto XI he develops the idea to explain buoyantly how, since he does not feel well, he is becoming more religious:

> *The truth is, I've grown lately rather phthisical:*
> *I don't know what the reason is—the air*
> *Perhaps: but as I suffer from the shocks*
> *Of illness, I grow much more orthodox.*

A final illustration from Canto XIII, Byron's racy account of English country life, will suffice to show how the poet broadens the application of this theme to include all history. The

> *polish'd horde,*
> *Form'd of two mighty tribes, the* Bores *and* Bored

sit down to a sumptuous meal, which Byron insists he will not describe, but then proceeds to do so in half-a-dozen stanzas:

> *I will not dwell upon ragoûts or roasts,*
> *Albeit all human history attests*
> *That happiness for man—the hungry sinner!—*
> *Since Eve ate apples, much depends on dinner.*

But then he adds, as if in an afterthought, there is one competitor to the importance of food to man, and that is money.

As he ruminates upon the question of human immortality, and this comes increasingly to his mind in the cantos written immediately following the death of Shelley, Byron is again unwilling to commit himself in the face of the undemonstrable and withholds judgment. When the Italian commandant of troops was killed in front of his palace at Ravenna, he gazed at this dead man

> *To try if I could wrench aught out of death*
> *Which should confirm, or shake, or make a faith;*
> *But it was all a mystery. Here we are,*
> *And there we go:—but* where?

He anticipates in a searching question Shelley's argument on the indestructibility of matter expressed in *Adonais:*

> *Nought we know, dies. Shall that alone which knows*
> *Be as a sword consumed before the sheath*
> *By sightless lightning?*

For Byron asks:

> *Can every element our elements mar?*
> *And air—earth—water—fire live—and we dead?*
> We, *whose minds comprehend all things?*

Finding no answer, he concludes,

> *No more;*
> *But let us to the story as before;*

and turns back again to

> *this unriddled wonder,*
> *The World, which,*

he says cheerfully, "at the worst's a *glorious* blunder." And though

> *'t is very puzzling on the brink*
> *Of what is called eternity, to stare,*
> *And know no more of what is here, than there,*

there is never in Byron a retreat into apathy or indifference. If he arrives at the familiar anti-Cartesian position that even to express doubt about extra-sensory knowledge is to commit oneself beyond what the evidence indicates,

> *So little do we know what we're about in*
> *This world, I doubt if doubt itself be doubting,*

he retains a resilient intellectual curiosity which he conveys to us with infectious enthusiasm:

> *I would solicit free discussion*
> *Upon all points—no matter what, or whose.*

If, then, we arrive in Byron's mature thought at a position of skepticism towards man's assured knowledge of ultimate realities ("But what's Reality?" he asks in Canto XV of *Don Juan,*

> *Who has its clue?*
> *Philosophy? No; she too much rejects.*
> *Religion? Yes; but which of all her sects?*),

we arrive at a position of healthy agnosticism, healthy because it implies a ceaseless ranging over the phenomenal world, sketching it, both good and bad, exactly as it goes. If he concludes, "For me I know nought," he immediately follows with these words,

> *Nothing I deny,*
> *Admit—reject—contemn.*

In this refusal to exclude there is something of Walt Whitman's exuberant philosophy of acceptance; it is a creative not a stultifying agnosticism, that places Byron with that other master of the desultory and the doubtful, Michel de Montaigne. Like Montaigne, he prefers to separate himself from the error of those who because they see, deem they are all-seeing. As Byron grew older and his core of certainty narrowed, he wrote in *The Deformed Transformed* that men are "themselves alone the real 'nothings' "; and yet we find no relaxation in the exposure of hypocrisy and cant, nothing of the frustration and hopelessness of a defeated man.

In a fear-stricken world such as ours, it is heartening to be able to find in Byron, himself the product of a postwar world no less unsettled than our own, a poet whose spirit was not vitiated by his doubts, whose most effete character, Sardanapalus, challenges us with his proud statement:

> *There's something sweet in my uncertainty*
> *I would not change for your Chaldean lore.*

12 | Byron and the Modern Spirit

LESLIE A. MARCHAND

IN A WORLD of scientific thinking and critical realism, is there a place for the romantic impulse, a seat where romantic literature may repose unapologetically? Is Romance necessarily an "illusioned view of the universe," as it has been called by one modern critic? Must one who sees value in Romanticism cling to a foggy imaginative fusion of the real and the ideal? Further, must romantic literature and the response to it disappear with the advance of scientific knowledge? Keats apparently felt that it would, for in *Lamia* he envisioned the beauty of the rainbow vanishing at the approach of "cold philosophy." And Wordsworth believed that "Our meddling intellect/Mis-shapes the beauteous forms of things," and was consequently willing to "close up those barren leaves" of science. Professor Fairchild has concluded in *The Romantic Quest* that "the craving for romantic illusion has become progressively thwarted with every advance in our understanding of nature." What is there left that has value for us in romantic literature once we have repudiated it as a kind of self–bootstrap-lifting, as a philosophy of wishful thinking—in other words, when we no longer believe we can mold the world to the heart's desire by merely "taking thought"? Does the romantic impulse become only feeble when we deny it transcendental powers? Must it now be limited to a sort of decadent "escapism," the reverse side of a disillusioned realism?

Romantic expression in the past was restricted by none of these considerations. The Middle Ages was not limited in its romance by disturbing fact, but could believe comfortably in its dragons and its heroes of romance, in its visions and its aspirations, heavenly if not earthly. The motivation of Renaissance enthusiasm, which gave free scope to the romantic imagination, was a belief in the infinite possibilities of man. Shakespeare voices it in Hamlet's apostrophe:

> What a piece of work is a man! How noble in reason! How infinite in faculty! In form and moving how express and admirable! In action how like an angel! In apprehension how like a god! The beauty of the world! The paragon of animals!

In the early nineteenth century it was the belief in the "creative power of the imagination" which carried the romantic writers to their highest flights of poetic achievement. And today, despite our disillusioning skepticism, we still respond to the appeal of these poets and all the great romantic writers of the past because of a common denominator in our natures manifested in different forms under the stimulus of various environments and needs. This universal psychological demand is constant whether we call it by names invented by Coleridge or by Freud, by Shakespeare or by a modern biologist. It is a desire, often subconscious, for a perfection which we do not find in our ordinary life —a desire which is not destroyed or made less poignant because we may happen to believe it is not achievable except in the mind. Shelley voiced most memorably that longing which lies at the heart of all romance: "We look before and after/ And pine for what is not."

But what have these elementary commonplaces to do with Byron? Precisely this, that of all the romantic writers, Byron came the nearest to expressing the modern temper which willingly or perforce is ready to face any of the facts that science can present. His recognition of the disparity between the mind's conception of perfection and what we actually believe is achievable in our personal lives or the life of man brings him closer to the twentieth century than any of his contemporaries. His appeal is strongest to those who recognize that a self-honest rather than self-deluding romance need not relegate the romantic impulse to a lesser importance in the life of modern man. Byron is most congenial to the person who may be reasonably aware of the limits of hope for the future of both the individual and the race in a world of hard facts and who yet has the capacity for literary and artistic appreciation of the ideal forms demanded by a *real* portion of his nature, and not comprehended in his most sanguine picture of the future of man and of himself.

It is here that Byron touches most intimately the modern world. The two chief aspects of his literary expression—his intense longing for an ideal which he did not find in life, and his constant measurement of the dream against the reality, with the melancholy disillusionment or ironic laughter which followed upon the disclosure of their incompatibility—are also alternate facets of the thinking minds of our century. It is because Byron refused to deceive himself into believing that the dream was other than of the mind's conception that he seems to speak our language more clearly than most of his contemporaries. In *Childe Harold*—which it has been the fashion among critics in this century to belittle—Byron has expressed with admirable clarity this view of the ideal as the mind's creation:

> *Oh Love! no habitant of earth thou art . . .*
> *But never yet hath seen, nor e'er shall see*
> *The naked eye, thy form, as it should be;*
> *The mind hath made thee, as it peopled heaven,*
> *Even with its own desiring phantasy.*

And again:

> *Where are the forms the sculptor's soul hath seized?—*
> *In him alone. Can Nature show so fair?*
> *Where are the charms and virtues which we dare*
> *Conceive in boyhood and pursue as men,*
> *The unreached paradise of our despair . . . ?*

Byron's modernity rests in his clinging to an ideal without deluding himself with a transcendental belief in "dreaming true," and in his insistence upon seeing the world as it is (not always steadily and whole, but generally with a vision unclouded by the wish) without losing his interest in the romantic dream or discounting it. The most completely realistic of all the romantics, he accepted the romantic urge as a part of human nature without pretending it was more than a dream.

It is true that he was more perturbed than we, who have grown up with the echoes, at least, of psychology and the new sciences of the mind ringing in our ears, by the failure of the dream to be real, but he recognized its origin and put a proper human value on it.

But it is in his critical attitude that Byron is more completely of our age. Goethe, Arnold, and all the serious spirits of the nineteenth century thought always of Byron as the author of *Childe Harold*. For us increasingly he is the author of that amazing "versified Aurora Borealis," *Don Juan* (and of course of those frank and freshly human letters which reflect the same realistic moods). His agnostic humility touches more sympathetic chords in our time than the philosophic certainties of other men. Here is a voice we recognize:

> *Newton (that proverb of the mind), alas!*
> *Declared, with all his grand discoveries recent,*
> *That he himself felt only 'like a youth*
> *Picking up shells by the great ocean—Truth.'*

And we hear the accent of the modern world again when he says:

> *If from great Nature's or our own abyss*
> *Of thought we could but snatch a certainty,*
> *Perhaps Mankind might find the path they miss—*
> *But then 't would spoil much good philosophy.*

Byron was more obsessed than we generally are with the mask that hides the face of reality in the world, but not more so, as he was aware, than the great masters of realism and the comic spirit in the past. "I hope it is no crime," he said,

> *To laugh at all things—for I wish to know*
> *What, after all, are all things—but a show?*

The broad, panoramic view of life which we get in *Don Juan,* even though it is seen through one temperament, gives us a clear vision of the world we know. And that view is predominantly a sane one even though the world it pictures is not. "They accuse me," Byron wrote, of

> *A tendency to under-rate and scoff*
> *At human power and virtue, and all that . . . .*
> *I say no more than hath been said in Dante's*
> *Verse, and by Solomon and by Cervantes;*

> *By Swift, by Machiavel, by Rochefoucault,*
> *By Fénelon, by Luther, and by Plato;*
> *By Tillotson, and Wesley, and Rousseau,*
> *Who knew this life was not worth a potato.*

The exuberant *lèse-majesté* of Byron's years of exile, when with a beyond-the-tomb freedom he cast off all reticence and social restraint and spoke the truth about himself and others with a rare frankness, finds a readier response in our day than in his. His baring of man's naked impulses and of society's foibles is wholly in the mood of the twentieth century. He can sum up the tragicomedy of man's nature in a thoroughly modern manner:

> *Yet 't is a painful feeling, and unwilling,*
> *For surely if we always could perceive*
> *In the same object graces quite as killing*
> *As when she rose upon us like an Eve,*
> *'T would save us many a heartache, many a shilling,*
> *(For we must get them anyhow, or grieve),*
> *Whereas if one sole lady pleased for ever,*
> *How pleasant for the heart, as well as liver!*

Or he can condense in a couplet a devastating social critique that sounds irreverently of our time:

> *And rash Enthusiasm in good society*
> *Were nothing but a moral inebriety.*

It is the honest realism then of both his flights to the realm of the ideal and his descent into the main currents of life which makes Byron seem our contemporary. The overstressed melancholy, the strained emotion, which belongs to his own day, we can overlook, for the clear voice of unstifled truth comes through to us as have the voices of all the untrammeled spirits in literature.

Whether or not we would care to live in a world inhabited exclusively by Byrons (and we might do worse), any more than we would care to live in a world made up entirely of Miltons or Alexander Popes, of Shelleys or Queen Victorias, doesn't affect the question of Byron's interest or importance to us. The world has always been refreshed by contemplating an honest man—even when in many realms it dared not individually or collectively be as honest. At a time when Byron's friends in London had been urging him to give up the frivolities of *Don Juan* and to write some important work of high seriousness, he replied: "You have so many *'divine'* poems, is it nothing to have written a *Human* one?" In the end it is the essential humanity of Byron that appeals to us.

v: Shelley

13 | Shelley the Artist

RAYMOND D. HAVENS

Shelley is one of the best artists of us all: I mean in workmanship of style. —WORDSWORTH'S REMARK TO HIS NEPHEW.

Prometheus Unbound . . . seems to me to have an even more certain place than I had thought among the sacred books of the world. —YEATS, *Ideas of Good and Evil.*

The only way to find out if a poet is immortal is to kill him; Milton and Wordsworth slain have risen; Cowley and Shelley are rotting in their tombs. —LESLIE FIEDLER, *Kenyon Review* (AUTUMN, 1950).

IF THERE is anything new under the sun it is not hostility to Shelley. Ever since *The Necessity of Atheism* and *The Cenci* burst upon a startled world, contempt and denunciation have been heaped upon their author and all his works. Both have been pursued almost continuously by those who dislike the kind of man Shelley is supposed to have been, the kind of ideas he held, and the kind of poetry he wrote. Furthermore the man and the ideas have frequently attracted more attention than the poetry, the evaluation of which they have seriously affected. This was true not only of the first critics but of "Matthew Arnold's very lofty lift of superterrestrial nose over the Godwin nest." [1] It is true today. T. S. Eliot has confessed: "I find his ideas repellent . . . . And the biographical interest which Shelley has always excited makes it difficult to read the poetry without remembering the man: and, the man was

[1] George Meredith's letter to William Sharp of February 13, 1888. See *Wil-* / *liam Sharp: A Memoir by his Wife* (New York, 1910), p. 134.

169

humourless, pedantic, self-centered, and sometimes almost a black-guard." [2] If then we are to arrive at any sound estimate of Shelley as an artist we must forget his elopements, his hallucinations, his treatment of Harriet and of Elizabeth Hitchener, his self-confidence and self-pity, his emotional instability, his vague, cliché denunciations of priests and tyrants, his attitude towards incest and other unusual sex relations, his vegetarianism, his devotion to intellectual pursuits, his strength of will, his kindness to the poor, his idealism, his purity of mind—we must forget all these, as well as the mystery of his Neapolitan ward, and concentrate on the poetry. This alone presents difficulties enough since it continues to have the power of arousing intense admiration and equally intense dislike, of calling forth, from poets no less than from critics, the most divergent opinions.

So wide a disparity is not surprising if the nature of Shelley's poetry is considered. For it differs not only from what is now in vogue and from what was contemporary with it but also from nearly all other English verse. To look in it for the realistic, the classical, the dry, hard, and firm, the particular and precise, the exact perceived detail, for irony or objective correlatives; to expect the probing of an individual soul, the narration of little unremembered incidents of daily life, a "Second Anniversary," a *Rape of the Lock, Fowre Hymnes,* or *Four Quartets,* is to ask, as Sir George Beaumont did of Constable, "Where do you put your brown tree?" It is to listen for arias in *Pelléas and Mélisande,* to seek photographic exactitude in a late Picasso or a sculpture by Henry Moore. No one, to be sure, need enjoy Shelley's lyrics. But no one should be deterred from enjoying them by critics who, believing with Dr. Johnson that they have established their principles of judgment on unalterable truth and rational deduction, are confident that "Art and diligence have now done their best, and what shall be added will be the effort of tedious toil and needless curiosity." [3]

"The road into Wordsworth's mind," Bradley remarked, "must be through his strangeness and his paradoxes, and not round them." [4]

---

[2] *The Use of Poetry and the Use of Criticism* (Cambridge, Mass., 1933), p. 80. This is not the impression that the man Shelley made upon those who knew him best: his wife, Hogg, Trelawny, and Byron. In discussing the bearing of Shelley's beliefs on the greatness of his poetry Mr. Eliot forgets that the views of life held by Lucretius, Omar, and Dante are so remote that they can be viewed dispassionately, whereas the ideas of Shelley with which he disagrees are still controversial.

[3] Dr. Johnson, *Rambler,* 92, 208; *Lives of the Poets,* "Pope," ed. G. B. Hill, III, 251.

[4] A. C. Bradley, "Wordsworth," in *Oxford Lectures on Poetry* (London, 1923), p. 101.

So the road into Shelley's art must be through what is unusual and implacable in it and not round about its widely accepted "beauties." Probably the most distinctive characteristic of Shelley's poetry is enthusiasm for abstract ideas. The hero is invariably the millennium; the purpose, "to familiarize the imagination . . . with beautiful idealisms of moral excellence"; the characters, not human beings or divine personalities, but embodied characteristics or ideas; the subject, the eternal struggle between freedom and tyranny in the political, religious, and domestic spheres. Always there tends to be preoccupation direct and immediate with the ideal, the universal, and the infinite. In these is the only reality; the rest is illusion, "the painted veil which those who live/Call life." [5] Even when the poetry comes down to earth, it is to deal with what is least earthly in phenomenal nature: clouds, winds, the heavens, the moon and stars, night, music, rain, streams, skylarks. And these are universalized: it is not any particular night or cloud or lark that inspires the song. A promising drama dealing with real persons and events, *Charles the First,* was never completed because Shelley lacked interest in history and patience with actuality. But with abstractions and universals his interest never flagged. It was an enthusiasm, a passion—an impersonal passion, be it noted—which stirred him as most men are stirred only by what they see and experience. Wordsworth's concern for the French Revolution was aroused by witnessing the farewells of soldiers on their way to the front; Shelley's by ideas— liberty, justice, brotherhood—and the hope that they might prevail.

This wedding of passion to the intellect gives birth to the enthusiasm for abstractions which is the distinctive quality of Shelley's poetry. The idea, the concept of a universal, takes fire and, at the best, rises into a flame clear and intense, "consuming the last clouds of cold mortality." So it is with *Prometheus Unbound, To Night, Mutability* ("The flower that smiles to-day"), "Life of Life! thy lips enkindle," "The One remains, the many change and pass,"

---

[5] Shelley's sonnet, "Lift not the painted veil." Cf. *Letter to Maria Gisborne,* 154–57:

> *and how we spun*
> *A shroud of talk to hide us from the sun*
> *Of this familiar life, which seems to be*
> *But is not.*

Even poems which start from a definite subject or occasion tend to pass—as do *Adonais, Hellas, The Mask of Anarchy, Ode to the West Wind,* and *To a Skylark*—to the universal and impersonal. Likewise songs that seem to be tied to no time or place or individual—*Rough Wind, that Moanest Loud, Time Long Past, The World's Wanderers*—may have been called forth by a particular occasion.

> *Alas! for Liberty!*
> *If numbers, wealth, or unfulfilling years,*
> *Or fate, can quell the free!*

and many other poems or parts of poems.

To be sure there are those who deny that anything of the kind takes place, who see passion without intellect, flame without idea. An eminent critic of the last generation heard in Shelley's writings only "the voice of enthusiasm, of unreasoned emotion"; [6] but this is because abounding description and imagery, lushness of style, and perhaps the personality of the author distracted his attention, as they have that of many others, from the conception they were intended to convey. That Shelley was more of a student and was more interested in ideas than are most poets is indubitable; yet to Mr. Leavis he "represents pre-eminently the divorce between thought and feeling, intelligence and sensibility." He "offers the emotion in itself, unattached, in the void. . . . being inspired was, for him, too apt to mean surrendering to a kind of hypnotic note of favourite images, associations and words . . . switching poetry on." [7] That is he keeps his thought, his intelligence, out of his verse. But Mr. Leavis also has been distracted by a style that he dislikes (and probably by ideas with which he has no sympathy and by his conception of the man who held them) from recognizing that there is plenty of brainwork behind, for example, *Prometheus Unbound, The Cenci, The Mask of Anarchy, Charles the First, The Triumph of Life,* the

[6] "Always his philosophy, whether magnified into a shadowy mythology or expressed in human drama, whether it be the love or hate of Prometheus or his own relation to mankind, is the voice of enthusiasm, of unreasoned emotion."—Paul Elmer More, "Shelley," in *Shelburne Essays* (New York, 1910), VII, 14.

[7] F. R. Leavis, *Revaluation* (London, 1936), pp. 8, 214–15. The first assertion seems to me true only if, like Mr. Eliot, by "feeling" we mean sensation and by "sensibility," the faculty which registers sensations. See F. W. Bateson's illuminating "Contributions to a Dictionary of Critical Terms, II Dissociation of Sensibility," *Essays in Criticism,* I (July, 1951), 302–12, and II (April, 1952), 207–14. Even this Mrs. Shelley would apparently have denied since in the passage quoted above she also seems to mean by "sensibility" the faculty which registers sensations. "A thought to Donne was an experience," Mr. Eliot affirmed in 1921; "it modified his sensibility" ("The Metaphysical Poets," *Selected Essays,* p. 247). Ten years later, however, he thought differently and confessed: "In Donne, there is a manifest fissure between thought and sensibility." See *A Garland for John Donne,* ed. Theodore Spencer (Cambridge, Mass., 1931), p. 8; see Bateson, as above, pp. 308–9. I should say that to Shelley a thought was an experience but an emotional experience which did not involve "a direct sensuous apprehension of thought."

Which of Shelley's poems "offer the emotion in itself, unattached, in the void," and how do they differ from other lyrics dealing with emotion?

Hymn to Intellectual Beauty, the sonnet *Political Greatness,* the *Ode to Liberty,* and even the youthful *Revolt of Islam.* Shelley's depth is not on the surface. His observation, his reflection, his learning are not paraded before us but they are there, and his emotion is not divorced from them. His poetry no less than his life reveals "the intensity of passion [which he gave] to his intellectual pursuits." [8]

One danger for the poetry of abstractions and universals is vagueness, and this danger Shelley did not escape. "The deep truth," he wrote, "is imageless." [9] Yet he was ever seeking to image or adumbrate such truth: in narratives, dramas, lyrics, and metaphysical comments. The result, since he kept his arguments for prose, is what many would term rhapsody, a kind of verse that, as Saint Paul said of the gospel, is "unto the Greeks foolishness." An illustration, which is indeed an excellent test of the appreciation of Shelley, is "Life of Life! thy lips enkindle." Of this lyric Clutton-Brock writes:

> No poetry could be more empty of fact. . . . It expresses with its music Shelley's passion for a perfection that he could not describe any more than a religious poet can describe Heaven. . . . It is not the sound alone that delights us but the inextricable connection between the sound and the idea; for there is an idea behind the emotion without which the emotion could not exist, and the poem could not have been produced except by a mind familiar with intense thought. It is not itself philosophy, but the result of a passionate experience of philosophy. [10]

For some persons—they are not and never have been many—this song is not only Shelley at his best, it is also the very essence of poetry. To a much larger group, which includes most of the critics of our day, it is euphonious mumbo-jumbo.

Shelley was frequently not at his best; and when the flame flickered and sank he, who conceived of the poet as all flame, as a "scorner of the ground," suffered more than most. Since he saw little value for the artist in anything save the creative moment, thus overlooking "the capital importance of criticism in the work of creation itself," [11] he

[8] Mrs. Shelley's preface to the 1839 edition of her husband's poems.
[9] *Prometheus Unbound,* II.iv.116.
[10] A. Clutton-Brock, Introduction to C. D. Locock's edition of Shelley's *Poems* (London, 1911), I, xiii; cf. C. M. Bowra, *The Romantic Imagination* (Cambridge, Mass., 1949), pp. 114–15; Herbert Read, *In Defence of Shelley* (London, 1936), p. 84.
[11] T. S. Eliot, "The Function of Criticism," *Selected Essays, 1917–1932* (New York, 1932), p. 18.

made few later corrections. Yet these were the more needed because, in his eagerness to capture what the creative moment gave, he wrote rapidly, loosely, and obviously. He also left a large number of unfinished pieces because the impulse from which they sprang died quickly and did not return and he was unwilling to force it.

Then too the contrast between his craving for the ideal and his acute consciousness of injustice and mutability—of

> *Virtue, how frail it is!*
> *Friendship how rare!—*

encouraged his preoccupation with the millennium. His sense of the contrast also explains his fondness for escaping into the elysiums pictured in *Prometheus Unbound, Epipsychidion,* and *Euganean Hills,* or into such vast, romantic landscapes as those described in *Alastor,* thus encumbering his poems with passages that are mainly decorative. Furthermore, his expression, whether he wrote letters, essays, pamphlets, or poetry, was naturally exuberant. The age too was exuberant and, being young and passionately devoted to beauty, Shelley often turned from "the very world" to depict in nature and in personality either the soft and idyllic or the grandiose: rebellious demigods or maids whose life is love, rugged mountains or bowers of bliss. He has no golden mean. His exuberance likewise shows itself in his style and diction, which lack astringency, tension, the relief offered by plain surfaces, the bite that comes from roughness, contrast, and conflict. At times they verge on the pretty, as in *Prometheus Unbound,* II.ii (the scene with the fauns and spirits), in Part I of *The Sensitive Plant,* or in lines like these:

> . . . *where the blue heavens bend*
> *With lightest winds, to touch their paramour;*
> *Or linger, where the pebble-paven shore,*
> *Under the quick, faint kisses of the sea*
> *Trembles and sparkles as with ecstasy.*[12]

The advice which Keats ungraciously offered was needed:

> You might curb your magnanimity, and be more of an artist, and load every rift of your subject with ore. The thought of such disci-

---

[12] *Epipsychidion,* 544–48; cf. 83–85, 108–11. C. D. Locock regarded *Epipsychidion,* 525–90, as "perhaps the finest lines in Shelley's most wonderful poem." See *An Examination of the Shelley Manuscripts in the Bodleian* *Library* (Oxford, 1903), p. 3. He said of *Prometheus Unbound,* II, ii, "For sheer beauty this Scene, and especially the opening lyric, may rank as Shelley's most perfect work." One wonders how many agree with him today.

pline must fall like cold chains upon you, who perhaps never sat with your wings furled for six months together.[13]

Verse came easily to Shelley and it came in a flood of words, too many of them adjectives:

> *Erewhile I slept*
> *Under the glaucous caverns of old Ocean*
> *Within dim bowers of green and purple moss,*
> *Our young Ione's soft and milky arms*
> *Locked then, as now, behind my dark, moist hair,*
> *While my shut eyes and cheek were pressed within*
> *The folded depth of her life-breathing bosom.*[14]

Only toward the end—he was not yet thirty—did he, under Dante's guidance, learn to curb his magnanimity, to condense, to be more vigorous, direct, and definite, yet more reserved in style. It is this that makes memorable *The Triumph of Life,* unfinished and obscure though it be:

> *Before the chariot had begun to climb*
> *The opposing steep of that mysterious dell,*
> *Behold a wonder worthy of the rhyme*
>
> *Of him who from the lowest depths of hell,*
> *Through every paradise and through all glory,*
> *Love led serene, and who returned to tell*
>
> *In the words of hate and awe the wondrous story*
> *How all things are transfigured except Love.*
> *(469–76)*

A characteristic expression of Shelley's exuberance is his imagery. So profusely is this poured out that many passages of his prose as well as his verse seem to consist of little else. In the first stanza of the *Hymn to Intellectual Beauty,* one of his early and less ornate pieces, he tries to express a difficult idea by comparing the visitations of non-sensuous beauty to summer winds, to moonbeams, to hues of evening, to clouds, to memory of music, and to anything which is dear for its grace and mystery; in the third stanza he adds that this beauty is like mist, like music made by night winds, or like moonlight on a stream. A similar

[13] Keats's letter to Shelley of August, 1820. [14] *Prometheus Unbound,* II.i.43–49.

succession, but of more elaborate similes, is found in lines 405–31 of Shelley's last work, *The Triumph of Life*. Images abound in *The Cloud, To a Skylark, Prometheus Unbound*, and, to a greater extent than is generally realized, in *Adonais*. Many of them are excellent: Byron, when *English Bards* has silenced his critics, stands an Apollo Belvedere smiling after the arrow he has shot; "flowering weeds, and fragrant copses" growing on Roman ruins "dress/The bones of Desolation's nakedness"; Time feeds on the mouldering walls of Rome "like slow fire upon a hoary brand"; the skylark sings and flies upward until almost invisible as the planet Venus fades at dawn, "Until we hardly see—we feel that it is there."

> *O Slavery! Thou frost of the world's prime,*
> *Killing its flowers and leaving its thorns bare!*

> in he~~n~~en-defying minds
> . . . *thought by thought is piled, till some great truth*
> *Is loosened, and the nations echo round,*
> *Shaken to their roots, as [are] . . . the mountains [by] . . .*
> *The sun-awakened avalanche! whose mass,*
> . . . *had gathered there*
> *Flake after flake.*[15]

Yet the very abundance of these images is their weakness. One may be elaborated through a series of lines and followed by another, which perhaps has a simile within a metaphor, until, although Shelley holds firmly to his thought, the reader is lost. The confusion is often greater because the figures are more elusive or more difficult to understand than the matters they are supposed to illustrate. They are never homely, as Shelley was in one of his letters: "Our memory . . . is for

---

[15] *Adonais*, 248–51, 436–67, 442–43; *To a Skylark*, 21–25; *Hellas*, 676–77; *Prometheus Unbound*, II.iii.37–42. To fit the last quotation into my series I have rearranged the lines.

In the preface to *Prometheus Unbound* Shelley remarks: "The imagery which I have employed will be found, in many instances, to have been drawn from the operations of the human mind, or from those external actions by which they are expressed." This is an interest-

ing illustration of Shelley's desire to escape the tangible, but examples—such as

Like music which makes giddy the dim brain
Faint with intoxication of keen joy
(II.i.66–67)

or I.801–6, II.i.2–5—are neither frequent nor peculiar to their author and have little effect on the character of the poetry.

ever scratching at the door of your absence." [16] Here is a metaphor that immediately and vividly makes its point and so lingers in the memory, as few of Shelley's images do. We tend to forget them not only because they crowd upon one another and are lost in the surrounding lushness but also because they are rarely vigorous. They are almost never startling, as are Donne's and those of our contemporary poets. They do not illuminate by bringing before us objects, ideas, or qualities which we have not associated with the subject compared. Rather they are what might be expected. In the main they deal with stars, moonlight, breezes, music, flowers—what used to be thought the poet's stock in trade—and do not altogether escape prettiness: "A light of laughing flowers along the grass is spread." [17]

They are rarely subjective, that is, the connection between the image and the matter it illustrates is one that might occur to others as well as to Shelley. They are not closely integrated with the thought, partly because so many of them are similes. Yet in intent most are not decorative but functional. They are due to preoccupation with universals and abstractions, to the wish to picture, not any particular cloud or wind or skylark, but the spirit which Shelley felt was embodied in every cloud, every wind, every skylark. Since he found it almost impossible to do this by ordinary means, he resorted to figures to suggest this universal spirit, approaching his subject now through one image, now through another.

The union of the love of nature with the fondness for abstractions is unusual enough, but to these Shelley added a passion for the Greeks and a "gift for the spontaneous creation of myths." [18] In consequence the sun, the west wind, and the cloud were to him not the conventional personifications of eighteenth-century odes but living forces rejoicing in their freedom, their strength, their beauty. Remarkable creations, they are characteristic of the happy, ethereal side of their creator. Like *The Witch of Atlas* they are pagan forces, leading their own serene lives, aloof from man, of whose toils, aspirations, and griefs they know little or nothing. This remarkable myth-making relationship to nature through which Shelley entered into what may be supposed to be the life and consciousness of a cloud or a brook is most clearly revealed in *Ode to*

---

[16] To Maria Gisborne, October 13 or 14, 1819. Shelley interjects apologetically, "if you will accept so humble a metaphor."

[17] *Adonais*, 441.

[18] Douglas Bush, *Mythology and the Romantic Tradition in English Poetry* (Cambridge, Mass., 1937), p. 135.

the West Wind, The Cloud, and the group written for his wife's myth-ological dramas: *Arethusa, Song of Proserpine, Hymn of Apollo,* and *Hymn of Pan.* But it is remarkably pervasive: *The Witch of Atlas* is an original myth of Shelley's, *Prometheus Unbound* is his recreation of a classic myth, and each of them contains many brief independent exam-ples:

> *From all the blasts of heaven thou hast descended . . .*
> *Cradled in tempests; thou dost wake, O Spring!*
> *O child of many winds!* [19]

One of these winds is called to life in the vivid lines:

> *When the chill wind, languid as with pain*
> *Of its own heavy moisture, here and there*
> *Drives through the gray and beamless atmosphere.*[20]

Mrs. Shelley said of her husband:

> He was unrivalled in the justness and extent of his observations on natural objects; he knew every plant by its name, and was fa-miliar with the history and habits of every production of the earth; he could interpret without a fault each appearance in the sky.

and later:

> His extreme sensibility gave the intensity of passion to his intel-lectual pursuits; and rendered his mind keenly alive to every per-ception of outward objects.[21]

This, to be sure, is the testimony of a devoted admirer; but there is abundant evidence in his poems and letters that Shelley cared deeply for nature and at times observed it closely. He wrote, for example:

> *The sun is set; the swallows are asleep;*
> *The bats are flitting fast in the gray air;*
> *The slow soft toads out of damp corners creep . . . .*
>
> *There is no dew on the dry grass tonight,*
> *Nor damp within the shadow of the trees;*
> *The wind is intermitting, dry, and light;*

---

[19] *Prometheus Unbound,* II.i.1–7.
[20] *Rain* (A fragment written in 1819), 2–4.

[21] Mrs. Shelley's preface to her 1824 and 1839 editions of the poems.

> *And in the inconstant motion of the breeze*
> *The dust and straws are driven up and down,*
> *And whirled about the pavement of the town.*[22]

Yet details as numerous and exact as these are rare in Shelley's many nature descriptions. The reason is partly that, like Monet and the French impressionists, he wishes to give the feeling of a scene rather than the individual elements that constitute it. But chiefly it is owing to his conviction that "a poem is the very image of life expressed in its eternal truth . . . the creation of actions according to the unchangeable forms of human nature, as existing in the mind of the Creator." "A poet," he held, "participates in the eternal, the infinite, and the one; as far as relates to his conceptions, time and place and number are not." [23]

> *Nor seeks nor finds he mortal blisses*
> *But feeds on the aërial kisses*
> *Of shapes that haunt thought's wildernesses.*
> *He will watch from dawn to gloom*
> *The lake-reflected sun illume*
> *The yellow bees in the ivy-bloom,*
> *Nor heed nor see, what things they be;*
> *But from these create he can*
> *Forms more real than living man*
> *Nurslings of immortality!* [24]

The poet observes nature but creates something very unlike it. This is likewise what Shelley did with Greek literature. He knew it well in the original, admired it greatly, and was much influenced by it; yet he wrote nothing that is really Greek. His *Prometheus, Hellas, Arethusa,*

[22] *Evening: Ponte al Mare, Pisa,* 1–12; cf. *The Sunset,* 9–20; *The Question,* 9–32; *A Vision of the Sea, passim; Marenghi,* 76–81, 1361–41; *Witch of Atlas,* 173–74; *Euganean Hills,* 49–54; *Julian and Maddalo,* 1–12; *Letter to Maria Gisborne, passim; Boat on the Serchio, passim.* The passage from *Prometheus Unbound,* I.740–49, quoted just below is unusually detailed since the bees are feeding on ivy blossoms that are not in the direct sunlight but in the light reflected from the surface of the lake. Most of the descriptions in the letters are generalized and literary but with occasional details like the

following: "the cytisus, a delicate kind of furze with a pretty yellow blossom, the myrtle, and the myrica. The willow trees had just begun to put forth their green and golden buds, and gleamed like points of lambent fire among the wintry forest."—Letter to T. L. Peacock, February 25, 1819.
[23] *A Defense of poetry,* ed. H. F. B. Brett-Smith (London, 1921), pp. 30, 27.
[24] *Prometheus Unbound,* I.740–49; cf. *To a Skylark,* 96–100: "Better than all measures [or] . . . treasures . . . in books . . . Thy skill to poet were, thou scorner of the ground."

and the rest are variations on Greek themes which at times use Greek forms, but are Shelley to the core. So in depicting character Shelley aimed to present "beautiful idealisms of moral excellence" and held *Prometheus* a "more poetical character than Satan, because . . . he is susceptible of being described" as "the type of the highest perfection." [25] "Real flesh and blood," he wrote, ". . . I do not deal in. . . . You might as well go to a gin-shop for a leg of mutton, as expect anything human or earthly from me." [26]

In other words Shelley idealized and universalized his embodiments of human nature or mythological personages and, though he often observed external nature closely, he generalized his descriptions of it. This is a dangerous practice for an artist in any field since it may lead to sameness, conventionality, vagueness, lifeless figures, and stereotyped scenes—painting that leaves few definite impressions on the beholder. Most of Shelley's admirers today would probably agree that he was unwise in consciously excluding from his poetry "real flesh and blood" together with vivid details of natural objects and scenes. In the lyrics neither persons nor settings need be made definite, for the mood, the emotion, is the main thing; this fact goes far towards explaining why these shorter pieces are more successful than the longer. And the longer works will usually be found to be best where there is no occasion to picture the world of nature or of man.

It is partly for this reason that his greatest achievement is *Prometheus Unbound*. Characteristically this work deals with the cosmic, the timeless, the eternal. It contains no characters that are human or divine but only abstractions: "Spirits," "Echoes," "Voices," and personifications; of forces, such as the spirit of life; of qualities, such as love, faith, hope, strength, the ideal and evil in man; and of natural things: ocean, the earth, the moon. Characteristically also it is original in form and in idea, lyrical even in most of its blank verse, ideal in temper, subtle in thought, impassioned in utterance. Since it deals with brave translunary things the action is slight and symbolic, much of it being internal; but from the noble, austere opening to the equally noble, triumphant close it is vital, rich, fresh, varied, alive.

Shelley has a few poems or parts of poems which not only abound in realistic detail but are unusual for him in avoiding abstractions in dealing with the concrete, with the definite in time and place, in em-

---

[25] Preface to *Prometheus Unbound,* eighth and second paragraphs.   [26] Letter to John Gisborne, October 22, 1821.

ploying a conversational language and style, as well as a tone not idealistic but matter-of-fact. These include *Julian and Maddalo, Letter to Maria Gisborne,* parts of *The Witch of Atlas,* and of the brilliant translation of the Homeric *Hymn to Mercury, The Aziola, The Boat on the Serchio, To Edward Williams,* and the last stanza of *The Magnetic Lady to her Patient.* The reason for the marked change, for using in these poems a subject matter, style, language, and prosody quite unlike that employed in *Prometheus Unbound, Alastor,* and *Epipsychidion,* is that Shelley is here following the neoclassical tradition of familiar verse and writing with the deftness, elegance, and casual ease of Prior or of Pope's epistles. Little of the kind was achieved by Blake, Wordsworth, Coleridge, or Keats, nor by Byron until he wrote *Beppo* and *Don Juan.* That Shelley did it so well is evidence of "poetic gifts, which were certainly of the first order," [27] and of versatility as unexpected as it is little recognized.

This versatility and Shelley's *art* in general are revealed most clearly in his prosody. For he handles with easy mastery not alone the standard English meters—blank verse, heroic and octosyllabic couplets, the Spenserian stanza, the sonnet—but *ottava rima* and the little-used *terza rima,* as well as the Pindaric ode and a great number of regular or irregular lyric measures which he invented or took over. In his shorter pieces he was inclined, as were Herrick and Herbert, to devise a new verse form to fit each mood, thought, scene, or incident to be dealt with. If he used stanzas, he varied them from poem to poem—regular or irregular, short and simple or long and complicated, now with a refrain, now without. So with the length of the lines: all might be long, all short, or both might be used as well as lines of irregular length. He employed couplets frequently, alternate rimes and internal rimes occasionally. Often he made the contrast between feminine and masculine rimes part of the framework of a stanza.[28] To be sure, in several of his best known poems, *The Sensitive Plant, The Cloud, Arethusa,* the prosody is facile, undistinguished, and loose, with obvious, pouncing rhythms. When however the words, the style, the vowel and consonant sounds, and the prosody are fused into one, as they often are, the result is pure poetry, subtle, haunting, unusual, yet seemingly simple. Swinburne praised the "ineffable effect . . . produced by . . . the

---

[27] T. S. Eliot, *The Use of Poetry and the Use of Criticism,* p. 88.
[28] See "Structure and Prosodic Pattern in Shelley's Lyrics," *PMLA,* LXV (Dec., 1950), 1076–87.

suppression . . . of a single syllable" in the lines "Is it with thy kisses or thy tears?" and "Fresh spring, and summer, and winter hoar." [29] Saintsbury, who found *The Witch of Atlas* "pure prosodic nectar," said of *Prometheus Unbound:* "In all the long procession and pageant of English poetry which it has been my good fortune to survey as I have been preparing and writing this History, nothing has ever presented itself, and nothing, I think, will present itself in such a combination of prosodic beauty and variety as this." [30]

Shelley's long poems have had few readers. That, to be sure, is the common fate of such works; some have a contemporary vogue but few save the greatest continue to be read except by students. Yet the desultory, fragmentary reading or neglect which has been the lot of Shelley's longer pieces aside from *Prometheus Unbound* and possibly *The Cenci* is very unlike the devotion given to *Childe Harold, Don Juan, Manfred, The Prelude, Hyperion,* and even *Endymion.* The reason is not obscure. Many of Shelley's works are distinctly difficult—the first canto of *The Revolt of Islam,* the fourth act of *Prometheus Unbound, The Triumph of Life,* and part of *Epipsychidion*—and all require a greater degree of concentration than most readers are willing to give. Even devotees of poetry, if they finish *Alastor* or *Julian and Maddalo* or *The Witch of Atlas* or *The Triumph of Life* or even *Hellas,* may have a feeling of bafflement, of uncertainty as to the author's intent. Then there is the lack of human interest and ordinary human concerns and, in *The Cenci* and *Epipsychidion,* a subject matter that is distasteful to many.

But the critics of our own day who condemn Shelley's more extended works, though they may praise his lyrics, are not troubled by difficult poetry, by incest, or the lack of human interest. They feel that the so-called major poems are vague, confused, wordy, dithyrambic, ill-constructed, and generally futile. Even in *Prometheus Unbound,* they point out that the last act is a late addition which suggests a masque and, like the second scene of the second act, contributes nothing but poetry, and a very different kind of poetry from that found in Act I;

---

[29] Swinburne, "Notes on the Text of Shelley," *Essays and Studies* (London, 1888), pp. 229–30. The lines quoted are from Shelley's exquisite but little-known *To Emilia Viviani* ("Madonna, wherefore hast thou sent to me") and from *A Lament* ("O world! O life! O time!").

[30] *History of English Prosody* (London, 1906–10), III, 108–11. Saintsbury calls attention (*ibid.,* pp. 106–7, 112), as have others, to Shelley's grave prosodic mistake of running over the tercets in *terza rima.*

that *Prometheus* holds the center of the stage for the first 655 lines
but thereafter is rarely seen or heard; and that several times a scene is
given over to characters who do not appear elsewhere. They object that
the first third of *Epipsychidion,* an ecstatic idealization of Emily, contains
passages which in thought, style, diction, and prosody are not in harmony
with the rest; that the central third contains a prolonged unintelligible
history of Shelley's love life, and the conclusion a bower of bliss and
the lovers' passionate union there. Such a mixture of rhapsody and
riddle, of exclamation, declamation, and escapism does not, they maintain, make a great poem. *The Cenci,* which has proved effective on the
stage, is, coming from Shelley, a surprising and often, particularly in
the Count Cenci scenes, a powerful *tour de force,* an impressive imitation of a seventeenth-century play. It has a unity, clarity, and a rounded
completeness that are rare in its author's works; yet our critics find it
unreal, declamatory, literary, and seldom moving. Few, they assert,
have returned to it willingly.[31] *Hellas,* a curious, interesting, undramatic
drama which has notable passages apart from the well-known choruses,
drifts from song to declamation, to philosophical meditation, and back
to song, but arrives nowhere. *The Revolt of Islam* with all its absurdities
and obscurities is the promising work of a rebellious young romantic
whereas *Rosalind and Helen* is gently futile and *Julian and Maddalo*
falls into two dissimilar parts: the first admirable, the latter (devoted
to the maunderings of a lunatic) a failure. In *Alastor* the wanderings
of an all-too-gentle poet furnish the occasion for extended descriptions,
often sonorous and impressive though heavy with adjectives, in the
course of which any "meaning" that may have been intended is lost.

No impartial judgment of Shelley's work is possible at the present
time. We are at once too near him and too far from him. But opinions
like these which stress chiefly the limitations of his longer poems are
presumably over-severe expressions of the contemporary reaction against
nineteenth-century romanticism. They do, however, raise doubts as to
Shelley's architectonics. Did he have any strong feeling for unity, for
structure, for a beginning, middle, and end? A number of his lyrics give
striking evidence of a sense of form [32] but of how many of his long
poems with all their admirable, even glorious passages can it be said:

---

[31] Saintsbury, an ardent admirer of
Shelley's, speaks of "the artificiality
which mars the whole" of *The Cenci*
(*ibid.,* p. 108); and Herbert Read, who
is enthusiastic over *Prometheus Un-*
bound, Epipsychidion, and *Adonais,*
condemns *The Cenci* roundly (*In De-*
fence of Shelley, pp. 23–26).

[32] See note 24.

"This is a unified, sustained, well-constructed work of art which is effective *as a whole*"? Such questions will be raised more insistently in the years to come and more emphasis will probably be laid, for example, on the inequalities of *Adonais* [33] while it may be that *The Witch of Atlas* will be treasured as an exquisite piece of fantasy touched with meanings. Yet if Shelley's weaknesses and limitations are most apparent in his longer works, it is in these that his intellectual side— his profound interest in politics, religion, and philosophy, his concern for liberty and the welfare of his fellows, his love of nature, literature, and art—is most fully revealed. There is a power, a breadth, and a depth here that no swallow flight of song can give, even if the lyrics, those included in the dramas as well as those published separately, show his inspiration at its purest, his art at its best.

[33] I refer especially to the relative tameness of a number of the early stanzas, perhaps a third of the whole, and not to comments like the following:

". . . the lines

Life like a dome of many-colored glass
Stains the white radiance of eternity

are not poetry; they express the frustrated individual will trying to compete with science. The will asserts a rhetorical proposition about the whole of life, but the imagination has not seized upon the materials of the poem and made them into a whole. Shelley's simile is imposed upon the material from above; it does not grow out of the material."—Allen Tate, *Reactionary Essays* (New York, 1936), pp. 84–85. One would like to know how Mr. Tate discovered these facts.

The Bottom of the Night

14

CARLOS BAKER

Follow, poet, follow right
To the bottom of the night,
With your unconstraining voice
Still persuade us to rejoice . . . .
                    —W. H. AUDEN, *In Memory of W. B. Yeats*

1

"IF YOU want me again," said Walt Whitman, "look for me under your bootsoles." In coming to the problem of Shelley's survival as poet-thinker in our own day, one would sometimes suppose that he were truly underfoot. But not in the sense that Whitman had in mind when he wrote the *Song of Myself*. For to the cursory by-passer, Shelley the thinker may look like a mere handful of historical dust. Overhead, perhaps, the invisible skylark may continue to sing its arrow-sharp notes, or the west wind may raise its thunderous voice of destruction and restoration, or the cloud may fall in drops that look something like tears. But Shelley lies dead beneath our bootsoles; there is nothing of him rich and strange enough to speak to our generation.

Why? Perhaps because Shelley the artist has seemed to operate in our time as the enemy of Shelley the thinker. More exactly, the failure of Shelley the artist to speak to us in the poetic idiom to which we are accustomed has prevented his achievement as thinker from being understood and appreciated. Our view of poetry has not been, technically speaking, the view of poetry which Shelley held to. If there are elements of his thought directly applicable to our times, they have not often been applied. In the age of streamlining we have not admired Shelley's vehicles of transport. Though their bickering wheels flash fire enough to catch our eye momentarily as they roll past, we have not liked their dimensions. This is, as Keats once said, poetry with a "palpable design upon us," and we do not like the design. We agree with Mr. Auden that "poetry makes nothing happen." The intellectual freight here looks like gossamer: we do not think, as they roll across the frontiers of our consciousness, that a systematic search of the contents of these vehicles would repay the effort. Until we have prepared a bill of lading, and then recognized that this is at least a permissible kind of celestial omnibus for this particular freight, the relevance of Shelley's thought to the modern predicament will not be apparent.

Perhaps we have turned away from Shelley's voice because it is said to have been shrill, betokening an emotional instability of a kind only too well known in our day. Yet there was Hawthorne, speaking of the otherworldly Jones Very and saying that "his voice is scarcely heard among us, by reason of its depth." Which is it, the shrill bat-screech which we shudder away from as from something eerie and insane, or the deeper voice of the poet-philosopher that we have never tried to understand because we found it impossible to adjust our hearing-aids to such deep tones? The relevance of his thought, the true resonance of his inner voice, can become apparent only to those willing to make the necessary adjustments, and the adjustments require an act of the imagination.

During the past twenty-five years, Shelley has been as much studied, as much written about, as any of the other poets of the second romantic generation. As new materials have become available it has become necessary to incorporate them into the total picture of Shelley, though in effect that picture has not changed very much from the one Professor Dowden made available to the scrutiny of Matthew Arnold. From Dowden's transcendentalist approach, Arnold extracted a descendentalist conclusion. He found difficulty, that is, in bringing together in his mind's eye Shelley's mode of life and Shelley's poetry. To account for the evident gap between the two modes, he was obliged to imagine the queer spectacle of something with luminous wings leaping upward, like a butterfly from a dunghill, out of the nasty little set of free lovers whose existence he shrewdly suspected between the lines of Dowden's official biography. Perhaps history will record that our greatest achievement was the *grounding* of Shelley—in his factual life, in his literary and his philosophical sources, in the intellectual background of the Europe of his time. We may have contrived to show him more nearly as he was: a fairly human merger of faults and virtues, of falsehoods and truths, neither demoniacal nor angelic, neither grub nor butterfly. But we have not, as a rule, been willing to say of him what Auden said of Yeats, "You were silly like us: your gift survived it all."

For all the effort, rightly and wrongly expended, Shelley remains in a state of partial eclipse. Mr. T. S. Eliot may quote him in *The Cocktail Party,* and even publicly withdraw a former opinion that Shelley can lay no serious claims to our attention. There may be some other searchlight beams playing just over the horizon of literary criticism, beams which point to the possibility of Shelley's gradual acceptance as a visionary poet of the stature of Blake and Coleridge. Yet we shall scarcely reach the state of full acceptance until Shelley's achievement is redefined in the critical idiom of our time—not once but often enough to disperse the prejudicial fog in which he is now partly hidden.

An example of the necessary kind of operation can be conveniently located in Mr. Auden's distinction between "occasional" and "mythological" poetry. In all good poems, says Mr. Auden, the reader is presented simultaneously with two kinds of experience. The first kind is a *historically unique* experience; it is unique in that this particular set of circumstances (the poem) has occurred in this particular order for the first and last time. The second kind is a *universally significant* experience; it is universal in that analogous experiences have always occurred and will continue to occur "to all men." [1]

If we use this distinction as a critical instrument, Mr. Auden continues, we find that "most poems fall into one of two classes, those in which the historic occasion is . . . on the outside, and the general significance on the inside, and those in which their positions are the other way round. In the first kind of poem, the overt subject of the poem is a specific experience undergone by the 'I' of the poem at a specific time and place." Here the universal significance, though present, is implied, not stated directly. "In the second kind of poem, the overt subject is universal and impersonal, frequently a myth, and it is the personal experience of the poet which is implied." Some poets (Auden cites Robert Frost) are pre-eminently "occasionalists." Others are

[1] W. H. Auden, Foreword to W. S. Merwin, *A Mask for Janus* (New Haven: Yale University Press, 1952).

"mythologists." (Auden names Valéry.) A third group (Yeats is Auden's example here) alternate between the occasional and the mythological types.

Like Yeats, Shelley is an alternator. The *Hymn to Intellectual Beauty* is. in Mr. Auden's sense an occasional poem. Other examples are frequent among the lyrical utterances of Shelley. And it may be fair to say that the whole strategy of disapproval which has befogged the reading of Shelley in this day has been to center attention on the "occasional" poems, and to condemn the experiences there recorded as too unutterably and uniquely unique (as well as emotionally flaccid). On the other hand there has been a tendency to forget or to underrate the fact that the great bulk and body of Shelley's work belongs to the poetical genre which Mr. Auden calls "mythological."

The constant element in Mr. Auden's distinction is the notion of "general significance," which is inside the event for the occasional poet and more or less overt for the maker of myths. The nature of the present subject is such that we are required to emphasize Shelley's general significance—if he has any—and to pay relatively little attention either to the "occasions" of Shelley's poems or to the interpretations of his "myths." If, in short, we are to emphasize the term *thinker* in the phrase *poet-thinker,* it is probably axiomatic that only so much of a poet-thinker can survive from age to age as is particularly engaged with problems which are of general concern.

Because Shelley occasional or Shelley mythological is not the poet for everyone, or even the poet for the majority, or even the poet for a very large minority, we return forewarned to the question posed by this essay: In what ways, and to what end, has he survived in our time? This is a different question from: In what ways *ought* Shelley to survive? Or what is there in Shelley which would be "good" for us if by sufficient explanation and interpretation his true voice could be made audible to a sufficient number? But certain provisional answers to the moral question may appear as we attempt to answer the factual one.

2

S H E L L E Y T H E thinker survives chiefly in three ways, all separate, all related. First, he survives through those of his latter-day disciples who are intent, as he was, upon preserving the integrity of the life of the mind, yet who have spoken to our generation in fiction and poetry with an idiom which does not fall as oddly on modern ears and eyes as Shelley's idiom does. Second, he survives (though often as an unacknowledged legislator) among all those to whom political liberty is a matter of primary concern, who would guard and nurture it wherever it exists, as they would seek to revive it wherever it has died. Third, he survives for at least some of those who wander in the no-man's land between full acceptance of the Christian faith and the twilight of irreligion which overspreads so large an area of the modern world. These last are the modern idealists, absolutists by temperament and conviction, who need some kind of foundation on which to erect a structure of necessary belief, but have found no such foundation in the institutions or the philosophies (political and other) which obtain in our day.

In his memorial poem to William Butler Yeats, Mr. Auden records imaginatively that moment when Yeats, having died, "became his admirers." Shelley became his admirers in 1822, and his immortality, so far as we are acquainted with it, is in the hands of those in each generation to whom his works have meaningfully spoken. Yeats happens to have been one of these—an original and searching mind, a poet of the philosophic persuasion, much of whose best and strongest poetry was written (like Shelley's) in terms of a carefully worked out cosmic system, though not to such a degree that his lyricism was thereby inhibited. Yeats could not feel content with Shelley's philosophic poetry until he had mastered, through Shelley's leading tropes, the groundwork of that idealistic system, and laid out the recurrent symbols like planks for a platform from which he could take the long view of Shelley's work. He recognized, as others have done and will do, that Shelley belongs to that small group of visionary poets whose works are the verbal manifestations or imaginative projections of thought-systems which seek to embrace and to account for man's total relationship to the cosmos. So far as these systems are of interest to thinking men, so long as modern man finds anything instructive in the contemplation of the various thought-systems of the past, Shelley's poetry, which is the partial imaginative incarnation of his system, will interest other men as it interested Yeats.

Shelley also became, after eighty years, his admirer E. M. Forster. Unashamedly and even aggressively, Forster championed the Shelleyan position in several novels and shorter fictions. His grasp of Shelley's "teaching" is well summarized in the account of the surrender of Lucy

Honeychurch in *A Room With A View.* "It did not do," Forster ironically writes, "to think, nor for that matter, to feel. She gave up trying
to understand herself, and joined the vast armies of the benighted, who
follow neither the heart nor the brain, and march to their destiny by
catchwords. The armies are full of pleasant and pious folk. But they
have yielded to the only enemy that matters—the enemy within . . . .
They have sinned against Eros and against Pallas Athene, and not by
any heavenly intervention, but by the ordinary course of nature, these
allied deities will be avenged." With just the necessary touch of irony,
Forster has expressed in a modern novel Shelley's most characteristic
philosophic message. To sin against Eros and against the Pallas Athene
is to release the "enemy within," and to enter the vast army of the benighted and the regimented who "march to their destiny by catchwords"
—those banal trap-words which are set for the unwary in every generation, and not least in our own.

Even Mr. Auden, who has somewhere indicated his detestation
for Shelley's works, is hewing precisely to the Shelleyan line in the
magnificent conclusion to his threnody for Yeats:

> *In the nightmare of the dark*
> *All the dogs of Europe bark,*
> *And the living nations wait,*
> *Each sequestered in its hate;*

> *Intellectual disgrace*
> *Stares from every human face,*
> *And the seas of pity lie*
> *Locked and frozen in each eye.*

> *Follow, poet, follow right*
> *To the bottom of the night,*
> *With your unconstraining voice*
> *Still persuade us to rejoice;*

> *With the farming of a verse*
> *Make a vineyard of the curse,*
> *Sing of human unsuccess*
> *In a rapture of distress;*

> *In the deserts of the heart*
> *Let the healing fountain start,*

In the prison of his days
Teach the free man how to praise.[2]

Yeats and Forster are only two of Shelley's modern memorials. It is possible to assert Auden's discipleship by a species of remote control, though he would probably discount anything like influence. Yet we do not need to insist on "influence"; what appears is mainly—though not simply—a fellowship in common purpose. Taken altogether, Shelley's modern admirers suggest one of the ways in which a long-dead poet can survive—by speaking to the gifted men of our time with so powerful and persuasive a voice that they are willing to serve as translators and interpreters for his convictions. This is precisely the debt that every generation of thinkers—whether they work primarily as artists or as thinkers—owes to the past which has helped to form them. I mean to translate, to interpret, and by these acts to render "modern" as much of the original doctrine as can be carried over without misrepresentation from age to age. What cannot survive in this way belongs to the past and is the business of the historian. What can survive belongs as much to the present as present men can make it belong.

We turn now to the question of Shelley's survival as a political "thinker." There is an instructive parallel here to the situation of the poet or the critic who pays his debt to the past by restating its positions in terms of contemporary need, and in the contemporary language. Free nations, like free critics, must constantly reinterpret their instruments of government. The history of constitutional interpretation in America is a constant restatement of those principles which the Constitution itself is designed to express and to preserve. We translate these principles into our idiom, and we reaffirm them in the light of our particular problems. It is a task analogically related to that of the literary critic who is trying to discover how much of Shelley's political thought is germane to our times.

Clearly, that part of Shelley's political thought which is concerned with broad ethical principles rather than with immediate and temporary political expedients is the only part which can survive in our time except for purely adventitious reasons. Seen in this dimension, Shelley's convictions on the causes and cures of human slavery are as modern as today's newspaper. Though perhaps only in the broadest sense, they

[2] *The Collected Poetry of W. H. Auden* (New York: Random House, 1945). Quoted by permission.

are released and operative among us. If we do not recognize them as
Shelley's, or feel that we need to return to Shelley to see them formulated, it is chiefly because the present does not ordinarily trust the
past sufficiently to accept, in what are called practical affairs, the
formulations that the past has made. The exception to this general
rule would be those formulations like the Constitution which have been
institutionalized, and are therefore constantly referred to. It is undoubtedly as well for all poets that in the nature of things they resist institu-
tionalization.

Mr. Auden is probably correct in his belief that poetry makes
nothing happen—at least not externally. Yet in another and internal dimension, as Shelley perfectly knew, poetry may be an important agent
in the development and strengthening of those ideas which support
political liberty from underneath. The tree of liberty must be period-
ically watered with the blood of patriots. This is on the level of the
"practical action." On the plane of ideological action, it is well for
the tree of liberty if its roots are fed with the words of poets. This is
Shelley's conviction on the political function of poetry—that it should
hold up ideals as constant reminders to men of what they might do and
might be if they acted in conformity with these ideals. The IF, of
course, is large and conditional. It was no part of Shelley's belief, after
the callow days of his youth when he busily attacked everything under
the sun, that men would act according to ideal standards, either immediately or even perhaps in the long succession of future acts and
days. Yet he persisted in his belief that constant reminders were necessary. All his "ideal" poetry was designed to serve, in various ways, the
end of liberty in human society.

There is no need to make a political prophet of Shelley, although
he had in common with Thomas Jefferson and other radical thinkers of
his day the conviction that a new kind of democratic process was at work
in Europe and America, particularly in the latter country. Like many
Americans and some Europeans he felt that this process might, after
many years, gradually tend towards an egalitarian society whose limits
were as wide as the human race. He was throughout his life—at first
somewhat shrilly but later very firmly and sanely—a consistent radical
in the cause of human freedom. But his true contribution to modern
thought on the maintenance and advancement of liberty is his insistence on the practical relevance of political idealism. In this he never
wavered. A Biblical text—"Where there is no vision, the people perish"

—might with perfect justice have been carved on his tombstone. Had this happened, the anti-fascists of Mussolini's capital could have come over to the Protestant Cemetery, as to a shrine, for renewal of inspiration throughout the 1920's and the 1930's.

3

IN THE THIRD place, as was earlier suggested, Shelley survives as a kind of exemplar for certain modern idealists. In particular, he seems to speak instructively for those who exist, like many of Arnold's protagonists, between a world of irreligion, where men must content themselves with secular substitutes for religious knowledge, and the world as it becomes visible in the light of faith. Under the second of these conditions, as Wordsworth put it, the individual's consciousness of his divine origin is "habitually infused through every image and through every thought, and all affections [are] by communion raised from earth to heaven." [3] Shelley's struggle to move from the first to the second condition places him, so to speak, on the threshold of modernism. His spiritual kinsmen are everywhere, though they are not everywhere either so articulate or so esoteric as he.

The status of man under the first condition was well summarized by America's most articulate transcendentalist. "A new disease," wrote Emerson in 1842, "has fallen on the life of man . . . . Our torment is Unbelief, the Uncertainty as to what we ought to do; the distrust of the value of what we do; and the distrust that the Necessity (which we all at last believe in) is fair and beneficent. Our religion assumes the negative form of rejection." [4] The one visible error in Emerson's diagnosis is the assertion that the disease is new. We should not be surprised to find these sentiments in the sermons of an Anglican clergyman in 1742. The words are equally applicable to the intellectual milieu into which Shelley was born in 1792. Nor would a serious social critic have disdained to utter the same words in 1942.

It is therefore in some such framework as this that Shelley's struggles to discover and establish the grounds of his own religious belief may be said to have a kind of exemplary interest for men in any age which is tormented by varying degrees of uncertainty, unbelief, or doubt. A modern theologian, Professor A. N. Wilder, has in fact cited

---

[3] *The Prelude,* Book XIV.   [4] *The Dial* (July, 1842).

the intellectual career of Shelley as a significant instance "of the desperate and baffled efforts of the modern world to reshape its faith to accord with new circumstances." Any such undertaking, Mr. Wilder continues, "involves both reinterpretation of tradition and dependence on the present divine *afflatus* by way of spiritual immediacy, and both are full of risks and temptations." [5]

We shall come to the risks and the temptations. Our immediate concern is with the undertaking itself, the *process* through which Shelley passed in order to arrive at his formulation of the doctrine of cosmic love. Professor Lionel Trilling has justly said that "the course of [Shelley's] philosophical growth is his claim to greatness and to the attention of our generation." At one time or another he seems to have entertained nearly all those secular substitutes for religious faith which variously engage the attention of so large a segment of today's civilized population. To say that Shelley attained in the end to a special kind of theism which served him as a working substitute for Christian doctrine is not to insist on its usefulness to anyone but Shelley. It is only to say that we can hardly fail to find instructive the process by which he reached his mature position. Up to a point, many of the processes in action among the individuals around us run parallel to the course of Shelley's philosophical development.

His religion took at first, in Emerson's phrase, the "negative form of rejection." The angry tub-thumpings in *Queen Mab* might fairly be labeled sophomoric if only for the reason that they were conceived and partly set down in what would have been Shelley's sophomore year had he not been dismissed from Oxford. He cerebrated very busily on the state of the world, and ended by rejecting institutional Christianity as well as all the forms priesthood and kingship take or employ. As fiercely as a modern Marxist he asserted that religion was the opiate of the people. His motto was Voltaire's negativistic "Écrasez l'infâme." To this youthful and somewhat overenlightened intellectual it was clear that if one were to cultivate a garden, the first task was to raze and haul away the dangerous and ugly structures which had accumulated on the grounds during centuries of superstition.

Simultaneously he embraced philosophical materialism. Intellectually, if not emotionally, he became an enthusiastic naturalist. God for most people was a kind of inferior Blakean Nobodaddy; for Shelley God was nothing but a name for the existing power of existence. The sov-

[5] *Theology Today* (Fall, 1948).

ereign power in the universe was a strictly materialistic Necessity. Mind was mainly, if not perhaps exclusively, a function of matter, subject to the same laws which govern the material world. Yet this position, no matter how confidently he announced and defended it at this time, was only the first of the way-stations along the path of his development. Sooner than most of his modern counterparts, Shelley found that he must reject it. He had presently concluded that materialism was a "seducing system" for young and immature minds. By the age of twenty-four it lay behind him.

The second of his way-stations was humanism. His ardent philanthropy remained as a constant—the task was still the rehabilitation of society. But Shelley was now no longer convinced that the laws of a materialistic Necessity would guarantee the arrival of an earthly millennium if only the institutions and customs of the *ancien régime* were successfully extirpated. Considering the native idealistic disposition of his mind, it is not astonishing to find him executing a philosophical about-face. Matter now became for him a function of mind, and it was within mind that all reforms and revolutions must take their inception. During the period when he was writing *Prometheus Unbound,* the key poem in the development of his humanism, he would willingly have subscribed to Blake's opinions in *Jerusalem.*

> *Each man is in his Spectre's power*
> *Until the arrival of that hour,*
> *When his Humanity awake,*
> *And cast his Spectre into the lake.*

The human mind now seemed to Shelley the central directive force in all social and moral progress. Man's inhumanity to man had haunted Europe since the decline and fall of Periclean Athens. Fear, hatred, and superstition—the Jupiter-Spectre of *Prometheus Unbound*—had enchained men's minds to the rock of the ages. Blake had called such chains "mind-forged manacles." They had been clamped on by common consent; only uncommon dissent could remove them. Human will, human reason, human love, and human imagination were the sovereign powers. Through the exercise of such powers, the Spectre could be cast down into the lake of burning marle. The necessary precondition was the revival of the spirit of free enquiry which had governed ancient Athens during the one true golden age which the world had known. Shelley was wiser now than formerly. "Take action" had been his early maxim. "Take thought" became the ruling passion of his middle years.

To follow Shelley through to the end of his short career is to find that he did not establish permanent residence in the second of his way-stations. His final years were devoted to the organization and clarification of a theistic position which subsumed (without, however, destroying) his humanism. This is the point at which Shelley devotes himself wholeheartedly to the "reinterpretation of tradition"—as he had done throughout his humanistic period—but also begins to assert very firmly his dependence on a "present divine *afflatus*." It is also the point at which the developing arc of Shelley's circular thought begins most clearly to intersect the completed circle of Christian doctrine. "Shelley's relation to Christianity and to Christ," says Professor Wilder, "is of absorbing interest and, as in the case generally of the Romantics and transcendentalists, is suggestive of the cultural problems of our immediate background. In brief, it is helpful to think of him on the analogy of the great heretics of the second century. His hatred of the God of the Old Testament, his antinomianism [faith is enough] combined with heroic devotion to love and freedom, his oracular view of the poet, his sense of the reality of evil and tragedy, his mythological reading of existence—all suggest the operation of the Christian faith in him, but in an errorist form." [6]

It does not fall inside our present task to develop the parallel between Shelley's thought and that of the second-century Gnostic groups. It might even be doubted whether Shelley could be called a *Christian* heretic except in the possibly jocular sense which permitted Jacques Maritain to describe Marxism as a Christian heresy. What is incontestable about Shelley's theism is that it was reached through the reinterpretation of tradition in the light of a conception of cosmic love, while the interpretation of cosmic love was made in the light of tradition. On the side of immediacy, it is clear that Shelley was asserting, as Emerson would do, that God *is,* not *was.* The supernal power is immediately available, however, only to those who have prepared themselves to meet it through intensive meditation upon the best which has been said and thought by the best and wisest of men. The fact that there is an available—and inexhaustible—reservoir of spiritual energy has been perceived by the great "poets" of the past. Their works have been informed by it, and the worth of their writings is to be measured by the degree to which they have understood and imaginatively em-

[6] *Ibid.*

bodied the idea of divine love. From the position, "Take thought," Shelley has now moved to a further affirmation: "Take into account the world's best testimony on the transforming power of cosmic love." In this way the poet corroborates authoritatively his own highest intuitions. Thus his humanism serves and intensifies his theism.

We come now to the risks and temptations which attend on such an effort to reinterpret tradition and to invoke the aid of the divine power immediately. Professor H. N. Fairchild has enumerated a number of these temptations.[7] One of the most important is Fairchild's assertion that Shelley, like Blake, twisted traditional Christian beliefs to fit his own personal religious philosophy. This is certainly true, although *selected* might possibly be a better word than *twisted*. Shelley rejected what he regarded as the elements of superstition which had attached themselves to Christian teaching, retaining only those parts which seemed to him demonstrably true and just. A second point is that Shelley recreated Jesus in the image of the Shelleyan hero instead of attempting to understand the thought of Jesus. Fairchild objects that under this kind of program Jesus becomes "merely one of the numerous mediators of Intellectual Beauty and Love." Shelley would have explosively denied the adverb *merely*, because in his view this form of mediation was man's highest function. In *The Triumph of Life,* the poem on which he was working at the time of his death, Shelley is highly selective. Although many of the great and wise have undertaken the task of mediation, the only perfect mediators the world has known are Jesus and Socrates. A third point is Professor Fairchild's belief that the sense of sin was foreign to Shelley's nature. Shelley certainly rejected the legalistic and pre-Christian concept of sin as defined, for example, in some parts of the Old Testament. Yet he would agree with E. M. Forster that the true sin is to turn one's back on Eros and the Pallas Athene, becoming thereby spiritually blind and deaf. If sin is reserved as a term for the act of turning away from the idea of God as Love and God as Perfect Wisdom (a position which finds support in both the Old and the New Testaments), Shelley was as ardent an enemy of human sinfulness as the most fiery evangelist. A final (and for Professor Fairchild a crucial) point is that Shelley "could conceive of no divine force sufficiently distinct from his own personality to exert the necessary upward pull." This remark cannot justly be applied to

[7] H. N. Fairchild, *Religious Trends in English Poetry,* Volume III: The *Romantic Faith* (New York: Columbia University Press, 1949), pp. 328-87.

Shelley the naturalist, Shelley the humanist, or Shelley the theist. In all these periods, though of course with varying emphases, Shelley recognized an Otherness quite distinct from his own personality.

A useful example is the *Hymn to Intellectual Beauty,* written at a period when Shelley had not yet fully worked out the mythology or the implications of what was to become his doctrine of divine love. Even here, the idea of Otherness is emphasized in the petitional note on which the poem closes. The poet avows his worshipful attitude not only towards the supernal beauty but also to all the "forms" which contain it. The prayer is that he may learn, through the mediation of this unseen power, "to fear himself, and love all humankind." This fear of self, which plainly means self-abnegation rather than self-worship, makes Shelley's position comparable to that of Blake in *Jerusalem.* Blake has made Jesus over into "one of the numerous mediators." Now he cries,

O Saviour pour upon me thy Spirit of meekness and love!
Annihilate the Selfhood in me: be thou all my life!
Guide thou my hand, which trembles exceedingly upon the rock of ages,
While I write . . .

Like Blake, Shelley wishes for the annihilation of selfhood. Unlike Blake, who is (perhaps unintentionally) deceptive in this respect, Shelley does not express his prayer in the terminology of the New Testament. Yet both poets are invoking a divine power distinct from their own personalities. It is doubtful if either poet would have asserted, as Professor Fairchild says Shelley did, that the mediators can "create" real and eternal truth. For both Shelley and Blake, the poet (broadly defined) is of all men the man who can see most clearly into the nature of divine love. Shelley's opinion, as recorded in the *Defence,* is that the poet's creation is only an attempt, always partially unsuccessful, to say what he has *perceived* of real and eternal truth.

Few Christians would be willing to accept Shelley's theistic faith as even a reasonable facsimile of Christianity. His faith is like a line running parallel to the Christian doctrine. The parallel lines do not meet except in the infinity of divine love. Yet it is undeniable that in the light of his own deepest convictions, and in esoteric symbols derived from tradition and gaining a fresh impetus from Shelley's imaginative apprehension of them, this poet gave repeated expression to an article of faith in which all Christians share: the centrality of Love in the structure of the spiritual universe. If we return to Mr. Auden's terminology and speak of the "historical uniqueness" of Shelley's poems, we should end by emphasizing his highly individualized contribution to modern thought. If, on the other hand, we emphasize his meaning, it is evident that the course of his philosophical development has a "universal significance" which can hardly be lost on the modern idealist. The not unhappy irony of Shelley's career as a thinker is that the young man who began his serious writing life with a pamphlet called (or miscalled) *The Necessity of Atheism* brought that career to a close while he was at work on a poem which might well have carried some such title as *The Necessity of Theism*. The difference between the two titles is the sum of what Shelley had learned in the interim.

While we are on the topic of retitling, it might be noted that the present volume of reappraisals could easily have been called *The Uses of the Past*, the name chosen by Professor Herbert Muller for his brilliant book on the value of the study of past societies in the comprehension of our own.[8] Unlike the theist and absolutist Shelley, Mr. Muller is writing from a position on the borderline between naturalism and humanism. Yet he founds his secularist faith upon the "adventurous" and exploratory mind in a manner with which Shelley, up to a point, would certainly agree. "The ideals of freedom, individualism, and the 'open society' " are to be attained, if they are attained at all, by means of "humanism, liberalism, rationalism, [and] the scientific spirit." Our business as rational beings, says Mr. Muller, "is not to argue for what is going to be but to strive for what ought to be, in the consciousness that it will never be all that we would like it to be." This sounds not unlike the voice of Shelley, speaking evenly and without shrillness from the bottom of the night which still enshrouds him: "Our present business is with the difficult and unbending realities of actual life, and when we have drawn inspiration from the great object of our hopes, it becomes us with patience and resolution [to accommodate] our theories to immediate practice."

[8] Herbert J. Muller, *The Uses of the Past: Profiles of Former Societies* (New   York: Oxford University Press, 1952).

Present Values in Shelley's Art

15

STEWART C. WILCOX

AS MUCH as any English poet Shelley suffers the limitations attendant upon romanticism. This principle of attendant limitation, however, has recently been so overemphasized that the question remains whether he has received a wholly fair hearing. Did his way of composing, when he was "lifted above the stormy mist of sensations," frequently enable him to write with a pure imaginative directness, with a spontaneous fire that even he could not keep at white heat? Or is his best poetry "impure" because it lacks the concreteness of Keats or the dramatic objectivity of Shakespeare? Is he so naive in knowing only half of life that his naiveté renders valueless what he does know? Is he so idealistic that his poetry is worthless for the pragmatical present? One set of modern replies to such questions as these may be inferred from a recent statement by W. H. Auden: "How glad I am that the silliest remark ever made about poets, 'the unacknowledged legislators of the world,' was made by a poet whose work I detest. Sounds more like the secret police to me." [1]

Beside this silly remark about a "silly remark" one may place a more sympathetic observation from Santayana:

> For in our analytical zeal it is often possible to condense and abstract too much. Reality is more fluid and elusive than reason, and has, as it were, more dimensions than are known even to the latest geometry. Hence the understanding, when not suffused with some glow of sympathetic emotion or some touch of mysticism, gives but

[1] "Squares and Oblongs," in *Poets at Work* (New York, 1948), p. 177.

a dry, crude image of the world. The quality of wit inspires more admiration than confidence. It is a merit we should miss little in any one we love.

The same principle, however, can have more sentimental embodiments. When our substitutions are brought on by the excitement of generous emotion, we call wit inspiration. There is the same finding of new analogies, and likening of disparate things; there is the same transformation of our apperception. But the brilliancy is here not only penetrating, but also exalting. For instance:

> *Peace, peace, he is not dead, he doth not sleep,*
> *He hath awakened from the dream of life:*
> *'Tis we that wrapped in stormy visions keep*
> *With phantoms an unprofitable strife.*

There is here paradox, and paradox justified by reflection. The poet analyzes, and analyzes without reserve. The dream, the storm, the phantoms, and the unprofitableness could easily make a satirical picture. But the mood is transmuted; the mind takes an upward flight, with a sense of liberation from the convention it dissolves, and of freer motion in the vagueness beyond. The disintegration of our ideal here leads to mysticism, and because of this effort towards transcendence, the brilliancy becomes sublime.[2]

Should poetry, then, reveal "inner" truth through imaginative inspiration or should its emphasis be upon "harmonia" instead of the object to be "imitated"? Wit is close to the center of imitation whereas intuition is the heart of imagination in its high romantic meaning. Because the poet of wit puts the intellectual before the emotional, it is not surprising that critics of "metaphysical" leanings have been unsympathetic toward Shelley.

A recognition of this critical dilemma is important, for more than any poet except Blake, Shelley emphasizes the sympathetic imagination. Walter Jackson Bate has admirably summed up the significance of the imagination in Shelley's art:

The imagination, said Shelley, thinks in terms of totalities rather than proceeding by artificial analysis; it grasps the inner activity animating the changing, evolving reality outside, reacts to the varying crosslights in it, and captures the qualitative value potential in them. It is in construing this value in terms of ultimate and universal forms that Shelley reached back to the Platonic tradition and tran-

[2] *The Sense of Beauty* (New York, 1896), pp. 252–53.

scendentalized his romantic, organic theory of nature. Hence the remark that poetry tries to reveal "the image [the organic concreteness] of life expressed in its eternal truth," and that poets, in disclosing this reality, are the ultimate teachers and "unacknowledged legislators of the world." To this aim, Shelley subjoined another classical tenet: in conveying an awareness of reality in its full value and meaning, poetry is formative and moral in the highest sense. And Shelley gave this tenet a characteristically romantic phrasing by putting it in terms of "sympathy," though the spirit of what he said is essentially classical. The "great secret of morals is love"—it is a "going out of one's own nature," a sympathetic identification with others. Now the "imagination" is the means by which we do this; and poetry enlarges the range and scope of the imagination, gives it knowledge and experience, sharpens its delicacy and readiness to react, and in general strengthens and exercises this fundamental "instrument of moral good." [3]

In the Preface to *Prometheus Unbound* Shelley states his central belief regarding the function of poetry: ". . . to familiarize the highly refined imagination of the more select classes of poetical readers with beautiful idealisms of moral excellence." Such doctrine rejects didacticism for indirect "teaching" which inspires moral emulation. Thus the reader's pleasurable responses, arising from his perception of intuitive truth, cause him to re-create the poem for himself. In this way, Shelley argues, the lover of poetry renews his spirit at the fountainhead of knowledge.

My critical position should by now be clear. I concur with Frederick A. Pottle that it is "simpler and a great deal more satisfactory to abandon as meaningless the search for an absolutely good style, and to agree that good taste in literature is, like good taste in language, the expression of sensibility in accordance with the accepted usage of the time . . . ." [4] In this view, the question becomes whether Shelley is successful in putting poetry to the function he was convinced it should serve. Since I do not believe we need to lose Wordsworth to regain Pope or to abandon Tennyson to recapture Donne, my comments upon his artistic accomplishment need no absolute justification. Furthermore, if unique qualities in his poetry do give it a present value, these should be more clearly apparent to a sympathetic than to an adverse critic.

[3] *Criticism: the Major Texts* (New York, 1952), p. 428.

[4] *The Idiom of Poetry* (Ithaca, 1941), p. 30.

Such an approach can recognize Shelley's attendant limitations without making them the basis of appraisal or condemning him for not doing what the essential mode of his artistic effort precluded.

Shelley, then, is a religious and prophetic poet, like Blake. He straightway outgrew the allegorical framework of *Queen Mab,* within a few years evolving the unique form of *Prometheus Unbound* in which to reconcile beauty with truth and unite them in his conception of Love. Superficially this form is a closet drama; actually *Prometheus Unbound,* generally conceded to be as high an artistic achievement as Shelley reached, transcends its formal restrictions. Philosophically, his central problem was to deal with good and evil on a cosmic scale while recognizing that the problem of evil is unanswerable. Richard Harter Fogle has perspicuously observed regarding Shelley's "idealisms" that they are "symbolic, in the modern sense of symbol adumbrated by Goethe, Coleridge, Yeats, and Croce. They are not arbitrary intellectual constructions, they are not exhaustible in terms of abstract ideas, but take on a life of their own from the imagination of the poet, difficult to define because entirely unprecedented and original." [5] In addition they are a whole, for as C. S. Lewis says of the fourth act: "It does not add to, and therefore corrupt, a completed structure; it gives structure to that which, without it, would be imperfect. The resulting whole is the greatest long poem in the nineteenth century, and the only long poem of the highest kind in that century which approaches to perfection." [6] *Prometheus Unbound* is a tremendous feat of the modifying imagination, an effort to say what is perhaps beyond statement. Image evolves from image, and symbol from both, until the ancient myth is sublimed into an archetypal pattern of spiritual death and rebirth. The life force of humanity unbinds and regenerates itself through universal self-will.

Since Shelley is an impassioned poet, his imagery uses the directly imitative power of language to arouse emotion. Thus his poetic logic is implicit rather than explicit and has to be felt as much as perceived. His best lyrics, for example, appear unformed, at times suprasensuous, which accounts for Keats's memorable advice: "load every rift of your subject with ore." But Shelley fortunately clung to his own mode, letting himself sing with such lightness and liquidity that he challenges music for comparison. Many of the songs in *Prometheus Unbound* (a remark-

---

[5] "Image and Imagelessness: A Limited Reading of *Prometheus Unbound,*" *Keats-Shelley Journal,* I (1952), 27.

[6] "Shelley, Dryden, and Mr. Eliot" in *Rehabilitations and Other Essays* (London and New York, 1939), p. 29.

able lyrical flowering—nearly two dozen are in form original with him) belong in this group, the most famous being Asia's

> *My soul is an enchanted boat,*
> *Which, like a sleeping swan, doth float*
> *Upon the silver waves of thy sweet singing* . . . .

Of all Shelley's works, the most typical of his playful fancy, one which utterly confounds the literal-minded, is *The Witch of Atlas.* We may agree with F. R. Leavis that overuse of words like *daedal, faint, inwoven,* or of rimes like *abysses—wildernesses* is a fault without denying Shelley the singing voice. Moreover, in spite of lapses into self-pity, as in the last stanza of *Remembrance* or the fourth of the West Wind ode, his lyrics are often carefully developed. "Such structure," concludes Raymond D. Havens, "does not happen. It is produced only by hard work. Indeed, while many of Shelley's songs have as little formal pattern as *Hark, hark! the lark* and *Full fathom five,* others are much more . . . . They are curiously wrought and evince . . . ingenuity and . . . care . . . ." [7] *Adonais,* a poem of middle length, likewise discloses these characteristics. Shelley's own comment is relevant: "It is a highly-wrought *piece of art,* and perhaps better, in point of composition, than anything I have written." Far from lacking the constructive sense in poetry, Shelley had a clear awareness of his architectonic purposes. An illustration is the superb conclusion, an unsurpassed Platonic assertion of spiritual immortality over mutability. Here Shelley transcends his own identity to fuse into one the most complex set of themes ever woven into an English elegy.

At the core of the mature Shelley lies what he termed Love. His conception is both ideal and real, for it means the mystical One as well as the physical relationship between the sexes. In between these extremes, Love is a bond between the eternal and temporal; and it is *eros,* the force or "plastic stress" which urges man to aspire, as well as all that exists to realize its particular form or nature. The psychiatrist Karl Menninger recently said in *Love against Hate:*

> One of the best definitions of love, and a very scientific one, was written by the poet Shelley: "That profound and complicated sentiment which we call love is the universal thirst for a communion not merely of the senses, but of our whole nature, intellectual, imagina-

---

[7] "Structure and Prosodic Pattern in Shelley's Lyrics," *PMLA,* LXV (1950), 1087.

tive and sensitive . . . . The sexual impulse, which is only one, and often a small part of those claims, serves, from its obvious and external nature, as a kind of type of expression of the rest, a common basis, an acknowledged and visible link." [8]

This altruistic belief of Shelley's largely explains his rebellion against what he considered uncharitable tyranny in political and religious institutions. He makes his point universally: "The highest moral purpose aimed at in the highest species of the drama, is the teaching the human heart, through its sympathies and antipathies, the knowledge of itself; in proportion to the possession of which knowledge every human being is wise, just, sincere, tolerant and kind."

If we ask finally what is Shelley's peculiar virtue as poet, I think two critics have come close to the answer. Richard Harter Fogle writes of *Prometheus Unbound:*

> Shelley is expressing not a surrender, not a passive emotion, but the result of intellectual effort pushed to its furthest reaches, with all the difficulties and dangers which are involved in it. He presents a full cycle of the confrontation, of the struggle, and of the victorious defeat of the human spirit at full stretch. What seems superficially to be formlessness and the shattering of order is really the synthesis of form and formlessness, of expansion and determination, of image and imagelessness. As such, it is the wholly consistent result of absorbing into art a system of thought [Platonism] which has not been, to put it mildly, without influence in the world, and is not lightly to be banished by even the most confident criticism.[9]

The second writer, Leone Vivante, has influenced T. S. Eliot, who states in his brief Preface to *English Poetry and Its Contribution to the Knowledge of a Creative Principle:* ["Vivante] has brought me to a new and more sympathetic appreciation of that poet . . . . Signor Vivante finds Shelley's poetic thought . . . in recurrent insights which turn up again and again . . . . These insights are what might be called the proper thinking of Shelley's poetry." [10] An example of such an insight is the following:

> If we say that we are one with a person, whom we love, we hardly say anything philosophically significant or unequivocal, unless or until the characteristic and surpassing value of this *oneness* is elic-

[8] *Love against Hate* (New York, 1942), pp. 280–81.

[9] "Image and Imagelessness," pp. 35–36.

[10] New York, 1950, p. x.

ited. It is by the term 'annihilation', as he most forcibly employs it, that Shelley expresses and reveals the real content and the very principle of this *oneness,* especially in its form-transcending character; while the full weight of his personality, and his philosophical insight, are contained in the expression itself:

> *We shall become the same, we shall be one*
> *Spirit within two frames, oh! wherefore two?*
> *One passion in twin hearts, . . .*
> *One hope within two wills, one will beneath*
> *Two overshadowing minds, one life, one death,*
> *One Heaven, one Hell, one immortality,*
> *And one annihilation.*
> —Epipsychidion, *573–87.*[11]

Shelley "starts with objects that are just on the verge of becoming invisible or inaudible or intangible," says Frederick A. Pottle, "and he strains away even from these." [12] This observation upon his imagery is support to larger claim of uniqueness in his art. Self-informed by its own creative principle, spontaneously intense but firmly rooted in abstraction, his poetry begins in sympathy and ends in infinitude. "Sympathy and infinitude—these are," says Herbert Read, "expansive virtues, not avowed in the dry air of disillusion, awaiting a world of peace and justice for their due recognition." [13] Shelley's attainment is that he does not wait upon analysis, but absorbs it and passes beyond to a poetical aspect of truth. When he succeeds the mode is wholly his own.

[11] *Ibid.,* pp. 127–28.
[12] "The Case of Shelley," *PMLA,* LXVII (1952), 601.
[13] *In Defence of Shelley and Other Essays* (London, 1936), p. 86.

16 | Shelley's Philosophy

HERBERT READ

SHELLEY WAS by nature an optimist. In his last years in Italy he used to wear a ring inscribed with the motto: *Il buon tempo verra*— The good time will come. During his short life he had more than a normal share of suffering, and he often expressed his disillusionment with mankind. But philosophically speaking he remained an optimist, and his poetry is inspired by the intensest faith in life. It is that which above all gives it relevance in our own disillusioned age.

In this respect he stood apart from most of his fellow romantics. Romantic philosophy, as expressed at its source by Schelling, and as interpreted in England by our greatest romantic philosopher, Samuel Taylor Coleridge, was not optimistic. It was deeply tinged by that reaction to the contemplation of human existence which takes the form of dread or anxiety, and from it developed, during the course of the nineteenth century, the two pessimistic creeds of nihilism and existentialism. Shelley was untouched by this turbid stream of thought. He knew Coleridge and had read certain of his prose works. He possessed some of the works of Kant, though there is no evidence to show that he had ever read them. There is no need, however, to pursue such negative evidence, for Shelley's real interests are not in doubt. His mind was fed, if not formed, by Plato among the ancients and by Godwin among his contemporaries. It was reinforced, as time went on, by the neo-Platonists, by Bacon, Hume, Berkeley, Spinoza, and above all by Rousseau, whose name he held sacred, whose imagination had, he said, "divine beauty," and whom he was to make the central figure in his last poem, *The*

Triumph of Life. All these thinkers contributed in some degree to that blend of idealism and rationalism which makes up Shelley's philosophy.

We must remember that Shelley's life lasted only thirty years. His mind developed precociously, but from his school days until 1815, that is to say, until his twenty-third year, it merely absorbed and reflected the ideas of others—notably those of William Godwin. The decisive change that came about in 1815 was due, no doubt, to an accumulation of emotional and financial worries during the previous twelve months. Shelley was finding the world a tougher place than Godwin had led him to expect it to be; and incidentally Godwin himself with his insatiable demands for financial aid was one of the agents of disillusion. But the greatest agency in this change in Shelley had been the passionate experiences of that year: his desertion of Harriet, his love of and elopement with Mary Godwin, and all the melancholy consequences of that defiance of social conventions. Life itself was in doubt, for in the spring of 1815 a physician had told Shelley that he was dying rapidly of consumption; abscesses had formed in his lungs and he suffered acute spasms. But relief was at hand. At the beginning of this same year Shelley's grandfather had died, and Shelley's financial worries suddenly came to an end. In the calm that succeeded the storm of 1814, and with the security provided by a settlement with his father, Shelley was able to retreat into solitude, and in this solitude not only was his health restored, but he succeeded in coming to an intellectual settlement with himself. The immediate result was *Alastor, or the Spirit of Solitude,* a poem in which Shelley's original philosophy first makes a tentative appearance. I say "tentative" because the philosophy as such is clothed in allegory, and Shelley himself felt bound to explain the poem in a preface. He draws a contrast between those "unseeing multitudes" who are selfish, blind, torpid, morally dead, and the "adventurous genius" who is "led forth by an imagination inflamed and purified through familiarity with all that is excellent and majestic, to the contemplation of the universe." This genius imagines to himself a Being or Power, all wonderful, wise and beautiful. "He seeks in vain," Shelley writes "for a prototype of his conception. Blasted by his disappointments, he descends to an untimely grave."

Alastor is not a very optimistic poem, one might conclude. But actually it is inspired by the strongest faith in the beauty and goodness of the universe, and in the love and joy which can be realized by communion with nature.

By solemn vision, and bright silver dream,
His infancy was nurtured. Every sight
And sound from the vast earth and ambient air,
Sent to his heart its choicest impulses.
The fountains of divine philosophy
Fled not his thirsting lips, and all of great,
Or good, or lovely, which the sacred past
In truth or fable consecrates, he felt
And knew.

It may be said that there is nothing very original about this philosophy, and indeed *Alastor* was written under the immediate influence of Wordsworth's *Excursion,* which had been recently published. But there are original notes, not only in the verse but also among the ideas expressed by the verse. For a plainer statement of these ideas we can refer to a series of moral and philosophical essays which belong to the same period as *Alastor.* These essays are important because they show that most of the ideas that were to be embodied in his later and greater poems, and in *A Defence of Poetry,* were already taking shape in Shelley's mind.

There is a critical slander which accuses Shelley of intellectual adolescence, muddled thinking, and obscure writing. I do not know on what evidence it is based—certainly not on these essays. Although they suffer from their incompleteness, they are remarkable by-products of a few weeks' poetic activity in a man's twenty-fourth year. Insofar as they are complete, they are acutely and logically reasoned; and even as fragments they must strike any unprejudiced reader as the expression of a curious and vital intelligence.

From the essay *On Life* we may take a statement of Shelley's revised philosophical position from which he was never to depart. "I confess," he says "that I am one of those who am unable to refuse my assent to the conclusions of those philosophers who assert that nothing exists but as it is perceived"; and he goes on to describe an "intellectual system" whose main outlines he no doubt owed to Berkeley:

It is a decision against which our persuasions struggle, and we must be long convicted before we can be convinced that the solid universe of external things is "such stuff as dreams are made of." The shocking absurdities of the popular philosophy of mind and matter, its fatal consequences in morals, and their violent dogmatism concerning the source of all things, had early conducted me to materialism. This materialism is a seducing system to young and superficial minds. It allows its disciples to talk and dispenses them from thinking. But I was discontented with such a view of things as it afforded; man is a being of such high aspirations, "looking both before and after," whose "thoughts wander through eternity" disclaiming alliance with transience and decay; incapable of imagining to himself annihilation; existing but in the future and the past; being, not what he is, but what he has been and shall be. Whatever may be his true and final destination there is a spirit within him at enmity with nothingness and dissolution. This is the character of all life and being. Such contemplations as these, materialism and the popular philosophy of mind and matter alike forbid; they are only consistent with the intellectual system.

Alastor, according to Shelley's own Preface, was designed to show the dangers of an exclusive concentration on such an intellectual system. He had discovered that the intellectual faculties—the imagination, the function of sense—"have their respective requisitions on the sympathy of corresponding powers in other human beings." And so arose Shelley's doctrine of sympathy or love, to take a central place in his philosophy. It is beautifully outlined in one of the prose fragments of 1815, but it was to receive its supreme expression in the poem *Epipsychidion,* written at Pisa six years later:

> *True love in this differs from gold and clay,*
> *That to divide is not to take away.*
> *Love is like understanding, that grows bright,*
> *Gazing on many truths; 'tis like thy light,*
> *Imagination! which from earth and sky,*
> *And from the depths of human fantasy,*
> *As from a thousand prisms and mirrors, fills*
> *The Universe with glorious beams, and kills*
> *Error, the worm, with many a sun-like arrow*
> *Of its reverberated lightning . . . .*

Shelley's philosophy of love, which caused so much dismay in his lifetime, is still too unorthodox, and most people would say too impracticable, to be acceptable even now, when the science of human relations and the blinder drift of public manners have led to more tolerance of what is vulgarly known as "free love." But there is nothing vulgar about the philosophy expounded in *Epipsychidion.* The only comparable work, by which it was much influenced, is Plato's *Sym-*

posium, and the one is as pure and noble in conception as the other, though Shelley himself compared his poem to the *Vita Nuova* of Dante. What Shelley meant by love in this poem is not in doubt—in his own words it is "the bond and the sanction which connects, not only man with man, but with everything that exists." But like Plato and Dante, Shelley was ready to insist that such love is not necessarily ethereal, but should be embodied in our human relationships.

> *We—are we not formed, as notes of music are,*
> *For one another, though dissimilar;*
> *Such difference without discord, as can make*
> *Those sweetest sounds, in which all spirits shake*
> *As trembling leaves in a continuous air?*

One of the 1815 prose fragments is entitled *Speculations on Metaphysics,* and another *Speculations on Morals;* but important as these are for an appreciation of Shelley's philosophical position, I pass them by in favor of Shelley's greatest prose work *A Defence of Poetry.*

The *Defence of Poetry* is again a fragment, about 15,000 words in length (and so concentrated in reasoning and so eloquent in expression that any summary seems like a desecration). It is the inspired expression in English of that "rare union of close and subtle logic with the Pythian enthusiasm of poetry" which Shelley found in Plato; and we may say of Shelley as he said of his master, that "his language is that of an immortal spirit, rather than a man." But like Plato's, it is a language that can express logical distinctions (with scientific method) and of this kind is the opening discussion of "those two classes of mental action, which are called reason and imagination."

Reason is defined as "mind contemplating the relations borne by one thought to another, however produced"; and imagination as "mind acting upon those thoughts so as to colour them with its own light, and composing from them, as from elements, other thoughts, each containing within itself the principle of its own integrity." There is nothing very original in this distinction—it is the normal contrast between the procedures of analysis and synthesis, between quantitive enumeration and value judgments. But Shelley goes on to assert that poetry is "the expression of the imagination" that it is the original faculty by means of which mankind, in the long course of evolution, has developed those harmonious laws from which society results. It follows that poets, or those who imagine and express this harmony in a vitally metaphorical

language, are in Shelley's words "not only the authors of language
and of music, of the dance, and architecture, and statuary, and painting; they are the institutors of laws, and the founders of civil society,
and the inventors of the arts of life, and the teachers, who draw into
a certain propinquity of the beautiful and the true, that partial apprehension of the agencies of the invisible world which is called religion."
Shelley then develops that theory of the correspondency of the beautiful and the good, of the aesthetical and the ethical, which Plato first
proposed:

> The great secret of morals is love; or a going out of our own na-
> ture, and an identification of ourselves with the beautiful which ex-
> ists in any thought, action, or person, not our own. A man to be
> greatly good, must imagine intensely and comprehensively; he must
> put himself in the place of another and of many others; the pains
> and pleasures of his species must become his own. The great instru-
> ment of moral good is the imagination; and poetry administers to
> the effect by acting upon the cause . . . . Poetry strengthens the
> faculty which is the organ of the moral nature of man, in the same
> manner as exercise strengthens a limb.

"The great secret of morals is love"—that may be taken as the
central tenet in Shelley's philosophy, and his greatest poems are illustrations of its truth—illustrations rather than demonstrations, for Shelley
had a horror of didactic poetry. The "bold neglect of a direct moral purpose," he wrote, "is the most decisive proof of the supremacy of Milton's
genius." Shelley's aim in all his poems is to administer to the effect
by acting upon the cause—by which he means inducing in his audience
a state of sympathetic response to the actions depicted in poetry. In
his Preface to *The Cenci* he said that "The highest moral purpose aimed
at in the higher species of the drama, is the teaching the human heart,
through its sympathies and antipathies, the knowledge of itself; in proportion to the possession of which knowledge, every human being is
wise, just, sincere, tolerant and kind." In this light we should receive a
dramatic creation such as the figure of Beatrice; for as he says, "imagination is as the immortal God which should assume flesh for the redemp-
tion of mortal passion." In other words, greatness of character is created
by constancy in love.

It may seem that Shelley's philosophy remains on a moral, even a mundane, plane, and does not attempt to answer those profounder metaphysical questions to which Coleridge and Wordsworth addressed themselves, and which are still with us. But this is not true: Shelley was a man totally aware of the human predicament. The unfinished *Triumph of Life* ends with the question "What is life?" and it was a question of which Shelley was continuously conscious. And he did provide an answer. That love, which he declared the secret of morals, he also regarded as the guiding principle of the universe. Again, he was following Plato and, more particularly, Dante. In the detail of his conception he is much nearer to Dante than to Plato, but as a confessed atheist he did not want to identify this "unseen Power" with a divine agency. He therefore gives it an "awful throne . . . in the wise heart," from which it springs to "fold over the world its healing wings." This universal love is clearly and defiantly humanistic in character; its "spells" are faculties within the titanic frame of man's imagination.

In order to be good, great and joyous, beautiful and free it is necessary

> *To suffer woes which Hope thinks infinite;*
> *To forgive wrongs darker than death or night;*
> *To defy Power, which seems omnipotent;*
> *To love, and bear; to hope till Hope creates*
> *From its own wreck the thing it contemplates;*
> *Neither to change, nor falter, nor repent.*

These are Stoic virtues, human aspirations, and I see no evidence anywhere in Shelley's work which would justify any more transcendental faith. At the end of *Adonais* he writes:

> *From the world's bitter wind*
> *Seek shelter in the shadow of the tomb.*

And though he uses words like "Heaven" and "Eternity," it is always in a metaphorical sense: they are attributes of the One, absolute, denied to the Many.

> *The One remains, the many change and pass;*
> *Heaven's light forever shines, Earth's shadows fly;*
> *Life, like a dome of many-coloured glass,*
> *Stains the white radiance of Eternity,*
> *Until Death tramples it to fragments.*

Resolute words, among the most immortal in our language; and they are followed by the relentless command:

>   *Die,*
> *If thou wouldst be with that which thou dost seek!*
> *Follow where all is fled!*

"That which thou dost seek" is identified with the Spirit of Beauty:

> *That Light whose smile kindles the Universe,*
> *That Beauty in which all things work and move,*
> *That Benediction which the eclipsing Curse*
> *Of birth can quench not, the sustaining love,*
> *Which through the web of being blindly wove*
> *By man and beast and earth and air and sea,*
> *Burns bright or dim, as each are mirrors of*
> *The fire for which all thirst . . . .*

A fire, a white radiance, a transfused glory, a plastic stress, the splendors of the firmament of time—Shelley uses many such phrases to describe the immanent Spirit of the Universe, the ultimate Reality. They are concepts of the imagination, remote from revealed religion, but implying an endless resonance of love, beauty, and delight.

VI: Keats

17 Keats's Style: Evolution toward Qualities of Permanent Value

W. JACKSON BATE

1

WITH THE decline of neoclassicism, poetry was faced with some relatively new problems and a new uneasiness about its value and function. The problems and the uneasiness have persisted; and the principal ways of meeting them have not changed radically from those the greater romantics adopted. Whether we like our legacy or not, the present literary generation is very much the heir of the romantics.

On the other hand, of course, much of the poetry as well as critical effort of the last forty years has been written in a spirit of conscious protest against the idiom of romantic poetry. Some of the rather confused distinctions which this militant protest created at its start seem now to have become domesticated into academic orthodoxy, and we have begun to take them for granted, as we do most domestic phenomena, without any very searching revision of our first impressions. We especially follow the confusion of poetic form with mere idiom, and feel that we are describing or analyzing poetry according to the first when we are really thinking only of the latter. We hold academic symposia now on differences in the "metaphysical," "Augustan," "romantic," and "modern modes"; and the word "mode," because it is open and fluid, gives us the feeling that we are being comprehensive. But it usually turns out to be restricted to special problems of metaphor, syntax, and phrasing. Like good Alexandrian rhetoricians, we have begun to play close to the ground.

No brief discussion of the style of a romantic poet can hope to improve on the situation. There are, after all, genuine differences between the idiom of the romantics and the poetry of the last forty years; and some of them are quite fundamental. But any discussion that could make place for these acknowledged differences, and then subsume them within larger considerations would involve a more pluralistic, leisurely, less compartmentalized procedure that would permit us to review the total achievement of a poet. This is particularly the case with Keats. He has worn very well. He has continued to stir the imagination of poets and critics for a century and a half. On the other hand, the idiom of much of his earlier poetry is hardly at the present time a model or even much of an encouragement. Indeed, to a good many younger readers, some of it is not even very congenial. Of course the language of his greatest poetry has always held a magnetic attraction; for there we reach, if only for a brief while, a high plateau where in mastery of phrase he has few equals in English poetry, and only one obvious superior. A very important part of the more general significance of Keats is the fact that he was able to reach that level. But this, by itself, is not enough to explain the large, at times almost personal, relevance that we feel. He is a part of our literary conscience. Leaving aside the poignant appeal (and with it the sense of difference) of his own peculiar circumstances—the fact that he started with so little, the manner in which he struggled his way into poetry, his early death, and the like—we sense that this gifted young poet was working his way through problems that any honest poet of the last century and a half has faced.

Nothing less than a fairly capacious and imaginative consideration of his achievement, then, could get very far in capturing, or even beginning to suggest, the relevance of Keats's art to poetry since his death, and especially during the last generation. Still, the assigned purpose of this essay is to concentrate briefly on the stylistic character of Keats's poetry. Hard put to compartmentalize in this way, I should be forced to resort to the term "honesty." Certainly this is what now appeals to us most when we think of Keats as a whole, especially in the context of the letters. And we feel this impression confirmed in his stylistic development. Considering his short life, there is no parallel to the diversity of styles with which he experimented. Yet it was never experimentation for its own sake. The experimentation moves constantly toward great honesty—greater openness to concrete life and the claims of experience, toward greater fullness and richness of expression, and at the same time a growing strength of control and sensitivity to the formal claims of poetic art.

2

T H E E A R L Y verse of Keats, down through the writing of *Isabella* (early in 1818), shows little selectivity of subject in either its themes or its imagery when it is measured by a really high standard. The impulse towards self-absorption in the object is associated with having the "soul," as he said, "lost in pleasant smotherings." It finds its outlet, that is, in a luxurious abandonment to the conventionally "poetic" objects and images that intrigued a youthful romantic poet, and that Keats found ready at hand in the verse of his mentor, Leigh Hunt, and in the poets Hunt held up as a model. This sort of poetry, as it is developed by Hunt and the youthful Keats, and as it is continued throughout the poorer verse of the nineteenth century, is essentially a reaction, of course, against neo-classic conventions: an attempt to substitute for the stock themes and stock diction of the preceding century a conception of "poetic" material even more confined, a diction equally liable to stereotype, and a versification—as Keats later learned—of equal monotony.

We need not retrace in any detail the characteristics of Keats's early diction and imagery: his use of y-ending adjectives ("sphery," "lawny," "bloomy," "surgy," and the like); the unfortunate predilection for adverbs made from participles ("lingeringly," "dyingly," "cooingly"), and for abstract nouns that have little intellectual content ("languishment," "designments," "soft ravishment"); the use of such conventional props in his imagery as "Pink robes, and wavy hair," the "silvery tears of April," and monotonously recurring nymphs with "downward" glances, the habitual appearance of objects with "pillowy" softness, and the frequently embarrassing attempts to introduce action ("madly I kiss/The wooing arms") into this smothering world of rose-leaves, doves, "almond vales," and "blooming plums/Ready to melt between an infant's gums."

These characteristics and their sources have been frequently discussed, are familiar to every student of English poetry, and have little interest to present-day readers except as a steppingstone in Keats's chronological development. And they are accompanied not only by a lack of structural control but by a deliberately cultivated slackness of manner—except in his early sonnets, written in the Petrarchan form and employing diverse and not too effective structural peculiarities drawn from Hunt, occasionally Wordsworth, and the Miltonic imitators of the late eighteenth century. One is almost tempted to conclude that if Pope, in his versification, went in one direction and employed a device to secure economy and tightness, then Hunt—and the youthful Keats—not only discarded it but, in some instances, deliberately adopted an opposite device. Examples of this would take us into the by-roads of prosody—particularly caesural-placing, where Keats followed Hunt very closely. It is perhaps enough to note how forcibly Keats, even more than Hunt, broke the couplet. In fact, when a pause is needed at the end of a line, he frequently put it at the end of the *first* line of the couplet, and then tried to run on the second line, without break, into the next couplet:

> *Full of sweet dreams, and health, and quiet breathing./*
> *Therefore, on every morrow, are we wreathing*
> *A flowery band to bind us to the earth,/*
> *Spite of despondence, of the inhuman dearth*
> *Of noble natures, of the gloomy days,/*
> *Of all the unhealthy and o'er-darken'd ways*
> *Made for our searching: yes, in spite of all,/*
> *Some shape of beauty moves away the pall*
> *From our dark spirits. Such the sun, the moon,/*
> *Trees old, and young, sprouting a shady boon*
> *For simple sheep . . . .*
>
> *Endymion, I, 4–15*

The style of *Isabella*, written a few months after Keats became twenty-three, shows an embarrassed and confused attempt by Keats to rid himself of the influences of Hunt and of the "sickening stuff" he later associated with Hunt's taste. "I shall have," he wrote, "the Reputation of Hunt's elevé. His corrections and amputations will by the knowing ones be traced." He had grown "tired" of the "slipshod" *Endymion;* his opinion of it was "very low," and he wanted to "forget" it. Abandoning the loose, run-on couplet he had taken over from Hunt, Keats selected the tight ottava rima stanza (perhaps better fitted for satire, because of the snap of its concluding couplet); and though the story has limited possibilities, to say the least, and though there is still (as he himself was to say) a mawkish sentimentality of phrase and image, the versification shows an energetic struggle to impose a disciplined control.

3

I T I S D U R I N G the year or more following the writing of *Isabella* that the maturer style of Keats developed so rapidly. Among the primary characteristics of this style is a suggestive power of image capable of securing from the reader an unusually intense emotional and imaginative identification. This quality has become widely recognized in recent years, particularly since the implications of Keats's own conception of the poet's character, and of his puzzling term, "Negative Capability," have been discussed. We need not here make distinctions between the romantic theory of sympathetic identification, in which the poet takes on, through participation, the qualities and character of his object, and the more recent theory of *Einfühlung* (or empathy), with its suggestion that many of these qualities are merely the subjective creation of the poet or observer, and are bestowed upon the object rather than descried in it. The poetry of Keats contains abundant examples that might be used to substantiate either, or both at once, as a guiding characteristic of his verse.

Certainly, in the verse written before *Hyperion,* a subjective element —more empathic than sympathetic—often characterizes this imaginative identification ("sweet peas, on *tiptoe* for a flight," the foam crawling along the back of the wave with a "wayward indolence"). But a more sympathetic in-feeling is equally apparent (minnows "staying their wavy bodies 'gainst the stream," lions with "nervy tails," or the organic in-feeling in "Ere a lean bat could plump its wintry skin"). The verse from *Hyperion* through the great odes is replete with such imagery, ranging from "The hare *limp'd trembling* through the frozen grass" to the agonies of the huge figures in *Hyperion:* "horrors, portion'd to a giant nerve,/Oft made Hyperion ache"; or

> through all his bulk *an agony*
> Crept *gradual, from the feet unto the crown,*
> *Like a lithe serpent* vast and muscular,
> *Making* slow way, *with head and neck* convuls'd
> From over strainèd might . . .
>
> *(I, 259–63)*

Such lines remind us of the passages in both Shakespeare and Milton that evoked so strong a sympathetic participation in Keats—as, for example, when he wrote in the margin beside *Paradise Lost,* IX, 179 ff., where Satan enters the serpent without arousing him from sleep:

Satan having entered the Serpent, and inform'd his brutal sense—
might seem sufficient—but Milton goes on *"but his sleep disturbed
not."* Whose spirit does not ache at the smothering and confine-
ment . . . the *"waiting close?"* Whose head is not dizzy at the
possible speculations of Satan in the serpent prison? No passage of
poetry ever can give a greater pain of suffocation.

Or again there is his enthusiastic mention, in one of his letters (November 22, 1817), of Shakespeare's image of the sensitive retreat of a
snail:

> *As the snail, whose tender horns being hit,*
> *Shrinks back into his shelly cave with pain.*

And we may recall Charles Cowden Clarke's story of Keats's reaction,
while reading the *Faerie Queene* as a boy, to the phrase, "sea-shoulder-
ing whales": as if raising himself against the pressure of the waves, "he
hoisted himself up, and looked burly and dominant . . . ."

This kinaesthetic gift of image, if one wishes to call it that, this
organically felt participation, is further revealed in Keats's ability to
bring into focus several diverse sense-impressions of an object, and—in
transmuting them into a single image or series of images—present a
more valid, rounded, and fully realized apperception. This unifying interplay of sense-impressions should not be confused with synaesthesia.
Keats's imagery, to be sure, is perhaps as richly packed with examples
of suggestive synaesthesia as any that can be found (*"fragrant* and
enwreathèd light," "pale and silver silence," "scarlet pain," "the *touch*
of *scent"*), and Keats's use of it had more effect on the synaesthetic
imagery of later English poetry than any other one model. But the really
distinctive quality in Keats—and a quality his Victorian imitators rarely
attained—is less the *substitution* than it is the *substantiation* of one
sense by another in order to give, as it were, additional dimension and
depth, as in "the *moist scent* of flowers," "embalmèd darkness," or in
making incense tangibly "soft" and visible:

> *I cannot see what flowers are at my feet,*
> *Nor what* soft *incense* hangs *upon the boughs.*

A further example is Keats's predilection for tactile qualities:
his craving for touch ("Touch," he wrote, "has a memory"), and for a
firm grasp of the concrete as it exists in space. Thus images directly or

indirectly connected with the sense of taste are sustained and deepened, in their vitality, through associations with tactile and muscular response: the "purple-stainèd mouth," the nightingale singing of summer "in *full-throated* ease," or the closing stanza of the *Ode on Melancholy,* with its

> aching *Pleasure nigh,*
> *Turning to poison while the* bee-mouth sips . . .
> *Though seen of none save him whose* strenuous tongue
> *Can* burst *Joy's* grape against his palate *fine* . . . .

This tactile strength gives a three-dimensional grasp to Keats's images. Perhaps the most notable instance is the famous "wealth of *globèd* peonies," in the same ode: here the hand is virtually enclosing the peony, further assuring itself of the three-dimensional roundness.

There is, in short, a *centering* in Keats's imagery of the various qualities of an object into a single apperception; and as a result the object emerges as a totality with its several aspects resolved into a unified whole rather than delineated or suggested separately. The use of strong tactile associations that give a firmer hold, a more definitely felt outline, is one means by which this centering of impressions, into an amalgamated whole, is secured and anchored. His general amassing and condensing of sense-impressions is another. And the result is an imagery that is less "synaesthetic," in the ordinary sense, than it is a gifted illustration of what Hazlitt meant by "gusto"—that is, a state in which the imagination, through sympathetic excitement, draws out and expresses the total character of its object. In this intense identification, the impressions made on one sense "excite by affinity those of another"; the object is grasped as a vital whole. And accompanying this sympathetic gusto, with its resolving of diverse impressions into a unified and immediate experience, is a discerning ability to sense organic motion, with a vivid fellow-feeling, and as an unfolding and continuing process. One is reminded of Severn's account:

> 'a wave . . . billowing through a tree,' as he described the uplifting surge of air among swaying masses of chestnuts or oak foliage, or when, afar off, he heard the wind coming across woodlands. 'The tide! the tide!' he would cry delightedly, and spring on to some stile, ·or upon the bough of a wayside tree, and watch the passage of the wind upon the meadow grasses or young corn, not stirring till the flow of air was all around him, while an expression of rapture made his eyes gleam and his face glow.

4

IT IS ESPECIALLY through a rapidly developed mastery of idiom and versification that Keats acquired the control of impact and the
formal sense of structure that restrains the concrete richness of his mature
verse and thus contributes to its massive and interwoven firmness. It is
here that the powerful influence of Milton—against which he was later
to react in some ways—had so salutary an effect, lifting him far beyond
the weak and fitful devices with which he had tried to tighten his
versification in *Isabella.* The first *Hyperion,* begun a few months after
Isabella, immediately reveals that no apprentice, at once so gifted and
eager, ever sat at the feet of Milton; certainly none ever learned from
Milton more quickly and with greater ultimate profit. To be sure, much
that he took over consists merely of the obvious mannerisms that all
Miltonic imitators have used. One example is the frequent use of the
adjective in place of the adverb ("Shook *horrid* with such aspen mal-
ady," "Crept *gradual,* from the foot unto the crown"). And there are
the "Miltonic inversions" with which Keats later thought *Hyperion* was
disfigured: the epithet after the noun ("omens drear," "palace bright,"
"metal sick"), and the verb before the subject ("Pale wox I," "There
saw she direst strife"). But other devices less mannered and more
generally helpful were adopted. Among them should be noted the
Milton ellipsis ("still snuff'd the incense, teeming up/From man to the
sun's God; yet unsecure"); a condensed asyndeton ("some also shouted;
Some wept, some wail'd, all bow'd with reverence"); and a use of
repetition more effective than the crude repetition that Keats had taken
over from Fairfax in his attempt to tighten *Isabella.* In versification,
Keats closely followed Milton, and acquired metrical qualities that were
to remain as a strengthening support in his verse. Chief among these
are an increased slowing and weighting of the line with spondees, and
also the use of the majestic sixth-syllable caesura, which Keats alone
among Milton's imitators seems to have had the ear to catch. A growing
sense of stanzaic structure is apparent in the *Eve of St. Agnes,* which,
in contrast to other eighteenth- and nineteenth-century poems in the
Spenserian stanza, often preserves the quatrain division that Spenser
himself used in the stanza (*abab bcbc c*). In his sonnets, Keats now
abandoned the Petrarchan form, which had been the dominant sonnet
form since Milton; and he went back instead to the Shakespearian

rhyme scheme, consisting of three heroic, or elegiac, quatrains and a couplet. But the sonnet was now only an incidental and casual form for Keats. If his poetic temper was still mainly lyrical, it was becoming too richly weighted to be couched in the brief space of the sonnet. In fact, he not only wished for a more lengthy form, which would permit a more leisurely development, but he desired a different rhyme pattern. In the first eight lines of the Petrarchan form, the three couplets (*a bb aa bb a*), he felt, had a "pouncing" quality, the second line of each couplet leaping out, as it were, to match the first. In the Shakespearian form, on the other hand, the three alternate-rhyming quatrains (the heroic, and in the eighteenth century the traditional "elegiac" quatrain) often had an "elegiac" languor as well; and the concluding couplet, with which even Shakespeare had difficulty, "has seldom a pleasing effect" (May 3, 1819). Keats wanted, therefore, "a better sonnet stanza than we have," and wrote an experimental sonnet, "If by dull rhymes," the theme of which is

> *Let us find out, if we must be constrained,*
> *Sandals more interwoven and complete*
> *To fit the naked foot of Poesy.*

After experimenting in the *Ode to Psyche,* he finally developed a ten-line stanza (in the later ode, *To Autumn,* eleven lines). This stanza is essentially constructed from the *disjecta. membra* of both sonnet forms, and was possibly influenced also by some of the ten-line ode-stanzas common in the eighteenth century. Avoiding the "pouncing rhymes" of the Petrarchan octave, the continual alternate rhyming of the Shakespearian form, and its concluding couplet, this new ode-stanza—though there are variations—consists basically of one alternate-rhyming quatrain (*abab*) from the three that make up the Shakespearian sonnet, with the addition of something like the ordinary sestet (*cde cde*) of the Petrarchan form. And here, in these closely knit and restraining stanzas, Keats certainly achieved a lyrical form "more interwoven and complete." In the odes, moreover, may be seen a masterful use of the assonance and vowel-interplay, first employed in *Hyperion* and continued throughout the *Eve of St. Agnes* and many of the sonnets, with an intricacy hardly equalled in the history of English verse. Keats informed his friend, Benjamin Bailey, that he had a "principle of melody in verse, upon which he had his own motives, particularly in the management of open and close vowels:

Keats's theory was that the vowels should be . . . interchanged like differing notes in music, to prevent monotony . . . . I well remember his telling me that, had he studied music, he had some notions of the combinations of sounds, by which he thought he could have done something as original as his poetry.

And when Keats turned to the writing of *Hyperion,* in the autumn of 1818, he began to make use of an elaborate patterning both of open and close vowels and also of assonance. This use of assonance and vowel-arrangement is extraordinarily complex at times, and cannot be described in any detail in this essay. A few examples of assonance patterning, however, may be cited:

1   2   3   1   2   3
And still she slept an azure-lidded sleep.
1 2   3   1   2   3
Nor let the beetle, nor the death-moth be.

Or, to take a somewhat more complicated example:

1   1   2   2
And bid old Saturn take his throne again.
3 4   3   4

Patterns of vowel repetition occur, in an even more complex manner, throughout series of more than one line, and easily substantiate Saintsbury's assertion that the deliberate and frequent use of assonance in English poetry starts with Keats.

5

W I T H T H E great odes, we are probably at the apex of Keats's poetic art. A discussion of the relevance of Keats's stylistic craftsmanship to the present day could quite justifiably turn into simply an explication of one or two of these odes. But the procedure taken here, rightly or wrongly, has been to stress the rather rapid experimentation with styles, the interests that led to it, and some of the more general aspects of Keats's development in this series of experiments. Hence, there would be place for only the briefest explication; and considering the care with which the odes have been examined, especially in the last twenty years, a short impressionistic explication would be presumptuous. Nor could we get very far in discussing the form of these odes even in general terms unless we spent time in reminding ourselves of the under part of the iceberg—of what was going on in the mind of Keats throughout the year before the great odes and especially the last two or three months of it.

But we can certainly note in these odes—especially the *Ode on a Grecian Urn* and the *Ode to a Nightingale*—what I can only call a successful intrusion of the dramatic. In each we are dealing with a miniature drama. In each the poet seeks at the start—in the *Ode to a Nightingale* shortly after the start—to identify himself with an object that can lift himself beyond a world of flux. In each there is a gradual disengagement, an inability to follow completely the implications of sympathetic absorption, and a return back (implicit in the *Grecian Urn,* more obvious in the *Nightingale*) to the world of process and the claims of the human heart. So, a century later with Yeats, there may be the paeans to Byzantium; but the drama lies in the return back—the descent down the ladder, as in "The Circus Animals' Desertion"—to the human condition, and the assertive, unstilled desires of the dying animal, from which "all ladders start." The structure of the odes cannot be considered apart from this drama. Nor can the massive richness and the courageous openness to the full concrete expression, be considered apart from the drama, especially at a time like the present when fear of the welter, the quick unpredictable decay or change of concrete life has so intimidated the imagination of writers. There is courage here, in this welcome of concrete amplitude by Keats; and the courage is not apart from the poetic art.

The poems of the summer and early autumn of 1819 add important nuances to the situation. The questioning, before the odes, of the value and function of poetry in such a world as we find ourselves becomes more articulate in the letters. Energetic changes in style and form follow. *Lamia* drops, for the time being, many of the stylistic qualities of Keats from *Hyperion* through the odes. We have now a fairly open allegory, in some ways impetuously ironic and mocking in tone, which had, he hoped, a new energy that would "take hold of people in some way— give them either pleasant or unpleasant sensations." As if in a deliberate attempt to put things at arm's length, he surprisingly reverts to the crisp heroic couplet (the "rocking-horse" meter he had once shied away from) of Dryden and Pope, though with a vivid color all of his own. The couplet is not so closed as in Dryden or Pope; but there are many closer similarities of a minor prosodic nature. Whatever else may be said of *Lamia,* it treats the effect of a Circian enchantment upon the impressionable mind of a young man (Lycius) who is open to the appeal of a magic world, and who is unable to withstand reality when it is pointed out to him. This general theme is closely related to the style which Keats, within two months, has suddenly evolved in contrast to the odes.

But at the same time he has begun to disengage himself from this new style, and to turn to still another, though the fragmentary form of the *Fall of Hyperion*—the revised *Hyperion*—hardly shows it to advantage. For, leaving aside all the psychological difficulties of this impetuous period, he was dealing with a discarded fragment. Little can be said about the style of this recast and warmed-up fragment except about meter and idiom. Stripped of its original allegory, the poem indicts the "dreamer" who makes poetry a means of escape from the concrete world. Keats strips the poem, too, of many of its Miltonic mannerisms. In the place of the grandeur of the first *Hyperion,* we have now a more mellow blank verse, Virgilian and half-pastoral in tone:

> *Still was more plenty than the fabled horn*
> *Thrice emptied could pour forth, at banqueting*
> *For Proserpine return'd to her own fields,*
> *Where the white heifers low.*
>
> I, 35–38

> *When in mid-May the sickening East Wind*
> *Shifts sudden to the South, the small warm rain*
> *Melts out the frozen incense from all flowers.*
>
> I, 97–99

Despite the uncertainty of the poem as a whole, there is a relaxed, even confident, quietness in the opening hundred lines or so of this revision. This opening can be said to suggest a style unlike anything else in the nineteenth century: a style towards which Keats might well have moved —or through which he would have passed to something else—had he continued to write for a few more years. Meanwhile, Keats's last great poem—the ode *To Autumn*—is, of course, a return to the full and dense richness that characterized the great odes of the preceding May, but a richness now harmonized and lifted to a serenity quite unequalled elsewhere in romantic poetry.

6

T H E R A N G E and variety of Keats's style are perhaps greater than can be found in other nineteenth-century English poets. This is a large tribute; the brevity of Keats's career makes it larger. This variety partly explains Keats's continued appeal despite changes of taste during the past century. Victorian poets, for example, could find in Keats a veritable treasure house of the qualities they valued. Even when the romantic emphasis on "suggestiveness" in poetry—on qualities in poetry that will stimulate the imagination into a creative activity of its own—developed into a cult of subjective revery, with the poem serving merely as a backdrop to one's own personal mood, Keats, particularly in the early verse, could furnish the Victorians with as striking a precedent or model as Shelley. More specialized developments in Victorian poetry could find in him an even better stimulus than Wordsworth, Coleridge, Byron, or Shelley. Among two such developments one may mention a tendency—as in Tennyson, or in a different and cruder way, Swinburne—to sacrifice metaphor and concentrated imagery almost completely in order to exploit the musical qualities of verse; and Keats, as was said earlier—though without sacrificing metaphor and image—offers as dexterous and skillful a use of sound, especially in assonance, as can be found in English verse since the beginning of the romantic era. Similarly, the pre-Raphaelites, with their interest in single pictures, and in their effort to string a poem about a set of hangings or tapestries, usually to the neglect of any organic development of the poem as a whole, could find in Keáts better examples to imitate than in any other romantic. Because Keats's images often attain remarkable clarity, as well as the condensation and the suggestive magic that the pre-Raphaelites liked, his poetry, more than that of the other romantics, remained popular with the Imagists when they revolted against pre-Raphaelite vagueness.

In the shift in stylistic taste, of which the revival of metaphysical poetry was a symptom, Keats was left relatively unscathed during the general barrage directed at nineteenth-century poetry. One explanation is the tensely braced and formal tightness of his mature verse, particularly the odes, which is hard to match in other verse of the century. Another is a growing experimental use of disparates and of sketched, suggestive metaphor in his phrasing: "branchèd thoughts, new grown";

lightning viewed as "crooked strings of fire" that "singe away the swollen clouds"; or the now famous cancelled stanza of the *Ode on Melancholy*:

> *Though you should build a bark of dead men's bones,*
> *And rear a phantom gibbet for a mast,*
> *Stitch creeds together for a sail, with groans*
> *To fill it out, blood stainèd and aghast;*
> Although your rudder be a dragon's tail
> Long sever'd, yet still hard with agony . . . .

This active associative suggestion through compressed metaphor, when joined with an emphatic in-feeling that is comparatively weaker in metaphysical poetry, provides us with an idiom that at its best approximates that of Shakespeare. The combination, at least, is rare since Shakespeare.

The point is the variety, and a variety that consists not only in a successive series of styles but also in the diverse appeal of formal and stylistic qualities that are coalesced in the greatest poetry of Keats. It has stood him very well throughout some rather serious changes in stylistic taste during the past century, and throughout the growing, self-conscious fastidiousness that Johnson describes as "elegance refined into impatience." It is possible that what we think of as current tastes in poetry may continue for another generation, further refined. In this case the best of Keats will retain its relevance. But it may be that we are about to undergo another shift, a shift into a new romanticism, more sophisticated, of course, and more formally conscious than the old, but, I can only hope, with equal courage and openness to amplitude of emotion and experience. Indeed it may be a natural human craving for courage and openness, sharpened by long claustrophobia, that will have prodded us into such a shift and sustained it.

Should this be so, it would be difficult to imagine any poet since the mid-seventeenth century who could mean more. The help, the encouragement—the desire of which leads us constantly to reshuffle and re-evaluate our predecessors, when we are not doing so simply as an academic exercise—will not, of course, come from using even the greatest verse of Keats as a model. He that imitates the *Iliad,* said Edward Young, is not imitating Homer. The relevance is in what we catch from the example.

18 | *Keats and His Ideas*

DOUGLAS BUSH

THE ANTI-ROMANTIC reaction of the last few decades left two poets relatively undamaged and even elevated—Blake, who had scarcely attained a secure place in the nineteenth-century hierarchy, and Keats, whom the nineteenth century had taken a long time to recognize in his true colors. The slowness with which the real Keats had emerged was not entirely the fault of poets, critics, and general readers, since they did not have all the materials for a just estimate; in addition to the all-important letters, the revised *Hyperion* was not printed until 1856 and was not generally available until 1867. While Keats's influence on the poetry of the century was probably more constant and conspicuous than that of any other romantic, his personal and poetical reputation underwent perhaps more changes than that of any other. At first his loyal friends propagated the notion that he had been hounded to death by the reviewers, a notion sentimentalized and embalmed in *Adonais* (in our age we may have gone a bit too far in minimizing the effect of the reviews). For some people the picture of a lily-livered aesthete was corrected by Lord Houghton's *Life, Letters, and Literary Remains* (1848), but the Keats of manly strength and sanity was attenuated or distorted through his becoming a tutelary genius of Pre-Raphaelite aestheticism. Then his personal and, less directly, his poetical character suffered again from the publication of the letters to Fanny Brawne, which upset even some of his special admirers. In our time, with a full body of poems and letters, with a better perspective, and with information enlarged in all directions, we think we have arrived at real knowl-

231

edge and understanding of Keats the man, the thinker, and the poet.

At the same time it can hardly be said that modern criticism has reached even a provisional judgment of Keats's poetical stature to which all students would subscribe. In 1925 Amy Lowell's loving, lavish, and amorphous work contributed to our view of the man, but the author's poetical predilections made her unable to see in the poet much more than an early Imagist. In the same year Mr. Murry, in his *Keats and Shakespeare,* so exalted the poet-prophet that—with all the fine insights that have marked his Keatsian criticism in general—he somewhat blurred the difference between the poetry Keats wrote and the Shakespearian kind of poetry he wanted to write. The next year brought a parallel sort of opposition: H. W. Garrod expounded the traditional Keats, the poet of sensuous luxury, and C. D. Thorpe presented the first full and satisfactory analysis of the new philosophic Keats, the deeply thoughtful and troubled student of life and poetry. A partly similar antithesis appears in two large treatments of recent years, N. F. Ford's *The Prefigurative Imagination of John Keats* (1951) and E. R. Wasserman's *The Finer Tone* (1953), although they are allied in their concern with Keats's romantic striving toward a vision beyond mortal limits. For Mr. Ford, Keats's chief poems, from *Endymion* onward, celebrate sexual love and sensuous beauty, immediate sensation being intensified by the ideal of a postmortal elysium in which earthly happiness is repeated in a finer tone; in Mr. Wasserman's subtle and, it must be said, relentless explication of Keats's symbolism, the "finer tone" is so philosophic that even *The Eve of St. Agnes* becomes metaphysical. Recent criticism, less full than the stream of the 1920's and 1930's, has been less concerned with general estimates than with analysis of particular poems, especially the odes. The question of Keats's stature, as I said, remains a question. It is clear that he has had little influence on the most representative modern poetry (though the pioneer Wilfred Owen was a devotee); while the neo-metaphysical poets would not find him usable, the neo-romantics may. On the other hand, some modernist poets and critics, in slighting or damning most of the romantic poets, have paid high tribute to Keats.

This paper is restricted—so far as it is possible to observe the restriction—to a survey of Keats's ideas, and the subject raises a number of related queries. We might ask what "ideas" in poetry are, and we remember that even Matthew Arnold pronounced "For ever wilt thou love, and she be fair" a moral idea. But, if we are not philosophers or aestheticians, it is better to assume that we know what ideas are and to consider more practical matters. Are the ideas in Keats's poetry central in our experience of the poems, or do they have only the historical and peripheral value of explaining elements in poetry that is cherished for quite different reasons? Does Keats's best work give modern readers the total effect of major poetry, or is it superlative minor poetry that stirs only our sensuous faculties, or can we divide it into major and minor on the strength of its ideas? Does his poetry live in itself and speak to us directly, or is it in part sustained by our respect for his personality and the rightness of his self-knowledge and aspirations? Does the poet get into his poetry the realistic experience and understanding of life revealed in the letters, or does he fall short of the full maturity and wisdom of the letter-writer? This paper does not undertake to answer such questions; it cannot do much more than amplify them.

As soon as we try to weigh Keats's aesthetic and philosophical ideas in relation to the poetry, we encounter at least two general elements of complication. One is the obvious fact that he did not start with a full-fledged set of convictions, that both poems and letters are a product and a record of some years of rapid development. The other complication is the no less obvious fact that even in his ripest maturity Keats had not achieved a settled and unified creed but was continually divided against himself. We must take account of both facts, though it involves the repeating of commonplaces.

Some of Keats's central ideas were present, if only in embryo, in his very early verse. The poems of 1814–16, with their frequent symbols of liberty and tyranny, give evidence of a schoolboy liberalism which was only to mature in later years. More important—and heightened by his sense of imprisonment in London and in medical studies— was a devotion to poetry and nature, and an eager recognition of their affinity, that resemble the intoxication of a young man in love with love. In *To George Felton Mathew* (November, 1815) and, with much more fervent elaboration, in *I Stood Tip-Toe* (latter half of 1816), Keats associates classical myth with poetry and nature; for him as for Hunt, myth is partly a Wordsworthian revelation of truth and beauty in nature, partly an ideal version of human experience (which was Wordsworthian too). Although as yet Keats's actual poetic world is mainly one of luxurious sensation and fancy, he is already possessed by the romantic faith in the imagination. Here, and in *Sleep and Poetry* of the same period, the poet, raised above reason through nature and art and the senses, must and can transcend human limitations and "burst our mortal bars." Only once, at this time, does Keats in some sense achieve that goal, in the sonnet on Chapman's *Homer* (October, 1816), which ends with the "gigantic tranquility" of a vision perfectly fulfilled and expressed.

Sleep and Poetry is the first full disclosure of conflicts between Keats's opposed instincts and ambitions. In the same paragraph he would "die a death Of luxury" and also win immortality by seizing like a strong giant "the events of this wide world." Dwelling happily in the realm of Flora and old Pan, he is resolved that he must pass these joys "for a nobler life," where he may find "the agonies, the strife Of human hearts." (The evolution Wordsworth had gone through is self-compulsive anticipation for Keats.) High visions of the mysterious and fearful world of imagination give way to a disillusioned sense of actuality, yet a vast idea rolls before him and he sees "The end and aim of Poesy." Under the banner of Wordsworth, Hunt, and Hazlitt, he attacks the Popeian tradition, but with his own special emphasis—"beauty was awake!" However, as if conscious of reaching beyond his grasp, Keats subsides, in the rest of the poem, into the untroubled pleasures of friendship and Hunt's pictures. But later, in the spring of 1817, art and nature of a less merely sensuous kind arouse partly parallel tensions: the grandeur of the Elgin Marbles brings home to him the heavy weight of mortality, and both they and the sea become symbols of an inspiring if unattainable beauty and greatness.

The ideas so far observed have been expressed in Keats's verse. When we follow the letters, meagre at first, up to the completion of *Endymion* (November, 1817), we find some more or less similar and some new attitudes. Haydon's resolute loyalty to his art in the face of difficulty draws an echo from Keats,[1] and that conviction is to be reaffirmed and enlarged, under the growing stress of experience, in many subsequent letters. In this same letter (May 10–11, 1817), Keats would like to think of Shakespeare as his tutelary genius; he is conscious of a horrid morbidity of temperament; and he sees the sun, moon, stars, and earth "as materials to form greater things—that is to say ethereal things." The sense of mortality is oppressive (55, 60); life is "a continual struggle against the suffocation of accidents" (59). In the notable

---

[1] *Letters of John Keats,* ed. Maurice B. Forman, 4th edition (Oxford University Press, 1952), p. 28. Hereafter page numbers in this edition are indicated in parentheses in the text.

letter to Bailey of November 22, 1817, when *Endymion* is done, we have the first enunciation of the doctrine of negative capability (though it is not so named until December 21), and the first clear statement, a very strong and all-comprehending statement, of Keats's conception of poetry and life:

> I am certain of nothing but of the holiness of the Heart's affections and the truth of Imagination—What the imagination seizes as Beauty must be truth—whether it existed before or not—for I have the same Idea of all our Passions as of Love they are all in their sublime, creative of essential Beauty. (67)

For evidence of this "favorite Speculation"—a main tenet of European romanticism—he refers to the first book of *Endymion* and the ode to Sorrow of the fourth book; and he cites Adam's dream ("he awoke and found it truth"). Then comes "O for a Life of Sensations rather than of Thoughts"—that is, "O for the life of the artist rather than of the consecutive logical thinker." As artist, Keats can live in the moment, in the setting sun or in the sparrow picking about the gravel. But the next sentence brings him to the resources of the human spirit in meeting misfortune.

Explicit or implicit in this famous letter are some of Keats's enduring articles of faith and also some of his central tensions or "unreconciled opposites." If we put the letter beside the just completed *Endymion,* it is perhaps not too much to say that the brief piece of prose is, as a statement of ideas, more arresting than the diffuse and wayward poem. For *Endymion* reflects not so much the fruitful pressure of conflicting and equally realized impulses, but the confusion that results from half-unconscious instincts breaking through a self-imposed and only half-realized ideal. The "Platonic" idealism of Keats's parable, the idea that the way to the One lies through loving apprehension of the Many, was a sincere conviction, but his metaphysical notion of unity or reality was much less real than his sensuous response to the actual and concrete (which is not to deny, with N. F. Ford, the allegorical intention). Keats conceives of Beauty, but he loves particular beauties, natural and erotic. The final identifying of Cynthia with the Indian maid is an equation in Platonic algebra, not an experience; and the handling of this climactic incident has far less authenticity than *Endymion's* moods of disillusionment in his quest of the Ideal. In the "Hymn to Pan," though Keats has some feeling for the One or the All, the strength of the Hymn is rather in its catalogue of particulars. The episodes of Alpheus and Arethusa and of the reviving of young lovers are romantically decorative and inadequate examples of humanitarian "friendship" and service. And while, according to the letter to Bailey, the "Ode to Sorrow" is intended to illustrate the belief that "all our Passions," as well as love, are "in their sublime, creative of essential Beauty," the Ode is too merely pretty (and, in the Bacchic pageant, too merely pictorial) to fulfill any such intention. In short, the young poet's sensuous and erotic instincts are much stronger than his Platonic instincts; and *Endymion* is assuredly an uncertain "first Step towards the chief attempt in the Drama—the playing of different Natures with Joy and Sorrow" (90; January 30, 1818).

A large proportion of Keats's great utterances on poetry and life are contained in the letters of 1818, and we may, abandoning chronology, recall some of them. The general axioms set forth in the letter to Taylor of February 27 (107) are ideals that Keats says he has not yet attained: namely, that "Poetry should surprise by a fine excess and not by Singularity"; that "Its touches of Beauty should never be half way," that they should leave the reader not breathless but filled with a luxurious content; and "That if Poetry comes not as naturally as the Leaves to a tree it had better not come at all." Such axioms are more or less alien from those of most modern poets, but, since they fit more or less perfectly the finest poems Keats was to write, we can only say that the house of poetry has many mansions.

Other principles, no less axiomatic for Keats, are often affirmed in other letters. One prime essential is intensity (Keats's striving, by every technical means, toward that complex end has been concretely demonstrated by W. J. Bate). Yet intensity seems to operate on such different planes that in itself it carries only an elementary criterion of value. In December, 1817, Keats had invoked *King Lear* as a great example of the intensity that is "the excellence of every Art" and is "capable of making all disagreeables evaporate, from their being in close relationship with Beauty and Truth" (70). We might accept that as an informal and incomplete but incontrovertible statement of aesthetic theory. In his letter, however, Keats had just been complaining, in a manner hardly preparatory for *Lear,* that West's picture had "nothing to be intense upon; no women one feels mad to kiss, no face swelling into reality." Then in January, 1818, sitting down to read *King Lear* once again, Keats could feel "the fierce dispute, Betwixt Hell torment [later "damnation"] and impassion'd Clay"—and in February he could begin such a decorative tissue of romantic pathos as *Isabella*.

Throughout 1818—though not so much of course in the accounts of the Scottish tour—the letters, and some poems copied in the letters, reveal positive or conflicting attitudes that are characteristic of Keats's mature view of himself, the world, and poetry. He recognizes the mixture of beauty and cruelty in nature, the mixture of good and evil in men, the superiority of disinterested goodness to works of genius, the necessity and the moral benefits of facing pain and trouble. As artist he fluctuates—and is aware of his fluctuations—between belief in the poetic efficacy of a wise passiveness, of sensuous and imaginative receptivity, and belief in the active pursuit of rational knowledge and philosophy. Some of these ideas get full expression in the letter to Reynolds of May 3, 1818. Here Keats sees all departments of knowledge as "excellent and calculated towards a great whole"; knowledge reduces a thinking man's heat and fever, eases the burden of the mystery, and strengthens the soul, though perhaps it may not "console us for the death of a friend and the ill 'that flesh is heir to.' " There follows the fragment of an ode to Maia, which is hardly a plea for philosophic knowledge. Then comes the extended comparison of Wordsworth and Milton. In the Keatsian hierarchy Shakespeare was of course the great exemplar of the supreme poetic endowment and attitude, negative capability, while Wordsworth and Milton were the great exemplars of poetry with a purpose and a message (and both had the attraction, for a young poet, of being more imitable than Shakespeare). Keats finds—if one may go on summarizing the familiar—greater concern with humanity and the human heart in Wordsworth than in Milton, though the fact testifies less to greater individual power than to a general march of intellect. (Keats's comments on Milton show, not unnaturally, no modern comprehension of Milton's thought and themes.) He speaks also of the axioms in philosophy that must be proved upon our pulses, of the wisdom that comes only from sorrow (and the skeptic in him adds that that may be folly). Finally, there is the account of the several chambers in the mansion of life, "the infant or thoughtless Chamber," "the Chamber of Maiden-Thought," where pleasant wonders become darkened by a sense of human misery and heartbreak—the point Wordsworth had reached in *Tintern Abbey*. But against this steadily deepening awareness of human suffering might be set such a remark as this, inspired by northern scenes: "they can never fade away—they make one forget the divisions of life; age, youth, poverty and riches; and refine one's sensual vision into a sort of north star which can never cease to be open lidded and stedfast over the wonders of the great Power" (154). At moments the senses can reconcile what the mind and the heart cannot.

In the many letters that come after this time, most of the critical and ethical ideas are reaffirmations, with similar or altered focus and emphasis, of those already encountered. The impersonal, non-moral imagination of the poet of negative capability is opposed to "the words-worthian or egotistical sublime" (226–27; October 27, 1818). This universally sympathetic and creative power is associated sometimes with particular objects and experiences, sometimes with "the mighty abstract Idea . . . of Beauty in all things" (239; October, 1818). "I never can feel certain of any truth but from a clear perception of its Beauty" (258; December, 1818). Keats summarizes Hazlitt on the non-moral character of the poetic imagination as differing from pure reason and the moral sense. Even the cruelty of a beast, or a quarrel in the street, may give pleasure, because the imagination enjoys excitement and energy, "the sense of power abstracted from the sense of good" (307–9, 315–17; March, 1819). But while the hawk and the stoat fulfill their predatory instincts, man is capable of the disinterested goodness that was supremely manifested in Socrates and Jesus; there is a continual birth of new heroism among human creatures. The working of human energies and human reasonings, though erroneous, may be fine, and in this consists poetry, though it is thereby less fine than philosophy, as an eagle is less fine than a truth (316). Keats lays much stress on enduring the buffets of the world, a theme that is elaborated in the picture of life and its adversities as a "vale of Soul-making" (334; April, 1819). This idea seems to be the very opposite of negative capability, since the chameleon poet has no identity, no ethical character, whereas men are not souls "till they acquire identities, till each one is personally itself." In this view of life as a series of trials Keats finds "a system of Salvation" more rational and acceptable than the Christian. Though he can still wonder more and more at Shakespeare and *Paradise Lost,* and "look upon fine Phrases like a Lover" (368), he still ranks fine doing above fine writing (373). Then comes a reaction against Milton that leads to the abandoning of the second *Hyperion,* a recoil from Miltonic "art" to "other sensations" (384, 425; September, 1819).

These have been scanty reminders of the growth and recurrence of some leading aesthetic and ethical ideas in Keats's letters, and we must observe, with equal brevity, how far they are embodied in the mature poems. Of the first *Hyperion* it is perhaps safe to say that—in spite of difficulties that critics have inclined to overlook—we comprehend intellectually, and in some degree emotionally, the ethical-aesthetic theme, but that the poem's chief power over us comes rather from the inlaid beauties of image and phrase and rhythm. For we are hardly stirred more by the sorrows of the fallen Titans than we are by such pictures as that of the dreaming oaks; even these incidental, "non-human" images refine "our sensual vision into a sort of north star." Oceanus' speech is certainly Keats's own testimony to the principle of beauty and the grand march of intellect in human history. The beauty, however, that Oceanus has beheld in the young god of the sea, and that Clymene has heard in the music of the Apollo who is not yet a god, seems to be beauty in the conventional romantic sense, the sense that it frequently bears in the letters. Yet Keats had quite early evolved the larger and deeper conception of beauty created by all our passions in their sublime, that is, a vision, refined by intense apprehension, of all the varied and painful stuff of actual life. It is of course the attainment, through Mnemosyne, of this vision of suffering that makes Apollo a god, a "soul," a true poet. Oceanus had approached that idea—

> O folly! for to bear all naked truths,
> And to envisage circumstance, all calm,
> That is the top of sovereignty—

but he had done so only parenthetically, as a prelude to the delivery of bad news, and that was not the theme of his speech. The speech as a whole might be said to represent the young Keats, Apollo's deification the mature Keats; and—granted that Apollo's "Knowledge enormous" takes in the downfall of the Titans—the fragmentary poem really establishes no substantial connection between the aesthetic or romantic and the ethical or tragic ideals of beauty. Nor is Keats able to dramatize Apollo's passing through the Chamber of Maiden-Thought and the vale of soul-making; his transformation is simply asserted.[2]

The total effect of *The Eve of St. Agnes* is in a way not unlike

---

[2] Although the two *Hyperions* have been relatively neglected in recent criticism, one may refer to Kenneth Muir's perceptive study in *Essays in Criticism*, II (1952), 54–75.

that of *Hyperion*. The theme—if we hesitate to climb all the rungs of Mr. Wasserman's metaphysical ladder—is young love in a world of hostility and age and death, but we are no more, and perhaps less, moved by the young lovers' feelings than we are by the sculptured dead in icy hoods and mails, the colored window, and a hundred other incidental items in the romantic setting, items of material, sensuous empathy. One is reluctant even to hint at disparagement of a uniquely rich and magical tapestry, and yet one remembers that comment on Robert Burton's account of love which might seem to have come from another man: Keats sees "the old plague spot; the pestilence, the raw scrofula" in the human mingling of "goatish winnyish lustful love with the abstract adoration of the deity." [3] Although Mr. Wasserman's view of *The Eve of St. Agnes* is not incompatible with Mr. Gittings' realistic —and dubious—argument for its genesis in the poet's having an affair with Isabella Jones, we may, looking only at the poem, see it as an example of romantic idealism shunning the inward troubles of "impassion'd clay."

The great odes of the spring were variations on one theme, a theme complex enough as Keats consciously conceived it and further complicated and intensified by his half-unconscious doubts of his own aesthetic resolution. The *Ode to Psyche* is devoid of explicit "ideas," except as its animating idea is the power of the imagination to preserve and transmute direct sensuous experience. That theme causes no conflict in *Psyche;* but conflict is central in the *Nightingale* and the *Grecian Urn.* In these two odes Keats feels not so much the joy of the imaginative experience as the painful antithesis between transient sensation and enduring art. He cannot wholly accept his own argument, because both his heart and his senses are divided. The power of the imagination, the immortality of art, offer no adequate recompense for either the fleeting joys or the inescapable pains of mortality. Keats's early desire to burst our mortal bars, to transcend the limitations of human understanding, becomes in the *Nightingale* the desire for death, the highest sensation, or an anguished awareness of the gulf between life and death. In the end the imagination cannot escape from oppressive actuality; far from attaining a vision of ultimate truth, it achieves only a momentary illusion.

In the *Grecian Urn,* the sensations evoked are almost wholly con-

[3] *Complete Works of John Keats*, ed. H. B. Forman (Glasgow, 1900–1901), III, 268.

cerned with young love (the great fourth stanza is logically a digression), and again Keats cannot convince himself that love and beauty on marble are better than flesh-and-blood experience, however brief and unhappy that may be. It is the underlying lack of satisfaction that inspires the unrelated picture of the little town, for ever empty of humanity, a picture almost forced upon the poet, as it were, by his recognition of the negative side of his theme. But he overrides his emotional skepticism (though it comes up again in "Cold Pastoral"), and ends with the positive statement of his most famous "idea," a statement that has been much questioned on the score of both meaning and artistic propriety. The meaning (and the meaning of similar utterances in the letters) may be simpler than some of the explanations of it. In a world of inexplicable mystery and pain, the experience of beauty is the one sure revelation of reality; beauty lives in particulars, and these pass, but they attest a principle, a unity, behind them. And if beauty is reality, the converse is likewise true, that reality, the reality of intense human experience, of suffering, can also yield beauty, in itself and in art. This is central in the poet's creed, if not all explicit in this poem, yet the undercurrent here prevents the urn's assertion from being the Q.E.D. it is intended to be. If the *Grecian Urn* and the *Nightingale* rise above *Psyche* and *Melancholy,* the reason is not only their artistic superiority but the complexity of their unresolved tensions. They were begun, so to speak, by the poet of sensuous luxury, but were taken over by the poet who had learned on his pulses the knowledge given to Apollo and could not escape from it.

Lamia, written in the late summer of this year, is, like *The Eve of St. Agnes,* a highly decorative story of romantic love, with a difference. The emotional simplicity of a tale of happy fruition has given place to a mixture of passion, dissonance, and tragedy; Romeo and Juliet have become, in a sense, Troilus and Cressida. *Lamia* is Keats's only completed poem that has caused real disagreement in regard to its theme and intention. To group various interpretations (some of them rendered in concretely and impossibly allegorical terms), *Lamia* is (1) a literal romantic narrative, with ethical overtones perhaps but with no general parable, a poem in which Keats was concentrating his forces on technique and popular appeal; (2) a condemnation of cold philosophic reason; (3) a condemnation of feeling and the senses; (4) a condemnation of a divorce between reason and feeling; (5) an incoherent expression of Keats's unresolved conflicts, emotional and philosophical; (6) a contrast between the immortal and perfect love of Hermes and the nymph and the mortal, imperfect love of Lycius and Lamia. It is assuredly not easy to harmonize the implicit or explicit contradictions in both the narrative and the author's comments within the poem, and inner conflicts that had troubled Keats before had lately been heightened by the course of his passion for Fanny Brawne and the problems of his mind and career. Keats had long had ambivalent feelings toward women and love, and "Bright star" and *The Eve of St. Agnes* had been quickly followed by *La Belle Dame sans Merci;* as poet, he had long fluctuated between the ideals of sensation and thought and between the ideals of poetic contemplation and humanitarian action. If we see in *Lamia* the condemnation of a sensuous dreamer (to put "the moral" crudely), we feel more sure of our ground because of our external knowledge of his ethical growth and his state of mind. Lycius' quest has stopped far short of Endymion's, and the beauty he embraces is sterile and corrupt. But does the poem, as a statement of its theme (whatever we take that to be), really come home to us, or does it remain mere romantic narrative and picture-making, on a lower level for the most part than *Hyperion* and *The Eve of St. Agnes?*

Keats's last important poems sharply define his poetic dilemma. There could scarcely be a greater contrast than there is between *To Autumn* (September 19, 1819) and *The Fall of Hyperion.* *To Autumn* is Keats's most perfect poem, but it has none of the tensions of the *Nightingale* and the *Grecian Urn.* Critics have said that the rich serenity of the ode has been "earned," in the sense that it finally composes and transcends its author's inner turmoil. The verdict, however, seems to depend more on biography than on the poem itself, and might equally well be rendered—if we look only at the poetic texts—in regard to the fragmentary ode to Maia, which was written at the beginning of Keats's troubled maturity. *To Autumn* does embody acceptance of the process of fruition and decay, yet can we extend that idea—as Keats does not—from the life of nature to the life of man? While the poem is the product of his ripest art, it expresses a recurrent mood; it is less a resolution of the perplexities of life and poetic ambition than an escape into the luxury of pure—if now sober—sensation.

That the ode was not a final resolution is made clear by the revised *Hyperion.* The *Fall*—on the one hand a new experiment in technique, a partial exchange of Milton for Dante—is Keats's last confessional poem, a last desperate effort to define the nature and function of poetry and his own position. The poem is much more difficult to interpret in detail than the odes, though recent criticism has largely neglected explication. After three years of experience and mature thought Keats is returning to the problem set forth in *Sleep and Poetry,* a problem which then had been mainly of the future but had, with increasing complexity and intensity, disturbed him ever since. In the simplest terms, there is the question of poetry versus humanitarian action, and —even if we exclude the cancelled lines—the question of the humanitarian poet versus "the dreamer." The poet of the *Fall*—there is no longer the *persona* of Apollo—is allowed to gain the height reserved for

> *those to whom the miseries of the world*
> *Are misery, and will not let them rest.*

But, he asks, since there are thousands of such, why is he here alone? The others, says Moneta, are not poets, visionaries and "dreamers weak," but active servants of humanity who do not desire or need to come. What benefit can poets do to the great world? Other men have their work, "sublime or low"; each has his distinct joys and distinct pains;

> *Only the dreamer venoms all his days,*
> *Bearing more woe than all his sins deserve.*

Is Keats saying that the poet of negative capability, who lives all men's lives, is subject to a curse, a futile fever of the imagination remote from normal, healthy life?

The debate is not directly continued—unless we admit the cancelled lines, which attempt to distinguish between the true poet and the dreamer—but something like a final answer is given through what the narrator discerns in Moneta's unveiled face and eyes,

> *a wan face*
> *Not pined by human sorrows, but bright-blanch'd*
> *By an immortal sickness which kills not;*
> *It works a constant change, which happy death*
> *Can put no end to; deathwards progressing*
> *To no death was that visage; it had past*
> *The lily and the snow . . . .*

Here, or in the whole episode, seem to be concentrated, and perhaps reconciled on a new plane, some of Keats's central perplexities—the fluidity of experience and the enduring truth of art; a vision of life that embraces but transcends all suffering, that unifies all diverse and limited human judgments *sub specie aeternitatis;* the supreme sensation and insight of death without death itself. Moneta's face and eyes reflect, in calm benignity, the knowledge that had rushed upon Apollo, and Keats is reaffirming the godlike supremacy of the poetic vision, but his conception has risen above mere negative capability to what suggests, to one critic [4] at least, Christ taking upon himself the sorrows of the world.

Whether or not Keats had thus moved toward the Christian "idea," at any rate his poetic criteria, which had never been low, had reached a level where not a great deal of the world's poetry could pass the test. There is no question of the modern validity of many of his aesthetic principles and observations, since many of his phrases have become part of our critical language. And, as parallels to his doctrine of negative capability, for example, we might recall Mr. Eliot's emphasis on the impersonality of the artist, or Yeats's "intellectual innocence." As for Keats himself, it may be added, it is not clear, at least to me, how far he had succeeded, or would have succeeded, in harmonizing his conception of negative capability, of the amoral artist, with his conception of the soul's need of acquiring, through the trials of experience, a positive ethical identity—and here we might recall Yeats's posing of "the choice" between "Perfection of the life, or of the work."

Even if in the *Fall of Hyperion* Keats was not repudiating much of himself, he leaves us uncertain about his final judgment of his own poetry. Our concern here has been with his ideas, and his poetry would be exactly what it is if all the letters had been lost. Some of his ideas and problems are directly embodied in the poems, sometimes they are between the lines, sometimes—as in *To Autumn*—they are temporarily forgotten or put aside. But their positive or negative importance is great. For most readers and some critics Keats remains a poet of miraculous sensuous apprehension and magical expression, and in much or most of his poetry his negative capability seems to stop well short of Shakespearian exploration of life and man, to be mainly confined to aesthetic sensation and intuition. But even if we share that conventional estimate, we must say that his poetry is not all of a piece. Keats's Shakespearian or humanitarian ambitions, his critical and self-critical insights, his acute awareness of the conditions enveloping the modern poet, his struggles toward a vision that would comprehend all experience, joy and suf-

[4] D. G. James, *The Romantic Comedy* (London: Oxford University Press, 1948), pp. 149–50.

fering, the natural and the ideal, the transient and the eternal—all this made him capable of greater poetry than he actually wrote, and makes him, more than his fellow romantics, our contemporary. And if these "ideas" did not get into his poems very often or very far, their overshadowing presence distinguishes his major from his minor achievements. Though his poetry in general was in some measure limited and even weakened by the romantic preoccupation with "beauty," his finest writing is not merely beautiful, because he had seen "the boredom, and the horror" as well as "the glory."

The Artistry of Keats:

19 | A Modern Tribute

CLEANTH BROOKS

MODERN CRITICISM is intimately bound up with the rediscovery of the poetry of John Donne and with a restatement of the virtues of metaphysical poetry. There have been bitter observations to the effect that modern criticism has been concerned only with those virtues and that it deliberately refuses to see any virtue elsewhere. The modern critic, so the charge runs, is on principle anti-Romantic. The charge is unfair, as an examination of the writings of the modern critics will speedily show. But in view of its alleged bias, it ought to be interesting to see what modern criticism has to say about the poetry of John Keats.

One point becomes immediately clear: John Keats is not one of the villains of modern criticism. Richard Fogle, in his recent defense of Keats and Shelley against the attack of the modern critics, found, when he came to Keats, comparatively little to confute. The last chapter of his book turns out to be quite simply a defense of Shelley. With the adequacy of that defense, I am not concerned here, though the differentiation that recent critics have made—consciously or unconsciously —between Keats and Shelley may have its own significance.

My second point is less obvious—or rather this second point is not so much a historical observation as a prophecy: the Keats of the Odes may well prove to be one of the heroes of modernist criticism. If the reader considers this to be hardly praise—as if Keats's merits had to wait upon their recognition by the critics of the present day—I am cheerfully ready to agree. There is a sense in which no critical system is finally important. One may concede this, and concede further that

246

criticism itself is judged and validated by its ability to recognize the fact of great poetry (though *what* is great poetry, we must never forget, is determined by an act of criticism). But I repeat my concession: for my concern here is not to vindicate the modern critics but to pay tribute to the artistry of Keats.

T. S. Eliot, in an essay that has been important for the development of modern criticism, characterized Donne's poetry as revealing the intellect at the tips of the senses. "A thought to Donne was an experience. It modified his sensibility."

What is important in this statement is the assertion of an integration of intellect and emotion—not the fact that Eliot makes *intellect* his first term, *senses*, his second. In describing the later poetry of Keats, *senses* will inevitably be our primary term. Critics have always emphasized Keats's sensuousness. But the connection between the senses and the intellect is there, and in the great poems, it amounts to an integration. In view of the poetry of the Odes, one could just reverse Eliot's suggested image of the intellect extended to the very nerve ends: with Keats, the nerve ends maintain contact with the intellect itself.

Put in this way, the concept may not seem very helpful. Isn't every true poet possessed of quick senses which are duly related to a central nervous system? And besides, didn't Keats himself see in the intellect an obstacle to the life of the imagination, complaining that "the dull brain perplexes and retards"? Yet Keats values knowledge, and for Keats the intensity of experience is not a blind blotting out of consciousness but a means of attaining knowledge—though a knowledge which transcends that accorded to the dull brain. Keats cultivates— almost like a connoisseur—"the wakeful anguish of the soul." No phrase is more characteristic of Keats. He refuses to drug it into insensibility —even in the *Ode to a Nightingale* where the heartache begins as a "drowsy numbness." The soul insists upon remaining awake and trying to understand its anguish, and indeed using its anguish as a means to understanding itself.

The foregoing comments, however, will hardly serve to pin down the basic matter in question: the specific sense in which Keats may be said to integrate intellect and emotion in his poetry. Perhaps the best way into the matter is through consideration of the central themes of the Odes. Take the theme of joy in beauty and melancholy at the loss of beauty. Keats is concerned with "Beauty that must die" (*Melancholy*), with Beauty caught and fixed by art (*Urn*), with Beauty that is transitory, yet apparently immortal (*Nightingale*). Logic and the dull brain would have it that the nightingale, though felt by the hearer in the Ode to be an immortal bird, is simply another instance of Beauty that must die. The nightingale, to be sure, may be abstracted from the transitory world of nature by the process of art. It might, for example, have been pictured on the urn, along with the happy boughs or the heifer lowing at the skies, but its immortality in that case would be the heavily qualified immortality of the other objects that go to make up the "cold pastoral." And in its duller moments the brain might propose additional difficulties: if unheard melodies are actually sweeter than heard melodies, how can the heard music of the nightingale move as it does move the hearer in the Ode? There, it is a kind of ecstatic culmination.

Our best counsel is not to ignore tactfully the apparent intellectual inconsistencies. It is rather to pursue vigorously the dialectic of the poetry. If we do so, we shall find that Keats's thinking is as acute and as responsible as any other poetic thinking—that, indeed, the thinking-through-images has gone beyond—not fallen below—such logic as the dull brain can manage.

Consider a relatively easy example. Keats's "April shroud" in the *Ode on Melancholy* is as characteristic of Keats as Donne's more celebrated shroud is characteristic of Donne. First of all, it is an *April* shroud, and the associations of joy and fruitfulness clash sharply with the more somber associations of the grave clothes. But the phrase is not merely a showy but incidental flourish of rhetoric. The "weeping cloud" covers the "green hill" with an April shroud, and the descent of the cloud is used to describe the falling of the "melancholy fit." But such a description argues that the melancholy is fruitful as well as sad. It catches up the references to "droop-headed flowers" fostered by the rain, to the "globèd peonies," and finally by implication, to the mistress herself, ultimate type of April and fruitfulness. Moreover, the phrase "April shroud" is already preparing for the collocation of joy and melancholy. The two are indissolubly joined. In our mortal world, birth and death are necessary to each other, and the taste of joy's grape, to the finer palate, has in it the most exquisite bitterness of melancholy. The phrase "aching pleasure" (line 23) points toward the same conclusion. Is an aching intensity of pleasure, pleasurable at all? It is and it is not. In any case, such pleasure is aching for its fulfillment, which is its obliteration in the love-death—an anticipation of death itself.

In the *Ode to a Nightingale,* this doubleness of death receives the most brilliant treatment that Keats ever gave it. Death is a horrible dissolution and falling away, but it is also the climax of ecstasy. It is alienation and separation but it is also integration and fulfillment.

The bird was not born for death. It cannot *know* what man, whose thoughts are from the beginning filled with a consciousness of impending death, cannot refuse to know. Lacking man's foreknowledge, merged in nature, the bird can express the wholeness of nature and can, in the poet's mind, itself participate in the unwearied immortality of nature. Man's self-consciousness is at once man's glory and his curse. It cuts him off from nature but this very detachment from nature makes it possible for him to *see* nature as a total thing, harmonious and beautiful.

I have elsewhere dealt in detail with this poem. In this brief note I have space for only one or two examples of the part separate words and images play in building up the dialectical structure of the poem.

In the fifth stanza, death is suggested: the darkness in which the flowers are invisible, among them the violets which are "fast fading"— and most resonant of all, there is the word *embalmèd.* Yet the imagined scene carries no overtones of sterility and coldness—no hint of "deadness." The "incense" is that of living flowers—the place is a place of growth and birth—of the "coming musk-rose," "mid-May's eldest child." The stanza looks forward to "Now more than ever seems it rich to die" in the following stanza, and helps to interpret it.

How different in tone are the references to death earlier in the poem—"Where palsy shakes a few, sad, last gray hairs"—or later, when the poem has come full circle, where the song of the bird is finally *"buried* deep in the next valley-glades."

Or consider a related theme as carried by the light-dark imagery of the poem and focused on the word *fade.* The speaker's desire is for a breaking down of the distinctions such as the dull brain interposes between man and nature. He would "fade away into the forest dim"; he would "Fade far away, dissolve, and quite forget" what he as man knows but what the bird has never known. The process of dissolution is suggested by the imagined movement away from the world of clear outlines and sharply drawn distinctions into a world of shadows and darkness. The nightingale sings in a plot of "shadows numberless." As he moves toward imaginative identification with the nightingale, he moves into a region of "verdurous glooms" and into the "embalmèd darkness." His fading into the forest dim is a merging of himself with the world of nature, but the price is death—felt as a rich consummation as he listens "darkling," but seen in its bleak and chilling aspect at the end of the Ode when the "plaintive anthem fades" and is "buried." He would fade into the bird's song, but at the end, it is the bird's song that fades away from him.

In the *Ode on a Grecian Urn,* attention is focused upon a different kind of immortality and a different conception of integrated wholeness. The nightingale—part of the world of becoming—though it will die, was "not born to die"—lives without consciousness of death. The figures on the urn were not born at all—are as dead as the deadest stone, and yet in a sense are alive as their flesh-and-blood counterparts cannot be alive. Their alienation from the process of becoming is the very means to the wholeness and fullness of being that they possess. The urn baffles the dull brain as the song of the nightingale baffles it: it teases us "out of thought."

Both nature and art, as Keats contemplates them in the Odes, insist upon the human predicament. Man is involved in nature and yet through his consciousness transcends nature. He cannot accept birth and death as inseparable parts of a total process without being reminded that he too is involved in the process, his very organs of perception and awareness "fastened to a dying animal," and if he would fix his vision of totality beyond the flux of change, it is only by some such act as that of freezing it in cold marble, itself lifeless. To immerse oneself in the flux of change is to forfeit knowledge of it. Immersion in nature is a dissolution of the self which ends in lack of consciousness: "To thy high requiem become a sod." To detach oneself from the process in pure contemplation ends in the contemplation of changeless but lifeless stone.

Keats, by the way, would not be in the least shocked by E. E. Cummings' lines that state: "A pretty girl that naked is/Is worth a million statues." The *Ode on a Grecian Urn,* so different in tone from Cummings' admirable little poem, has absorbed and digested into itself that, among other related notions. The Odes are tough-minded, not soft and self-indulgent or prettified or—as Cummings' Bowery tough would put it—fancy. They deal an even-handed justice between the claims for the pretty girl that naked is and for the marble maidens that embellish the urn.

I have studiously avoided using such terms as paradox and irony, not because I do not think that these terms fully apply, but because these terms have raised so much opposition among the lovers of Romantic poetry that I do not want to risk obscuring my point. It is the point that is important—not the terms as such. In the Odes there is an integration of intellect and emotion. Form *is* meaning. The thinking goes on through the images and receives its precise definition and qualification from the images.

This last generalization is a conclusion to which I, at least, have not come speedily or easily. I must apologize for past blunderings and misreadings, occasions on which I felt that Keats was confused or careless and that his images were used as mere surface decoration. But the blunders have turned out to be my own, not the poet's, and even Keats's apparently casual choice of a word has usually vindicated itself.

Is one to say, then, that Keats was a monster of prevision, carefully working out the intellectual ramifications of his poems, adjusting this image and that to the precise development of a preconceived intellectual scheme? Not at all, though in view of what we know of Keats's revisions, few will want to insist upon the hypothesis that he composed hastily and unthinkingly. But I have no theory to offer concerning Keats's psychology of composition. My case for the intricate coherency of the Odes is based upon the texts of the poems themselves. What I think we can say—and probably must say—is this: that the imagery, however spontaneously it may have come to Keats's mind, was shaped, consciously or unconsciously, by that mind to a precision that is beautifully exact. The poems seem to me inexhaustibly rich. Even if the sensuous detail was the conscious preoccupation of the poet, the detail as given is more than that: it teases us *into* thought—not into vague ruminations, but into amazingly precise and profound thinking about the nature of man. Donne could say "This ecstasy doth unperplex . . . and tell us what our souls are." Keats's celebrations of ecstasy are no mere swoonings: they "unperplex" us in the same fashion.

Keats's Thought: A Discovery of Truth

20

J. MIDDLETON MURRY

THE MOST characteristic movement of Keats's thought first appears distinctly in a letter to Bailey of November 22, 1817. Bailey had been deeply offended by a letter from Haydon. Keats, without any intention of criticizing Bailey, told him that after three days' acquaintance with Haydon, he knew his character well enough not to be surprised or shocked by such a letter; nor was it a matter of principle with him, when he did know Haydon's character, to drop his acquaintance, though with Bailey it would have been "an imperious feeling." He goes on to distinguish between the man of Genius and the man of Character: the man of Genius has not "any individuality, any determined character," or "proper self." He has only lately come to understand this, and the understanding has increased his "humility and capability of submission." How entirely sincere he was in this is evident from the fact that he is claiming no superiority for the man of Genius over the man of Character. On the contrary, he is deliberately setting Bailey's character above his own.

He then declares: "I am certain of nothing but of the holiness of the heart's affections and the truth of the imagination." In trying to expound what he means by the latter, he explains that he is "the more zealous in this affair because I have never yet been able to perceive how anything can be known for truth by consecutive reasoning. Can it be that even the greatest philosopher arrived at his goal without putting aside numerous objections? However it may be, O for a life of sensations rather than of thoughts!"

After this letter, the main lines of this pattern of thinking recur continually in Keats's letters. A month later (December 21, 1817), as the result of a conversation with Dilke, he identifies the quality which goes "to form a man of achievement, especially in literature, and which Shakespeare possessed so enormously—I mean, *Negative Capability*, that is, when a man is capable of being in uncertainties, mysteries, doubts, without any irritable reaching after fact and reason." This, he says, "pursued through volumes would perhaps take us no further than this that with a great poet . . . the sense of beauty obliterates all consideration."

Two years later, as the result of a speculation on Dilke's character, he comes to the conclusion that Dilke is "a man who cannot feel he has a personal identity unless he has made up his mind about everything. The only means of strengthening one's intellect is to make up one's mind about nothing—to let the mind be a thoroughfare for all thoughts. Not a select party . . . Dilke will never come at a truth so long as he lives, because he is always trying at it." That was on September 24, 1819, when the *Ode to Autumn* was written and Keats's brief and dazzling poetic life was virtually over. Halfway between that moment and that of the letter to Bailey is the declaration to his brother George: "I can never feel certain of any truth but from a clear perception of its beauty"; and that to Woodhouse: "As to the poetical character itself (I mean that sort of which, If I am anything, I am a member . . .) it is not itself—it has no self—it is everything and nothing—it has not character—it enjoys light and shade; it lives in gusto, be it foul or fair, high or low, rich or poor, mean or elevated— it has as much delight in conceiving an Iago as an Imogen. What shocks the virtuous philosopher delights the chameleon poet. It does no harm from its relish of the dark side of things, any more than from its taste for the bright one; because they both end in speculation" (October 27, 1818).

This is not the occasion to trace in detail the growth and development of this body of thought. One can only emphasize a few of its important peculiarities. The chief, perhaps, of these is that it is not, in the ordinary sense of the word, a body of *thought* at all. Keats is aware of this from the beginning. Not only does he declare for "a life of sensations rather than of thoughts"; but he asserts that he has never been able to understand how truth could be reached by consecutive reasoning.

But by "sensations" Keats means something very different from what is ordinarily understood by that word. "Sensations" include two at first sight unrelated experiences: first, the "affections of the heart," which are sacred; and, second, the perceptions of beauty by the imagination, which, he says, must be truth.

To take the second first. Keats asks: Can the greatest philosopher—the master of consecutive reasoning—arrive at his goal, which is truth, without having to put aside numerous objections? By this he means that consecutive reasoning depends on the continual elimination of one term of a contradiction. How can that lead to truth, when reality is full of contradictions? This criticism of philosophy he develops shortly afterwards into his doctrine of Negative Capability. The imagination accepts the contradictions of reality, and finds beauty in their co-existence: and this discovered beauty is the sign of truth.

This metaphysical doctrine of Keats has a manifest ethical corollary. One must be patient and submissive towards the vagaries of one's fellow men. No more than the law of contradiction can be imposed on the large universe of experience, can rigid principle be applied to the behavior of one's friends. Here, a twofold attitude is apparent: one, of detachment and delighted contemplation of the "light and shade" of the world of human beings; the other, of tolerance towards the idiosyncrasy of those to whom one is united by the bond of friendship, or love. The formation of this bond is something which happens, a process with which we must not interfere by exercise of the conscious will. "The sure way, Bailey, is first to know a man's faults and then be passive—if after that he insensibly draws you towards him, you havè no power to break the link" (January 25, 1818). At this point, "the holiness of the heart's affections" comes into play. Then, just as the law of contradiction is not imposed in the large field, so we do not "care to be in the right" as against our friends. He criticizes Reynolds for standing on principle in his quarrel with Haydon. "But then Reynolds has no power of sufferance; no idea of having the thing against him" (January 13, 1818).

All this makes an impressive body of doctrine—the more impressive because it is seldom explicitly formulated, and then only partially. There are few, if any, of the longer letters of Keats in which some aspect of this total attitude does not find expression. It is, in the deepest sense, natural to him: much less a conscious philosophy, than a gradual and spontaneous unfolding of his own "experiencing nature." Fundamental to it all is an instinctive submission to experience. Instead of maintaining the ego against the outer world, instead of diligently building it up as a construction of character and principles, Keats feels himself to be passive and receptive—to the point, at one moment of intellectual awareness, of declaring himself to be (in contrast to the "egoistical sublime" of Wordsworth) a member of the poetical character which "has no self—it has no character"; and, at another moment of intense immediate experience, of feeling himself "annihilated" in a room full of company. Sometimes, when the pressure of experience was so heavy and painful as to be almost intolerable, the period of annihilation was prolonged into what he called an *agonie ennuyeuse*. One such period immediately preceded the writing of the great odes, and culminated in the famous passage on the world as "a vale of soul-making."

In this passage Keats's doctrine of the self flowers into fullness. He expounds, with affectionate urgency, to his brother a thought that had lately come to him as the result of an agonized pondering on the pains of human life and the fact of death. He finds his new thought difficult to utter. "I can scarcely express what I but dimly perceive," he says, "but yet I think I perceive it." It is one of those

> *solitary thinkings, such as dodge*
> *Conception to the very bourne of heaven,*
> *Then leave the naked brain.*

In order to express it at all, he says he has to take for granted that human nature is immortal. He does not mean that he is making the assumption that human nature is immortal, and arguing from that premise. He is not arguing at all. He is trying to grasp, to utter and convey a total intuition which has come to him, and which cannot be expressed except in terms which involve human immortality. That is part of the intuition itself.

What Keats suddenly perceives is the necessity of a world of pains and troubles to the creation of the human soul. What he means by the soul is peculiar, and important. Men are not born with a soul. They come into the world as sparks of the divine intelligence, or atoms of perception; but "they are not souls till they acquire identities, till each one is personally itself." In other words, the soul is the true self; and it is achieved or created by the submission of the Intelligence, or Mind, to the Heart, which "must feel and suffer in a thousand diverse ways" in the world of pains and troubles which is seen to be necessary to this process of soul-creation. That is to say, by the continual responsiveness of the understanding to the feelings—by which he means those deeper non-intellectual experiences which he has hitherto called "sensations"—Mind and Heart cease to be in conflict and are united in the Soul, or true Self. Thus, the antinomy between Thought and Sensation, by which Keats had originally been baffled in his letter to Bailey of November 22, 1817, is overcome. And it is overcome in a manner of which he had a premonition when he confessed to Bailey his inability to conceive how the operation of pure thought could arrive at truth. "However it may be, O for a life of Sensations rather than of thoughts!" His prayer had been granted. His life had been, and was yet to be, packed with "sensations," in his own deep sense, so full that it could contain no more: neither can we who have the "sensation" of imaginatively participating in it. Yet he declares, concerning the Heart which receives this "sensation": "Not merely is the heart a hornbook, it is the Mind's Bible, it is the Mind's experience, it is the teat from which the Mind or Intelligence sucks its identity. As various as the lives of men are— so various become their souls, and thus does God make individual beings, souls, identical souls [i.e., possessing a sense of their own identity], of the sparks of his own essence."

This is a profound religious intuition. I know of none profounder; and I believe it to be true. That confession would be irrelevant, except that I suspect that such an intuition, if it is to be understood at all, must also be believed. It is either nonsense, or a revelation. But I think it must be allowed to be significant that the illumination by this revelation, or the delusion by this nonsense, immediately preceded the composition of Keats's most perfect poems.

But my concern here is simply to draw attention to the manner in which, by this intuition, Keats's former difficulties concerning the self are resolved. Originally, in his letter to Bailey, the distinction had been between the man of Character (or Power) who possessed "a proper self" (that is, a self of his own) and the man of Genius, who was without "any individuality, any determined character"; and Keats, for all that he could not help expatiating on the nature of genius because it was his own, regarded the man of Character as superior. He was a little uncertain about this. But, after a similar hesitation, he reasserted it more positively two months later in a letter to his brothers (January 13, 1818).

So I do believe—not thus speaking with any poor vanity—that works of genius are the first things in the world. No! For that sort of probity and disinterestedness which such men as Bailey possess does hold and grasp the tip-top of any spiritual honours that can be paid to anything in the world. And moreover having this feeling at this present come over me in its full force, I sat down to write to you with a grateful heart, in that I had not a brother who did not feel and credit me for a deeper feeling and devotion for his uprightness, than for any marks of genius however splendid.

Keats's reverence for moral integrity and "disinterestedness" came from the heart. But, alas, he found that Bailey did not possess it. He came, too, to the conclusion that very few even of the benefactors of humanity had possessed it: "some meretricious motive has sullied their greatness—some melodramatic scenery has fascinated them." The men of Character, the possessors of a proper self, are egotists after all: whether their egotism be of the common and familiar, or the subtler intellectual kind. In the latter it is not *the* truth, but their truth, to which they are devoted. Yet the men of Genius are passive and receptive, are neutral, and have no self at all.

Suddenly it is revealed to him that through his very receptivity, his painful capacity for annihilation, the man of Genius, completely responsive to "sensation" in the pains and troubles of the world, can and does achieve a true Self. By his submission and humility, he suffers himself to be shaped by God. In him the Mind, obedient to the deliverances of the Heart, puts off its false pride, learns from the Heart, and is united with it in a new and individual being: a true Self, or a finally created Soul. The triumph of the ultimate integrity is his.[1]

---

[1] Keats meant by "the heart" the emotional being, primarily in its capacity for love and sympathy. Love and sympathy were for him, by nature and essentially, disinterested: as he had put it in *Endymion*, they were "self-destroying." Egoistic love is a contradiction in terms. And this remains true whether love is cast down by the experience of pain, misery, heartbreak and oppression in the world or happy in the momentary ecstasy. On the other hand, the mind seeks to operate in abstraction from this emotional experience: it generalizes, and forgets the individual; it tends to "make up its mind" and to ignore the contradictions of reality. Keats was not, of course, thinking of the strictly scientific mind which checks its hypotheses by constant experiment—not of the mind as it operates in the realm of "natural philosophy," as the sciences were called in his day; but as it operates in the realm of "moral philosophy"—or life-wisdom. Here, in Keats's view, the mind inevitably imposes a pattern on reality instead of being patient of it. It goes against the grain of the mind to suspend judgment, to be passive and receptive; it must

It lies in the nature of this illumination that it cannot give rise to a new pride. All that it offers is a conviction, or a faith, that the path to true individuality lies only through continued humility, continued submission, to the experience which the Heart alone can receive. If pride should take possession, it means that we have strayed from the path. Pride took possession of Keats in the summer of 1819: once more the conflict between his Mind and Heart became intolerable and internecine. But he knew that he had lost the track. With the advent of a new trouble—the financial disaster of his brother in America—came a new submission, a new courage, a new gaiety of heart: and the *Ode to Autumn*.

There is, surely, a great Beauty in the Truth he had discovered: it is an exquisite example of the operation of his own instinctive criterion: "I can never feel certain of any truth but from a clear perception of its beauty." And, though he himself was never, after the autumn of 1819, to emerge unclouded from the submission to his own suffering, except at the very moment of death, to those who revere his humility, his courage, his achievement, falls the realization that in the totality of Keats, in that wholeness for which he strove at so great a cost, is revealed the full meaning of his own dictum: "The excellence of every art is its intensity, capable of making all disagreeables evaporate from their being in close relationship with beauty and truth."

There are not many perfect poems in the English language; and Keats was the author of more of them than fall to the fair share of a man who died at twenty-five. But the life of Keats is as perfect as his finest poems, and it is greater than they, for it includes them. And in that is revealed the divine justice, wherein Beauty and Truth are one. This strange immortality Keats had earned: because, though he revered the works of genius, with a passion felt by few, he recognized that "probity and disinterestedness" were still more worthy of reverence. Because he clung to this, he reconciled them both, and became an example to us that the pinnacle of poetry is inaccessible save by the poet who pursues moral beauty as well.

---

judge. Thus it is, in this realm, as naturally egoistic as the heart is naturally non-egoistic. Only when the mind is submissive to the heart—to the sorrows and joys which are inevitable to love, understood in its widest sense—that is, when the mind comes instinctively to reject conclusions which do violence to primary emotional experiences, does it, in union with the heart, become a soul: the vehicle of Truth, which is at the same time Beauty—though, alas, a tragic Beauty.

INDEX